More BYGONE DAYS

Moonshine, Dancin' and Romancin'

REGINALD "DUTCH" THOMPSON

ACORNPRESS

More Bygone Days: moonshine, dancin' and romancin'
Copyright © Reginald "Dutch" Thompson, 2021
ISBN 978-1-77366-080-6

Canadian Cataloguing in Publication Data
Thompson, Reginald, 1817-
More Bygone Days: Moonshine, Dancin' and Romancin'
Editor: Lee Ellen Pottie
Proofreader: Hannah Reinhardt
Design: Cassandra Aragonez

Printed in Canada byMarquis

Library and Archives Canada Cataloguing in Publication

Title: More bygone days : moonshine, dancin' and romancin' / Reginald
"Dutch" Thompson.
Names: Thompson, Reginald, author.
Identifiers: Canadiana 20210360771 | ISBN 9781773660806 (softcover)
Subjects: LCSH: Prince Edward Island—Anecdotes. | LCSH: Prince Edward
Island—History—Anecdotes.

Classification: LCC FC2611.8 .T465 2019 | DDC 971.7—dc23

The publisher acknowledges the support of the Government of Canada,
the Canada Council for the Arts and the Province of Prince Edward Island
for our publishing program.

P.O. Box 22024
Charlottetown, Prince Edward Island
C1A 9J2
Acornpress.ca

ACORNPRESS

Dedication

This book is dedicated to my grandparents, all born in the 1890s, who lived through so many changes in the world around them. They taught me to make the best of what I've been dealt:

Maud (Prowse), war bride and midwife, and Eldon ("Straw") Thompson, First World War veteran;

Hilda (Henderson) registered nurse and midwife, and Joseph Howe Cunningham on whose farm I spent many joyful summers.

1st WW veteran Eldon & Maude (Prowse) Thompson, war bride & midwife

Joseph and Hilda (Henderson) Cunningham, RN & midwife

Acknowledgements and Thanks

Many thanks to my publisher Terrilee Bulger, my editor Lee Ellen Pottie, proofreader Hannah Reinhardt, book designer Cassandra Aragonez, Acorn general manager Genevieve Loughlin, and CBC radio host and legend Matthew Rainnie who was one of the first to hear these stories.

Huge thanks and love to my best friend and wife Jill Birtwistle, especially for putting up with all the jokes about her in the book.

And, to the hundreds of kind folks born between 1890 and 1925 who invited me into their kitchen for a cup of tea, and then shared their memories and stories, thank you. Your voices have been my best friends for over thirty years. Between us, we're keeping a bit of history alive.

Contents

Flo Arbuckle Turner, born 1900, Ponds NS

Witty, spontaneous, courageous, and a great sense of humour: that was Flo Turner, Amy Bryanton, and Kathryn MacQuarrie Wood. They were from different backgrounds but were similar in character. They were born at the beginning of the 20th century when women's place in society was shifting in their favour. Finally. The right to vote, the ability to choose their soul-mate, and, in Flo's case, the power to leave an abusive relationship.

Flo Arbuckle Turner was unforgettable. She was a century baby, born in 1900 in Ponds, eastern Pictou County. She worked hard all her life, starting off when she was a teenager cracking steaming hot claws in John Doyle's lobster factory in Lismore. Thirteen-hour days at a dollar-a-day taught her the value of money. When the lobster season ended, Flo and her pal Christine headed to D.D. MacDonald's big general store, high on the hill overlooking the Northumberland Strait, to buy some new "togs."

> When we were through working in the factory, we would have $45.00 from our summer's wages. Thirty dollars a month. That was pretty big. This night,

1

Christine MacKinnon and I were going to get new togs for the summer. We both needed a new outfit. So, we busted into the store this night, with the horse and wagon, tied the horse to the post, and, of course, there was a lot of people there. There were benches for the men to come in and sit on; a place to go and spend the evening. There was a bunch of young fellas there – we knew them all – and some elderly people, too. So, anyway, out comes Jim D.D. where we were waiting. 'Now, ladies,' he said, 'How are you, tonight?' We said, 'We're fine.' Jim D.D. MacDonald was a very comical fella, you know. He was full of business and full of fun, and he would take a joke and make a joke, too. He went around the counter and asked, 'Well now, what can I do for you?' The whole wall was nothing but boxes with all ladies' lingerie and fancy underwear. Ladies' shoes, everything was there, whatever you wanted. Well, we wanted to get some new undies.

Two teenage girls buying underwear in front of a room full of their neighbours... in 1916. Courageous. Foolhardy, maybe, but certainly courageous.

So, we were kind of bashful. All the boys were sitting around looking on, you know. Christine said, 'I want some panties.' 'Yes,' he said, 'You want some panties. What colour?' 'Oh, it doesn't matter about the colour. We just want panties.' 'And now,' he said, 'Here's ones for the elderly people, and some of the young people might wear them too. Do you want them open or closed?'

"Open" meant underwear with a flap at the back. Handy if you were in a hurry.

Well, this is what he hollered out to us, and, by God, we were so damn embarrassed, we were sorry we went in there. Anyway, down came the boxes, and he opened them all up and he was holding the panties up, and the whole crowd was looking at them, wondering which ones we were going to pick out. Oh, my God, I'll never forget it. It was the limit. It was the limit.

The following week, all decked out in their new togs, Flo and Christine headed for a dance and open-air picnic where a First World War veteran, home recovering from his wounds, saved the day.

We got all dressed up to go to the picnic, spent the whole day. There might be 10 families cooking for the picnic. There was a big tent set up, right beside the dancing stage. You could dance there all afternoon. Great fun. Lots of entertainment, but not like they have today, dropping them into a tank of water. That was never heard tell of. There was a Scottish dance hall and one for ordinary-speaking people. Two stages. The pipers would be playing at one for the Highlanders, and all us young people would have the other platform for dancing. Piano or organ and two or three violin players. If you wanted piper music, you went over to the other stage. A lot of people spoke Gaelic.

The hills and hamlets of eastern Pictou County, next to the Antigonish County line, were named for places in western Scotland: Eigg Mountain, Knoydart, Lismore, Dunmaglass. The old language and traditions persisted stubbornly well into the 20th century in this new world of transplanted MacDonalds, MacGillivrays, MacKinnons, and MacEacherns.

No cars then. Everyone came in horse and wagons. That day, at the picnic, Danny MacDonald from out here in Ardness had come home from War One. He was quite a guy, was Danny. He tried awfully hard for me to be his girlfriend, but he was a Catholic and I steered clear of Catholics. There wasn't much intermarriage then you know. Nothing.

See?

Anyway, Danny used to run in races, he boxed, did a

3

lot of sports, and he always won wherever he went. This day, the place was black with people. And Danny said, 'There's a fella out there on the road having trouble with his horses.' Two black horses and they were just wicked. And the fella couldn't hold them, and away went the horses with the wagon, and nobody in it. Everybody yelled and screeched, and Danny went out the gate, running, and he ran down the road about a mile and a half, and he jumped into the back of that wagon, and then he jumped from there out onto the horses' backs. He jumped onto the horses' necks, and he held them, and the horses started to slow up and slow up and slow up. And they stopped.

He got hold of the reins, turned the horses around, and brought the wagon back up to the man from Antigonish who owned the team. Well, my gosh, the fella gave Danny $50 for bringing the team back safe. He gave him $50. 'Here,' he said, 'I owe you this.' I'll never forget it. If the horse had tipped the wagon, well, the horses would have been killed and Danny, too."

The only downside was after that adventure no one paid any attention to Flo's new togs. And there was a Catholic running around with $50 in his pocket: Danny MacDonald, First World War veteran, and the hero of the day.

Flo was independent, and didn't worry about social conventions. She married Ted Turner, considered the smartest guy around, but a heavy drinker. The day he and a pal found a five-gallon of keg of rum washed up below the lobster factory, and trashed their house trying to feed fence posts into the kitchen stove, was the day Flo packed up her children and moved out, something women just didn't do in those days. Flo moved in with her dad, farmed, fished salmon, and on Saturday nights, organized chicken raffles and card games to support herself. The last time I visited Flo, she was up on her porch roof mending the shingles. She was 95.

Amy Adams Bryanton also bought clothes from the money she earned from her first paying job: picking potatoes for a neighbour in Spring Valley, PEI.

> You started at seven o'clock in the morning and you picked until six in the evening. And if you were one potato behind in that row, you were two potatoes in the next row, and soon you were a basket behind. You had pick like the deuce all the time to keep up.

Amy was born in 1914. In those days, a horse-drawn beater digger threw the potatoes out of the drills, scattering them like, well, the deuce.

> Those fellas who drove the digger just went around and around, and if you weren't done they went around anyway.

The beater digger looked like a big steel whirly-gig, and if young Amy couldn't keep pace, then the potatoes in her row would be buried under the next spray of dirt and potatoes.

> We'd pick enough potatoes to buy our clothes. We were getting a dollar a day. I picked for three or four years before I got two dollars a day. That's all we ever got, was two dollars a day. We had the Simpson's and Eaton's catalogues at that time. The best shoes in the catalogue were $1.98. And they were real good patent leather shoes. $1.98. And then, we'd buy a coat; the best coat in the catalogue was $14.00. School started in August so you could get time off. We got two weeks off in the fall to pick potatoes. After a while they didn't do that. They got too mean. They didn't give us any time off.

Not often you hear someone complain about not getting a chance to bend over in a muddy potato field for 12 hours a day. Amy and her schoolmates – and their parents – appreciated the chance to make a few extra dollars.

Here's why:

> My father was getting 75 cents for a 75-pound bag of potatoes. A penny a pound.

Amy never called herself an entrepreneur, but that's what she was. When she was in her 70s and 80s, she set up a recycling booth at the Kensington dump. She greeted everyone from an old lawn chair, convincing them to take things she'd fished out of the dump that they really didn't want to take home with them. Many people left with more than they'd arrived. Amy made her own cough syrup out of the tips of spruce boughs, and she boiled cherry bark for a spring tonic, recipes passed down from her Gramma Caseley. She bottled leftover goose grease from the Christmas dinner and took a big slug every day to "keep things working." She was Janus, one eye in the past and one on the future, always scheming, and she continued to do so right up to the end. She lived to be 104, and she ignored the bumps along the way.

> One time when we were bigger, my brother and I thought we'd put in an acre of potatoes. I suppose we were 15 years old, just the time we'd be wanting to do something on our own. So, we put in these potatoes between us, Green Mountains. If there's too much wet weather, they'll rot. So, we had an acre of potatoes in, and thought that was great. In the fall of the year, my grandfather Caseley said, 'You should pick them now. You can get 45 cents a bag for them.'

They were 75 cents a bag the year before. But this was October 1929. Miles away, on Wall Street, the stock market had just crashed, and the swift decline in farm prices didn't take long to head north to Spring Valley, PEI.

> Forty-five cents. We thought, well, they should be more than that. We'll wait. So, we waited. But we didn't get any more than the 45 cents. And the weather was wet and the potatoes went half rotten. So, we didn't even get

45 cents a bag for them. We never grew any after that. That ended it. Yeah, that ended it.

Amy didn't begrudge the hard work and the wasted effort. She was always able to laugh at herself, perhaps her most endearing quality. And she had plenty. Wilber Bryanton took note and courted her with his boss' driving horse.

I never had too many boyfriends. Wilber worked different farms, and then he'd borrow their horse, and this night – he was working for Stanley Ramsay – he had Stanley's horse and Stanley always used to preach, 'Watch that horse, because he'll run away every chance he gets.' Wilber came up to our place this night, and I used to make up rhymes about him. Just rhymes, I couldn't tell you any of them now, but just made-up rhymes about him. So, we're going down the road to Seaview with this horse that Stanley used to be preaching would run away, and it was cold. Fall of the year, horse and wagon, and we had the buffalo.

The "buffalo" was a buffalo skin folks wrapped themselves in to keep warm when out with the horse and wagon or sleigh. After the buffalo herds were wiped out, "buffalo" evolved to mean any fur or hide or heavy blanket.

So, I had the buffalo all tucked in around me, and I was making up rhymes and when I made up rhymes, I wouldn't let Wilber see me because I'd laugh, see. I'd just turn my back to him, and I had my back half-turned, and he was turned the other way too. He accidentally gave me a bump, and out I went, out over the side of the wagon. The side of the wagon was no more than seven inches high, what. Out I went, all wound up in the buffalo, and fell in between the wheels. And the horse just stood there. Yep. The horse just stood there. The horse that used to run away all the time. So, Wilber gathered me up and I got back on the wagon, and away we went. I didn't say any more rhymes that night. Ahh, we used to have a lot of good times.

"Good times" could have been Kathryn MacQuarrie Wood's motto. Kay was born in Hampton in 1907; one of the Hampton MacQuarries who, in my opinion, proved good breeding produces big brains. One of her home remedies was using banana peels to cure a migraine, and her father claimed to have cured himself of the Spanish Flu in 1919 by taking nips of moonshine. Like Flo and Amy, Kay could do it all: make soap, knit, quilt, and tell a funny story.

> In the wintertime, they used to have quilting parties and hooking parties. And the ladies of the district would all come to help. They'd make supper and you could hear all the news of the day there.

For years, Kay wrote a breezy column for the *Journal Pioneer* while running several tourist cabins on her farm in Victoria-by-the-Sea. Her big house with the side turret had been built by Charles Palmer, a 19th century shipbuilder. Kay's kitchen overlooked the bay where one day in 1933, she saw a fleet of Italian seaplanes land on their way home from the Century of Progress Exhibition in Chicago. Kay loved history, and collected many stories for her heritage books and newspaper columns.

> Later, when the telephone came in to being, we had one of the first telephones in Hampton. The office was in Crapaud and my cousin Amy Howatt was the operator. She knew everything – every baby that was born and who was going with somebody else and shouldn't be. She knew all the gossip of the country.

Between Kay and Amy, there weren't many secrets in central Queens County, especially since the phones were all on party lines. Listening in was a way of life.

> Our ring was four short rings. If she would ring and I didn't happen to be home, she must have been psychic, because as soon as I'd get home, she'd ring and she'd say, 'Where were you?' She always knew everyone's business.

The Woods had their house wired for electricity after running the poles and wire themselves from the dam in Tryon. Their house had been so well-constructed by Mr. Palmer's shipwrights, the electrician had a hard time running the wires between the wall studs, so he cut two holes in the baseboard, taped the wire to the tail of one of Kay's barn cats. He put a bowl of cream at the far hole, and the cat wormed its way through the maze of timber, and out the far hole next to the tasty cream. Kay said when the electrician left, he stole the cat.

In 1928, Kay married Howard Wood, also known as H.B. For years, they ran the big barn-like ice rink across from their farm, home of the Victoria Union men's and women's hockey teams. Kay said she rarely went into Charlottetown, because the nearest train station was miles away in Breadalbane, but also because Wright's General Store in downtown Victoria had everything they needed, even a milliner. The hat-maker was Mimi MacDonald from Crapaud, and, in later years, people were allowed to go upstairs to the store's attic where Mimi constructed her hats. This was also where decades-old clothes that hadn't sold in the shop were stored. Folks were allowed to borrow whatever caught their eye to wear to the fancy dress skating parties Kay and H.B. put on at the rink. Kay wasn't above entering the best-costume contest, and, the last time I visited, when she was well into her nineties, she was all dolled up and wearing a pair of bright red sequined ballet slippers. As always, she was gorgeous, and couldn't wait to get and give all the news.

Kathryn Wood, Amy Bryanton, and Flo Turner: three great women, not replaced in the hearts of those who knew and loved them.

Roy Clow, 2nd WW veteran

The earth just shook. There was a roar like thunder. The teapot moved that far on the stove. But the people in New Glasgow thought the coal mines blew up in Stellarton.

Pictou County, NS, was a coal-mining centre, so it was a natural assumption that one of the many coal mines in the area had had yet another explosion.

Over the years, almost 700 men died in the mines – a third from the explosions. On the morning of 6 December 1917, teenager Flo Arbuckle was visiting family in New Glasgow, NS. Flo and just about everyone else immediately thought of the Allan mine in Stellarton, considered by mining engineers to be the most dangerous coal mine in the world because of the huge volumes of volatile methane gas lurking in the county's coal seams.

Uncle Bill was on a roof – that's what he did, putting roofs on buildings. Tarring roofs. He climbed down and he came home. He came in and said, 'My God that must have been awful.' There was nobody on the streets of New Glasgow. Not a soul. Everybody got into the first door they came to. He said, 'I don't know what it is.' Just then who came in the door but Bill Livingstone. He was married to my father's sister. 'You know,' he said, 'There was an explosion in Halifax. It took Halifax off the map. Halifax is almost wiped out.' And that's what it was. You could hear it from here. It blew big anchors out of the middle of the harbour onto the streets.

The initial reaction to the explosion was natural considering coal mines' reputation. Halifax is over 100 kilometres from New Glasgow. There wouldn't be another man-made explosion as powerful as the Halifax Explosion until 1945.

Nova Scotia is both blessed and cursed with an abundance of coal. The methane-leaking seams in Pictou County are 13 metres thick in some places, and thousands of men had made a living by going down in the mines, as they did two counties over in Springhill, Cumberland County. Leo "Sailor" MacDonald had coal miners in his family. Leo managed to land a surface job, but even as a Springhill policeman and eventually the chief of police, he knew only too well the tragedies of the area's rich coal mines.

I think our Number Two coal mine in Springhill was the deepest mine in the world. In some places, we had nine-foot seams and the coal was as just as hard and shiny as a silver dollar. But the coal was gassy, worse than Pictou County. Very bad. We had 'bumps.' The floor of the mine comes up and the ceiling comes down and if you happened to be in between you were squeezed like a rat. Oh, you're gone.

Bumps. Quite a euphemism. Leo escaped the mines but his brother didn't.

A lot of good men were fatally injured in the coal mines. The one in 1956: there were 79, I think, killed. My heavens, we had probably 300 policemen here at that time. Mounted police, the city police. I have 46 years of police work, continuous service. You took the bitter with the sweet. It wasn't all sunshine. My brother was killed. My wife lost seven people very close to her. Charlie Burton was her uncle and he was the main cog out there. He was a mine official. Oh yes. Terrible. Those mining disasters, those mine explosions, they just cleaned our town out. We had a lot of fine, fine young fellas killed. The very best.

As chief of police, one of Leo's duties – unofficial I'm sure, but because he knew everyone in town, it was a job he felt honour-bound to do – was breaking the bad news to the dead miners' families. Over the years, they shared a lot of tears.

Springhill coal was first mined on an industrial scale in the 1870s. Twenty years later in 1891, the town suffered the first major disaster followed by the two devastating "bumps" in 1956 and 1958. In 1957, misery piled on when a huge fire destroyed most of the downtown core of the town.

Nova Scotia coal was shipped by the schooner-load down the eastern seaboard and across to PEI Railway firemen, who kept the steam engines rolling, preferred Springhill over Cape Breton and Pictou County coal, so Springhill coal was rationed in spite of the firemen's cry: "Give me some more of that Springhill." The vessels hauling potatoes and turnips to the coal-mining towns like New Glasgow and Glace Bay usually returned with the holds loaded with coal. Coal merchants like Larges, Weeks, and Pickards were perched on the Charlottetown waterfront. Roy Clow was born in Murray Harbour North in 1917. As a young lad, he'd hitch up the mare and dumpcart, and head to Montague to make few extra dollars. Very few.

I'd get a dollar for the horse and myself all day, and work from shortly after daylight 'til dark. I'd drive the horse all day long for a dollar. It was hellish good coal, too. It was real hard, nice, shiny black coal. They'd fill a big tub in the hold, give the rope a jig 'OK' – and sometimes the horse would back up and the tub would hit the tailboard of the cart and upset.

Half the coal would go overboard, and then the captain would curse me and curse everybody he could see. 'Look at my good coal, you young so-and-so. Hold that horse steady.' I couldn't hold the friggin' horse: I was seven or eight years old.

Miles from the pit-face, Roy and Maisie, the mare, were working just as hard on the surface as the fabled pit ponies were down in the mines. Roy was working hard, making a buck here, another there, because back at the farm, his father was terminally ill. Roy and his brothers were running the farm, fishing the gear, and taking whatever jobs were available. The 1920s and '30s weren't easy in the Maritimes. Roy delivered coal to several schools around Montague including his own one-roomed school in Murray Harbour North. The teacher never mentioned his absence from class.

◆

This night we were over practising for the Christmas school concert, and Keir Duggan found some dynamite in the coal.

At the other end of PEI in Spring Valley, north of Kensington, a coal-burning stove also heated the school. Amy Bryanton, born in 1914, recalled a terrible accident that was probably caused by an overlooked blasting cap when she was in grade four.

He had this little stick of dynamite and he put it on the hot stove, the pot-bellied stove that burnt coal. So, he put it on the stove and he hit it with a poker. I don't know what his idea was, but he hit it and it still didn't blow, so he did it the third time, hard with the poker. And it blew all right. It blew the fingers off his right hand.

Keir had discovered the blasting cap/dynamite in the coal shed out back of the school. The explosion brought the teacher running.

In those times – that was in the winter – the roads weren't plowed. People were travelling with horse and sleighs. Keir just dropped everything and they ran up to Fred Profitt's, who lived right handy. They took him to the doctor. But that was an awful surprise to everybody, what?

Probably more to some than others. The doctor, probably old Dr. Champion in Kensington, couldn't do much except cauterize the fingers and hope for the best. The hand eventually healed, and Keir went back to school. Amy said,

He had to learn to write with his left hand. After that, Keir worked in the post office.

Speaking of not plowing the roads and travelling by horse and sleigh, one of the last blacksmiths in Pictou County was Raymond Patton from Ponds. Raymond was the son of a blacksmith. One December day in 1926, Raymond's father Scott hitched up the horse and headed to the Albion coal mine, 30 kilometres away in Stellarton, because he needed a load of coal for the forge. He followed the trail of small trees that had been frozen into Merigomish Harbour marking the shortcut across the ice to town. Just another day in the lives of ordinary people, father and son.

He left home before daylight in the morning, good ice, the track was bushed, and he got on the harbour down here at Barney's River bridge and followed the bushed track right up to Pine Tree. There was a place he came off the ice there, and he got into New Glasgow about noontime. There was a livery stable down at the north end of New Glasgow known as Church's, and you could put your horse in there, and have it fed and watered. When the horse got through eating, he hitched up the sleigh and he went out to Albion Mines between Westville and Stellarton. I'd say about four miles more he'd have to travel to get out to the mine. They put the coal on the sleigh – it was a good junk of a sleigh too, probably take half a ton, I guess – and they didn't bother weighing it, they just asked him for a dollar.

Then he headed for home. He came down the ice and, by gosh, it came to snow that night. And the ice is a bad place if there's a drift of snow. Everything looks the same and you lose the track. Anyway, it was after dark – it would be about eight o'clock – I can see him coming up the hill yet. I was watching out to see if he was coming, knowing it would be bad out on the ice. I was old enough to know that. And I could see the horse coming by itself, coming up the hill. My father was walking behind the sleigh. So, he must have just got cold sitting on the sleigh, and he got off and walked. Yeah.

When I look at that little story, nothing really happens, but the details – feeding the horse, not weighing the coal, paying a dollar – and the tiny element of tension Raymond injects into it – seeing the horse first – makes it a lovely vignette. I can picture young Raymond sitting at the window with the kerosene lamp, anxious for his Dad's safe return.

I'm proud to say Raymond was a cousin on both my mum's and dad's side of the family. He was a bachelor, lived alone in the family home, an unpainted cedar-shingled farmhouse high on a hill overlooking the Northumberland Strait. He learned to play the fiddle sitting with his parents outside Luther MacDonald's dance hall near the Barneys River bridge he mentioned. He was never allowed in the dance hall – liquor and women – but when you wanted the straight goods, you went to Raymond. I failed to ask if the coal for the forge was a special type. A farrier on the Welsh/English border told me one time he preferred a variety of hard coal he called "breeze." This was in the 1980s, and, as the coal mines in Wales inevitably shut down, breeze got harder to find.

♦

Blacksmithing, like coal mining, is mostly obsolete. As are the skills the Francis family from Fortune, PEI, honed over the years. Like the blacksmith, they also made a living from horses, making wagons and sleighs, including the Francis cutter considered the Cadillac of sleighs. Lorne Francis was the last to run the business, taking over from his uncle and his father Harry who, rather cheekily for a sleigh-maker, also drove a truck and always had a fast car.

> I learned to drive on a '30 Nash. I never had a test. I never had a licence. When I was 12 years old, Dad took me out of school. He was sick that year, and he had a couple of schooners loaded with coal and had taken orders. They came in to Annandale wharf, and he took me out of school, and we had a new half ton truck, and I hauled coal off those schooners with the half ton along with another fella from Souris who had another half ton truck. They dumped the coal in with tubs and we delivered it around to all the people who had ordered it.

An updated version of Roy and Maisie the mare, except:

> And that's where I learned to drink rum. I remember getting a couple of long-neckers of rum off that schooner. Big long-neckers with the hollow up in the bottom. I remember the bottles. And the top was waxed in, sealed. Of course, I was just trying this rum, see.

"Long-necker" is a new one on me. Long-neckers, dollar-a-day wages, bushed ice, and one-roomed school Christmas concerts... all connected in one way or another to coal. Does anyone today remember the heavy smell of coal smoke in the air on a frosty winter's night? Heavy, pungent, gritty.

Let's put everyone to bed: Lorne went back to school, but that wasn't the end of the rum. His dad Harry recovered, became a Massey Harris dealer, and sold a tractor to a farmer tired of hitching up the horse to haul five-and-ten-gallon kegs of illegal rum up from the shore landed from a Newfoundland schooner. Amy Bryanton lived to 104 and passed on to me a score of home remedies gleaned from her Grandmother Caseley, including the salt-herring-on-the-feet cure for pneumonia. Roy Clow ran a little rum, was a Second World War veteran, and became my best pal. Flo Turner caught the Spanish Flu exactly one year after the Halifax Explosion, survived, taught herself to play the piano and to paint landscapes, and, when she was 95, I found her up on her roof repairing the shingles. Raymond Patton spent a day showing me how cedar shingle a house, how to make the corners square, and was insulted when I offered to pay him cash money, opting instead for one of my mother's roast beef dinners.

Leo "Sailor" MacDonald chased rumrunners in the Pugwash area, coincidentally where Ann Murray, another Springhill native, now has a home. Leo's son followed him as the Springhill Chief of Police. Leo earned his nickname playing baseball back in the 1930s and '40s with the famed Springhill Fencebusters. Mining towns fielded a variety of sports teams, a distraction from the colliery and the inherent hardships of daily life in a coal town. In 1910, Stellarton even boasted a cricket team. I wonder how many miners played.

And Springhill. The 1958 disaster in Springhill ended the coal mining. The round-the-clock coverage of the rescue operations put the town on the map, in a macabre way. Thanks to Ann Murray, the town now has more positive connotations. Ann Murray, like coal, also has a PEI connection: she taught physical education in Summerside, and got a leg up in her singing career at Johnny Reid's bar and lounge in Charlottetown, sharing the stage with fellow artist Gene MacLellan, and helping to launch his career with "Snow Bird."

In 2015, Springhill's abandoned coal mines were flooded, and now provide geothermal heating for the town. Light, in a way, at the end of the tunnel.

Frank Reid pack peddler

The Rawleigh man. The pack peddler. The Watkins man. The Avon lady. Welcome visitors who travelled PEI's country roads. You can still buy Rawleigh's double-strength vanilla extract and Rawleigh's antiseptic salve with turpentine... online. Folks in rural PEI back in the bygone days looked forward to those travelling salesmen – and they were mostly men – who brought a bit of the outside world into their kitchen. Clarisse Gallant, born in 1913 in Oyster Bed Bridge, knew the thrill of seeing a strange wagon or Model-T Ford – better still, if they were carrying a big pack over their shoulder – coming up the lane:

> I remember especially the Rawleigh man. He was a Corcoran from Piusville... and he always stayed at our home. There was a lot of story-telling going on when he'd come in. It was always a joy to see him. We'd give him his supper and a bed overnight, his breakfast, and then he'd take off. About once a month, quite regularly. He travelled by horse and wagon or horse and sleigh. We always bought something from him – medicated ointment, a big flat round box – I

think that's still on the market. And vanilla and different staples around the house. He'd always give us a freebie then because we'd given him lodging.

You didn't charge for the lodging?

No. No.

One of the best-known pack peddlers, so-called because of the big pack they carried, was Frank Reid from the east end of Charlottetown. Frank had emigrated to PEI from Lebanon in the 1890s, and like his compatriots around the Maritimes, he took to the road selling everything from ribbons and bolts of cloth to penny candy. Many of the pack peddlers eventually bought a horse, and later a car or truck. Many of the corner stores in Charlottetown were financed by pack-peddling. But Frank Reid stuck to Shank's Mare, carrying his big wooden pack on his back. On Monday morning, Frank would get on the train in Charlottetown and head west, and start walking back towards home. The next week, he'd go east on the train, and if he was successful, arrive home with his pack empty. He slept in kitchens across the Island, and his son, the entrepreneur and empresario Johnny Reid, told me that during Old Home Week, Frank was thrilled to be able to repay his rural benefactors:

Some of the people used to come and stay with us, the people who were good to my father. We didn't have many rooms. We'd have to sleep downstairs on a couch and put them in our bedroom. If they were in town and had some time to spend, they came down to our place and Mum would give them a meal while they were waiting for the train. Dad would come home with eggs he'd taken in exchange; a couple of chickens, already plucked, in the bottom of his wooden box. Bags of potatoes – he'd have to go back to the train and pick them up. He'd bring home canned lobster, canned chicken – people were doing their own canning out there. He'd make a trade – if they didn't have any money, he'd take food instead. And it would feed us. Right up until he had the stroke, he was out there walking. When he took the stroke, he'd be in his 80s, 81 or 82.

During the week while his dad was on the road, Johnny's mother sewed aprons with little pockets for Frank to put them in his pack to sell, 35 cents each. They never stopped working. Money was scarce. Johnny and his mother would walk the railway tracks picking dandelion greens for salads, and his mother would send Johnny to the corner store to get *ten cents worth of bologna, sliced thin*. That line pretty much sums up the Great Depression for many people. He told me his parents had one vacation, when they went "up to Boston" to visit a sister. I wonder if out of habit Frank slept on the couch beside the kitchen stove.

Commercial travellers were also pounding the Island roads, making the rounds to the many general stores that dotted rural PEI. They sold everything from soap – Harry Lapthorn – to hardware – Charlie Bell – to candy – Jim Montgomery who was known far and wide as "the Candyman." He sold an unusual combination: penny candy like coconut haystacks, chicken bones, and French bonbons, as well as Macdonald's tobacco. Export A cigarettes with its highland lassie logo was one familiar product. Royal White, who was born in 1916, met the Candyman when he was a young lad growing up in Murray River:

> Mother run the hotel, my father run the schooner, and in the wintertime, I drove the commercial travellers. A bed was a dollar and a meal was, I believe, 50 cents. Yeah. She got the commercial travellers. Jim Montgomery? Yes, yes, gracious, yes. And who was the other fella who had the small feet and used to sell drugs? Jimmy Montgomery, good gracious, yes. And Sterling Beaton from Beaton's Wholesalers.

Who was the fella with the small feet who sold drugs?

I can't remember his name, but he was smart, and

he knew he was smart. My father said to him one time – he spelled out such and such a word – and asked, 'How do you pronounce that word?' And this fella with the small feet – he thought he was awfully smart – he pronounced it right away. 'Well,' my father asked, 'How would you spell such and such a word?' He never raised his head at all. He knew he was caught.

Just to clarify, it's bad enough having small feet and being branded a smart aleck, but the drugs the mystery man was selling were things like horse liniments and castor oil.

♦

Another Beaton used to make the rounds in eastern PEI: Herbie Beaton would buy trinkets at stores and re-sell them door-to-door for a few pennies more than he'd paid for them. Kind-hearted homemakers invited Herbie in for a warm meal and a bed at night. In Munns Road, up at the north-eastern end of the Island, Boswell Robertson learned a few of the facts-of-life from travelling salespeople:

Tom Michael was one of those fellas from the foreign countries – they used to travel around with a big pack on their back. Lordy, I don't know how they did it. I don't know how they walked, but they did. Tom Michael was this fella's name – he used to come around here. And the Kays travelled too, and the Dows travelled. We had nothing but poverty, but my mother was a very, very hospitable woman, and there was no one ever left there cold or hungry. There was a lot of people that stayed when we were growing up. My father drove commercial travellers and sometimes he couldn't go, and I used to have to go. I was only a young fella. You see, they came up here on the train, and you'd pick them up and take them to all the stores you could get to in a night.

Them days, I think there were 11 stores around here, but we'd only get to about half them in a night. Mum would give them supper, and a bed and breakfast, and I'd take them back up here to the train. I think she got three dollars for that, and if it was two [travellers], it was five dollars, and if it was three, it was seven dollars. Now you imagine that for money.

But that wouldn't include all the driving around with the horse and sleigh.

Oh, yes, that was everything. Yes, sir.

Would these fellas have sample cases?

Yes. And they always had liquor. And cigarettes. Some of them were scared of their wives, which was a good thing. They wouldn't drink at home – they'd come up here. They all didn't drink... but I remember one fella by the name of Elmer Dunning. He was a terrible nice fella and he loved to drink when he'd get up here. I never saw him 'out of the way.' He could always walk.

Mr. Dunning travelled for the Eastern Hay and Feed Company. One day, a customer smelled liquor on his breath and exclaimed, "You smell like a Christmas fruitcake!" Better than being known for your small feet.

◆

Many of the commercial travellers graduated to driving a company car, but winter travel was dictated by the banks of snow on Island roads, so for four or five months of the year, train travel lingered even after the Second World War. Frances Reid Clinton remembers one of the ingenious ways PEI geography was taught when she was in school back in the 1930s:

There was a schoolteacher from Georgetown who taught at Suffolk school. We went down to see her once. It was a big trip, like you were going to Mexico or somewhere now. One of things she taught us was all those little stations. She'd start at the eastern end of the Island, and you had to name every station. There was Elmira, Souris, Mount Stewart, Tracadie, Bedford, Suffolk, York, Royalty Junction, Winsloe. And then there was Borden and Carleton Siding – it was like a geography lesson.

What was it like when the Rawleigh man came to visit?

He was a very jolly guy. He would put his horse in at our house for the night. We'd give him a meal. I guess there was an exchange of "products" for the meal. Then he'd sit around and tell us stories. Big Santa Claus and Little Santa Claus would be one of the stories. And how the sea got its salt was another: some machine fell in and they couldn't get it turned off. Stories like that. A very pleasant guy, and we looked forward to him coming. He probably only came once a year. His name was Corcoran; he'd be from Piusville. We thought he was old, but he probably wasn't.

Would you see any pack peddlers?

Yes. You'd trade – I think they bought horse hair. My mother would get a square of oilcloth in return. They were traders. Yeah.

Everyone saved their horsehair: some was used as a binder when plastering walls, and some was used as stuffing in furniture. Several folks mentioned a travelling tailor who went by the name of Tarbush. Frances loved to see him coming down the lane, because he was a ventriloquist, and sitting around the stove after a hot meal, suddenly the dog or the wood box would start talking. Kids loved him.

These days, we book our rooms on the Internet, and can read reviews and check out photos of the rooms and facilities in motels around the world. No more ads like the Queen Hotel in Summerside used to run, claiming the rooms were so clean you could walk around in your bare feet. The hotel would send a horse and sleigh to meet you at the Borden ferry, and, after registering, hot tea and a plate of oysters awaited. And for dessert, if you were lucky, the Candyman was down the hall with his big sample case full of coconut haystacks.

Those Invaluable Mothers

Margaret Townsend Crozier

Mothers. What would we do without them? Take Margaret Brown Crozier from Sherbrooke, PEI She was one of those courageous women who never made it into the history books or received a medal for bravery. Yet, at the time of the 1918-19 Spanish Flu epidemic, which killed hundreds of Islanders and millions around the world, she put her life at risk to help those in need. Her daughter Margaret was proud to share her mother's stories.

> I remember my mother going to one of the neighbours, and staying with them and sitting up all night with them. Two children died. I remember Mother telling how the mother was standing at the grave of the second child and the husband took her arm and said, 'Come on now, let's go Mother.' And she just couldn't leave.

The unfathomable anguish of burying your own child. Margaret senior somehow escaped the wrath of the Spanish Flu. Margaret junior ironically witnessed a similar tragic scene soon after.

> The first year I got out of college with my teacher's permit, I went to Enterprise, Ontario, to my sister Marion's. Her husband was the minister (there) cut and there was a family there who had lost their two children in that 'flu. They wouldn't even let the minister visit them, they were so bitter. They wouldn't have anything to do with the church. They had no faith at all. Lost their faith completely.

◆

Lona Acorn was born in 1913 in Vernon River, and lived to be 103. Her father had a mail route – horse and wagon, horse and sleigh. And her mother ran the rest of the show.

> She must have been a hard worker: in charge of the post office plus looked after eight children. It was really busy in the post office at Christmas. Eaton's catalogues. You can imagine when the Eaton's catalogues came, how heavy the mail bags would be, and how heavy the mail was. And some of the mail boxes weren't all on the right side of the road, but you had to go to the left side too. Some of the people had mail bags and, when you got there, you had to open the bag and see if they were mailing a letter, take it and the three cents. It all took time. And very little pay. I think my mother got $48 for three months. They only paid you every three months for running the post office, and she was there on call from morning until night, not like they have hours nowadays. She worked all the time.

Women's work still is under-valued. Women in Canada earn about 80 cents to every dollar a man makes. The percentage was even lower in the 1920s and '30s. But ask most men and they'd tell you they loved their mothers and wives, and would do anything for them. So I have to wonder what's stalling equal pay legislation.

> I grew up in the east end of town. They called it Hell Street. That's going back a lot of years.

Johnny Reid had a reputation around Charlottetown as a no-nonsense businessman and entrepreneur. The son of Lebanese immigrants, Johnny started off selling French fries out of a back-yard shed on Dorchester Street around the corner from the railway station. He parlayed that into a restaurant and bar, along the way helping launch the careers of Stompin' Tom Connors, Gene MacLellan, and Ann Murray.

> I was born down there. I was brought up down there. I stayed with my mother until she died. She died in 1982, and then I moved out to New Haven even though I had already built a house out there. I never lived in it. My wife would stay, but I'd come home. I wouldn't leave my mother by herself. The first Christmas we were out there – if my mother was going to stay home, I was going to stay with her. After she died on March the 20th, I don't think I left her house until that summer. I stayed there. I don't know... it was hard to leave when you've lived there all your life.

The soft side to Johnny Reid, the man who bragged he never forgot a face. If he threw you out of JRs Lounge, you were gone for good.

> I lived with her all my life and I wouldn't leave her when she was older. No, she brought me into this world and she looked after me. She was good to me, and she was a great mother.

When Johnny was a boy, times were tough. He and his mother Alice would pick coal along the railway tracks to feed the stove, and dandelion greens to feed the family. His father, Frank, was a pack peddler. He lugged a huge pack around the Island, leave on the train first thing Monday morning, then walk from farm-to-farm selling trinkets, and bolts of cloth, and penny candy. Frank returned exhausted on Friday's last train or his feet. So, Alice raised the family more-or-less on her own.

Alice had always wanted a vegetable garden and, when he was a young, Johnny decided she would have one. He had, shall we say, a certain reputation with the Charlottetown Police Department, which involved bootleg alcohol and resulted in the burning desire for the police to nail Johnny red-handed.

> I was buying moonshine and selling it to the bootleggers. I'd go out and haul it for $10.00 a gallon and sell it to them for $15.00. So, I was making $5.00 a gallon and as long as you didn't bother anybody... well... And I didn't bother anybody. If anybody bothered me, I'd retaliate. So, I never had any problems. I had some booze hidden in my – Mum's – backyard and this guy called the cops, but the booze was gone by the time they got there. So, what I did, I made out like I was burying something in the yard, see. And the guy called the cops again, and they came down and they were digging, and joking with me saying, 'Are we warm?' And I'd say, 'No. It might be over here.' So, they kept digging, and finally I said, 'Thanks very much. My mother wanted me to dig a garden there and I couldn't get anyone to dig it for me. Thanks very much.'

Johnny stood beside his mother at the kitchen window, watching the police, united in the pursuit of garden peas and carrots. Not sure what happened to the squealer. The worst he could expect was to be banned from JRs lounge, a cruel and much-dreaded punishment in the 1960s and '70s.

♦

Don Anderson took a different path to success. Don was born in 1927 on a farm overlooking the bay in St. Peters. He became the long-time general manager of the PEI Potato Marketing Board, negotiating contracts and agricultural trade disputes around the world. He once told me that in their 65 years of marriage, he never once heard his parents raise their voices in anger with one another. Maybe it was destiny, because Don's mother, Florence Nightingale Anderson could predict the future by reading tea leaves.

During the Second World War, Dad had his cattle in the ROP – Record of Performance – and, at that time, the milk inspector would come to the house. He would have to take three milkings and then test your whey and cream. This man's name was McInnis and he was from Souris. I was sitting at the kitchen table and he said, 'Mrs. Anderson, I hear you read tea leaves. I'd like to have my cup read.'

So Mother read Mr. McInnis's cup, and she said, 'Now Mr. McInnis I know you're anxious to finish up your work for the month and you're going from here to D.J. Mullin's in St. Peters' – who had Ayrshire cattle – 'and then get on the train and go to Souris. I know you're anxious to get home, but you may have some difficulties. And then when you get home, you may have some disagreement with a neighbour or a close friend.'

Well, a big storm came up, and Mr. McInnis was delayed because the train couldn't get up, so he was delayed getting to Souris. We also heard that when he got home, he went to a barber shop and got into an argument with the barber. Quite a disagreement.

A month or two went by, and Mr. McInnis came back for another milk testing. So we were sitting down at the table again in the evening and I said to Mother, 'Mother, maybe Mr. McInnis would like to have his cup read again.'

Mr. McInnis jumped up from the table, 'Oh good God, no!' He ran over to the sink, emptied his cup out, and put water in it so there was no tea leaves in it for her to predict anything.

My wife had her tea cup read when she was young, and was told she'd marry into money. We're still waiting.

♦

My dear friend Edith Whitlock Pryce also read tea leaves. Edith was born in Charlottetown and, when her Mum died, young Edith was raised by her Nanny and Grampy Whitlock. Her father Edgar sold and repaired tires on Kent Street. Edgar was a great old lad, a good friend of my father's who was also in the tire business, and they often went fishing trout together.

> My Dad was a great fisherman. Loved fishing, ohh yes. Oh, that was a wonderful pastime. Any time of the day or evening, Sundays – it didn't make any difference.

My father loved to fish, too. He'd work until noon on Saturday, and then he'd head off trout fishing, and leave my Mum home alone with six sons, the youngest five raising the roof. But as self-indulgent as my father might have been, Edgar takes the cake. The wedding cake.

> That reminds me. My dad told me that when he and my mother got married, they decided they'd go fishing. She was a Dingwell from the Fortune area and her uncle owned a fishing pond. So, they decided on their wedding day to go fishing. Dad always had cars – at one time he had seven, probably all Pontiacs – and so they drove out to the uncle's pond and he wouldn't let them fish. He turned them away because this was their wedding day. Oh, boy, was Dad upset. You know, in those days people were funny.

Yeah, funny. Not sure what the bride and groom did instead, although Edith was born nine months later.

Robbie Robertson and Clive Bruce and dory Clive built

You took a dose of salts for almost anything except a cough. Or castor oil. Some people used to say it was poison, but Dr. Brehaut used to say it was great. He said it should be worth $5 a pound. It was good medicine. The girls got castor oil, the boys always got a dose of salts. And that 'moved' you. I'll tell you, that moved you. It cleaned you out alright. It wasn't safe to take it if you had a cough. You mostly felt better too for some reason. I don't know why.

I do. You were just thrilled you didn't cough. That was Milton Buell born in 1907 in Abney halfway between Murray River and Murray Harbour South, Dr. Lester Brehaut's territory.

Boswell Robertson:

All of them was home remedies. I don't think there's anything better for you than cod liver oil even today.

It'll help so many things wrong with you, and it'll help if there's nothing wrong with you, too.

Home remedies have been around since Adam ate the apple and needed a dose of salts to rid himself of sin. In the 1930s, Helen Creighton, Nova Scotia's renowned oral historian and author, recorded an old Scottish home remedy cure for tuberculosis: eat a white egg from a black hen. It didn't work, but neither did many "scientific" cures for the dreaded "white plague," which included bleeding and the fresh air treatment wherein patients were confined to open rooms and verandahs in all weathers for hours on end.

In 1918, when Celia MacEachern McCloskey's family in Hermanville were suffering from the ravages of the Spanish Flu, eggs caused a minor riff between neighbours:

> We were at my grandfather's and we moved all the beds into the parlour. I begged my mother to let me get up and when I got up, I couldn't stand I was so weak. They kept the parlour nice and warm. Woodstove. Good friends of ours died. Terrible. The doctor [Sullivan] came around as much as he could but he was worn out. Mother didn't get it and she went to get a dozen eggs from a friend to try and get us to eat something and she charged her $2 for the eggs. She had sympathy, didn't she. Ha. There wasn't sympathy, but she had to live and she had to feed the hens.

Eggs were usually a-penny-a-piece back then. Twentieth century drug companies have taken a page from that "good friend's" playbook.

Milton Buell:

> The main medicine in those days, if you got wounded one way or another, was always kerosene. Put some kerosene oil on it and wrap it up. And if you had a bad cough, it'd be kerosene oil and sugar. Half teaspoon of sugar and put five or six drops of kerosene oil on it and swallow it. It didn't taste too bad.

They called it coal oil then. I don't think it was from crude oil, I think it really was a coal product. That's what we used to get to burn in the lamps.

Milton is bang-on. Coal oil is slightly different from kerosene – one's produced from coal, the other from petroleum. Ingesting a few drops of coal oil probably didn't cure the cough, but it wouldn't kill you either. Too much might though. As Oscar Wilde quipped, "everything in moderation, even moderation."

◆

Agnes Sheehan was born in 1908 in Bear River:

One day, Daddy decided he'd get a drink of water and there was another bottle behind the kitchen door that we had for kerosene. And I don't know for what reason he picked up the kerosene bottle and took a drink of it. He was all but gone. Yep. He was gone too far by the time I got him to Souris for the doctor [A. A. Gus MacDonald] to pump his stomach. Daddy lived on tomato soup for a long time. That's all he could keep down. That's what brought him around.

Agnes became a valued member of the community: a midwife who also dressed corpses, sometimes both the first and last person to touch someone. After her father's misadventure, when out working in the fields, either Agnes or her mother always took the brown kerosene bottle with them.

Midwife Mary MacDougall birthed Celia McCloskey in 1911. Many midwives practiced a few home remedies, which illustrated just how desperate people were before the wonders of modern medicines. "Salt herring went around your neck or on your feet for pneumonia. Why not?" Why not indeed when all else has failed. One treatment that's stood the test of time and science is cod liver oil. To their chagrin, Celia and her siblings were dosed every day: "Cod liver oil tasted awful. Terrible terrible terrible!"

The Omega-3 fatty acids in fish oils are now promoted to improve your health "from your brain to your toes" as one company advertises. Capsules, fruit drinks, and smoothies now mask the fishy taste of cod liver oil, but in bygone days, "terrible terrible terrible" was the usual reaction after swallowing raw cod liver oil.

> Cod liver oil – that was the real McCoy. And it worked. It was rendered by the fishermen. It wasn't refined, and how clean it was...well, your guess is as good as mine.

Eddie Easter was born 1905 in Hamilton, PEI, on the shores of Malpeque Bay. So who was making all the cod liver oil?

> I was 17 when I started fishing. I had a 24-foot boat. If we sold the fish fresh to MacLean's store, we only got 25 cents a 100 pounds for hake. And the cod, we got 20 cents for the small cod, 35 for the medium, and 50 or 60 cents for the large cod. Fresh, for 100 pounds.

Clive Bruce, born in 1910 in Red Point in northeastern PEI, fished for 70 years, everything from 100-pound cod fish – worth about 25 cents total after it was gutted, dried and salted – to a 1000-pound tuna that he sold for $10 to a man who fed it to his silver foxes. At one time, the Gulf of St Lawrence off PEI's north shore teemed with cod and hake. The livers were thrown into an open barrel to rot in the sun, the oil separated from the "gunk" and floated to the top. The oil was skimmed off and put in bottles from teddies, about a pint, to gallon jars.

> Fish was a good price during the First World War. Then, when the war was over, the bottom just dropped out of it.

One of the best days I ever spent was the time I picked Robbie Robertson up in Souris and we went "up country," as Robbie put it, to have a chinwag with his old fishing pal, Clive. They were both in their 90s and, between them, had

125 years of fishing under their belts. Robbie was born in 1904 and had 13 brothers and sisters. Their mother died in 1906 and some of the younger children were "farmed out to relatives." His father was a fisherman, and was known as Johnny Jim the Bear Killer because he shot at least 14 bears that were killing farmers' sheep with his trusty muzzle-loading musket. He'd fished the Grand Banks in a Lunenburg schooner and, like his father and brothers, Robbie spent decades at sea. "My father was strictly a fisherman and hunter. He wouldn't even set foot in the barn."

His sons did the farming, what little there was of it, since they were fishing out of dories like their father by the time they hit their teens. When we landed at his house, Clive invited us in. Before I had the tape recorder plugged in, he was off at a gallop leaving Robbie and me to catch up:

> **Clive:** Along the north shore after a bad storm, the farmers used to go down with a dung fork and a horse and cart, and fork the lobsters and cod and hake and herring into the cart and spread it on the land. There was that many fish, they'd get caught in the storm and get driven ashore. I sold hake to MacLeans, 40 puncheons of hake. I dried and salted them all. They were like shingles. I took them to MacLeans [Matthew and MacLeans General Store in Souris] and they only gave me $1.25 a quintal[1]- that's 112 pounds. We were paying $22 for 2,000 pounds of salt.

> **Robbie:** Yeah, they weigh about half from fresh to dried.

> **Clive:** We saved the livers all in a great big puncheon. With two plugs. Open the bottom plug and all the dross and water and blood came out. The oil came out the top plug. When we got 45 gallons of oil in a gasoline drum, we'd ship it to Halifax and that

---

1 A quintal was 112 lbs but only considered a hundredweight to allow for spoilage.

paid for our fishing boat's gasoline for the summer. To fish for a week, all it cost us was 24 cents with a four-horsepower Acadia engine. With the government tax rebate for inshore fishermen, a gallon of gas only cost six cents to run the one-cylinder gas engine; it only took four gallons a week to run the engine. That's 1926 or '27 all the way up until '39. Then we started getting bigger boats and bigger engines.

I remember one time in the 1930s, another fella was fishing with me and we got five cents for a haddock. The haddock weighed, I suppose, 10 pounds. You know what we did with that money? We couldn't cut the five cents in two, so we went up to the store and bought a chocolate bar and broke it in two. Now, that's how bad it was in the 1930s.

Robbie: I saw cod weigh up to 85 pounds, split. Heads and tails off, guts out, no backbone. Ready to salt.

Clive: Ray MacSweeney came into North Lake with 29 fish, codfish, the heads and tails off, that weighed one ton. I know you don't believe me but that's the truth. Guts and heads was off them. One ton of fish. I saw Jerome Chapman with three codfish, dried, and they just made the 112 pounds. The three codfish dried. Robbie knows that's the truth. If Robbie wasn't here, you'd think I was telling lies or romancin', but Robbie knows I'm telling the truth.

Robbie: You wouldn't tell lies.

Clive: It wouldn't do me any good.

Robbie: I wouldn't bring him over here if I thought you were going to tell him lies.

"Romancing," what a great expression. By the end of the afternoon, my head was spinning, full of stories from these two wonderful gentlemen.

I often wonder if Jessie Nicholson MacKinnon was romancin' when she told me this: "We always took cod liver oil and Scott's emulsion, that white stuff. Didn't taste too good. There was one guy in school, they called him 'Fish,' because they could smell the cod liver oil off him. It was coming right through his skin."

Another fine lad, from the same neck of the woods as Robbie and Clive, was Second World War veteran and fisherman Gus Gregory from Chepstow:

> The first cod liver oil that I remember was just rendered locally. It was in barrels and there were holes bored in the barrels, and all the old water and stuff would run out. There was an old fella by the name of Ryan from the north side, a great storyteller, and he noticed the rats in the fall were getting pretty well starved out down around the fish plant. But there was one rat that looked a lot better than the others. He was smarter and pretty good-looking, and Ryan wondered what he was living on, so he watched the rat late one evening and the rat backed his rear-end up to the cod liver oil barrel, shoved his tail in through the hole and swished it around and licked his tail. That's where he was getting his food – the oil out of the barrel. Knowing rats, it could be possible, but knowing Ryan and his stories... well, he was a great story-teller.

Clive might call him a romancer.

◆

Down in the southeastern corner of the Island, Jane Harris Fraser was born in 1912, the year the Titanic hit an iceberg and sank. Coincidentally, her uncle Tom Bartlett ran the

Cape Bear Marconi Station, set up to advise vessels of ice conditions in the Northumberland Strait. He was the first man in Canada to hear the Titanic's distress signal.

> I still have the poetry for Jordan's Emulsion somewhere: 'Jordan's Emulsion, sweet and pure, nature's ever ... I can't remember ... cure.' It was made by my old Uncle Ricky [Richard Jordan]. He was my great, great uncle. He was my great grandfather Edward Jordan's brother. They lived in High Bank for quite some years, and then I think they moved down to Guernsey Cove. It was made from cod liver oil, rendered, but I guess it was good.

In Whitman Daly's 1967 family memoir, he jokingly refers to Jordan's Emulsion: "Quite often, laughingly, people would quote, 'Jordan's Emulsion, sweet and pure, never fails to kill or cure.'"

The label on the bottle read:

> Richard Jordan's Emulsion sweet and pure,
>
> It never fails to cure.
>
> To Christians, it should not be given
>
> Who wish to die and go to heaven,
>
> But those who dread the other place
>
> May be restored in any case."

Catchy.

Also connected to Richard Jordan was Ada Baker MacKenzie, who was born in Beach Point on November 11, 1918, the day that the First World War ended. After the Second World War, Ada fished cod and hake with her husband, Chester. Her father was Stanley Baker and her mother was Phoebe, who had nine children, made bread twice a day, and sewed clothes out of the empty 98-lb flour bags:

> Mum was a Penny, one of William Penny's daughters.

There was nine or ten in their family. Hedley Penny was her brother. Uncle Hedley. They had 15 children, Aunt Lottie and Uncle Hedley. He had a lobster factory most of his life, out on the Back Shore they used to call it, out where the brook runs out before you come to the Cape [Bear]. Different ones had factories there. And then Hedley moved, and put his factory here [Beach Point] in either 1927 or '28. He rendered cod liver oil down here and shipped it, and then they got a chemical that they put in it after they dumped the cod liver in the barrels, and it would render the livers without you doing it – cooking – by fire.

There was a fella, Horey White, who lived up along the shore, where the graveyard is, up above that, he always rendered his by fire, and sold it. There was good sales for it, a lot of people gave it to their horse, racehorses, in the winter, and it was shipped away besides because it was done up clean.

Not that it matters, but when they dismantled the Cape Bear Marconi Radio Station, Hedley Penny bought two parts of the three-section steel tower for masts on his schooners. The third mast wound up in Beach Point where Chester MacKenzie – when he wasn't out fishing – would shimmy up to hang a warning flag off the top when a storm was approaching.

Ada will get back to Uncle Ricky eventually:

I took Scott's Emulsion. We used to buy that in the stores. There was a man on the back of the bottle with a big codfish on his back. Oh, that was good. It had a peppermint flavour, teaberry-like[2]. I said peppermint but it was teaberry. Wintergreen, I guess, is what they had in it.

Richard Jordan made his emulsion down here at

---

2   Teaberry is an evergreen used for flavoring and tastes like wintergreen. It was used by east coast Indigenous Peoples to treat back pains, rheumatism, fever, headaches, and to reduce bleeding from cuts.

Beach Point and then he'd go around selling it. Chester said every day he went down to visit, and Richard would give him a spoonful of his emulsion. The livers were cooked right fresh, and the oil taken off, and then cream and eggs and wintergreen flavouring went into it. One time, Chester picked teaberries or teaberry leaves, but they weren't a strong enough flavour for Richard. It was thickened and flavoured, sweetened. Chester said there was cream in it, and it was good he said. But nobody ever asked. His grandson, I guess, Elmer Stewart, used to go down, and he'd be making it sometimes with Richard. Nobody knows what happened to the recipe.

Chester MacKenzie was born in 1912 and Richard Jordan was married to Chester's grandmother.

I'll tell you the story of how Chester's grandmother married him. Richard went with her years ago. She used to come over here to visit up in Gladstone. She married a man called Barrass and they went over to the Eastern Shore (Nova Scotia) to live and she had seven daughters. When her husband died, Richard wrote to her and asked if she'd be interested in seeing him again. His wife was dead then, too. And she said, 'Old flames are easily kindled.' So, they got married in the end. Willard, that's Richard's son, she was an awful good mother to them. He used to see Chester and me, and he couldn't praise her up enough.

So, the fella she was married to made the emulsion. Oh, he made a lot of emulsion. He had his little place he made it in, and he made it for years, and peddled up through the country, horse and wagon. It was 50 cents for a little bottle. The bottle was made to look like Scott's Emulsion. The same as that.

The Scott's Emulsion bottle had a fisherman with a five-foot codfish engraved on it. The label listed its "active ingredient" as cod liver oil and stated it was "four times easier to digest then cod liver oil." It was concocted by Samuel Bowne of

Scott and Bowne, a pharmaceutical company based in New York City. Like Jordan's Emulsion, it was sweetened and flavoured, and preferred over plain, and sometimes rancid, cod liver oil. Even so, many people, children especially, still found it hard to swallow.

> Scott's Emulsion-cod liver oil: when I was really small, we didn't have a fridge, so we put it between the storm window and the inside window, and that kept it really chilled.

Bernice Delory was born in Georgetown, and named for her aunt who was a nun. Her mum, Cecilia Cullen, grew up on a farm in Sherwood near what became, in 1940, a Second World War Royal Air Force base, and, eventually, the Charlottetown airport. Her grandmother Cullen [née Landrigan] died in 1918 of the Spanish flu. Bernice worked for the Red Cross and taught swimming at the St. Vincent de Paul Orphanage, the Catholic orphanage across from St Dunstan's University in Charlottetown. The women who attended St. Dunstan's had their residence in the orphanage, which was another way Bernice got to know the children as well as she did because she played with them every night.

> There's a funny story about Scott's Emulsion: I was working at the orphanage in Charlottetown. At that time, there was well over 100 children. At meals, the tables sat six and some tables sat eight, and I'd go down and eat with the children. But the Sisters ate in their own dining room. When I'd go down, the kids would say, 'Sit with us. Sit with us.' So finally one day, one Sister asked me, 'What are you doing that they all want you to sit with them?' Nothing, I said.
>
> She said, 'Are you telling them stories?'
>
> Oh no no no.
>
> 'Are you giving them anything?'

42

Oh no no no.

What I was doing was drinking their Scott's Emul-sion for that day. They hated it and I didn't mind it. So, I'd go to a different table — there was at least 12 tables — so I figured they'd only miss the Scott's Emulsion one day out of 12.

It might be a stretch to call cod liver oil and the two emulsions "tonics."

They'd pull the bark off a wild cherry tree and boil that, and give it to you. And talk for a bitter taste. But it cleaned your blood up good. Sulphur'd clean your blood, too.

Boswell Robertson explaining the spring tonics he took as a kid on Munns Road. A daily dose of sulphur and molasses for a week was the go-to tonic for most families, like siblings Marjorie and Harry Heffell from Travellers Rest:

You could shake your socks over the stove and the sparks would be flying up! The sulphur would go through your system, and you could take your un-derwear, on a cold winter's night, shake your shirt-tail, shall we say, over the stove and the sparks would hop and jump.

Sulphur also had a nasty habit of going "through your sys-tem" in other ways too. One former schoolteacher told me the stink in the one-roomed schools during tonic season was one reason for the introduction of March break. She may have been romancin' me, but I don't think Janie Llewellyn MacQuarrie ever told a lie. Janie was born 1917, and lived in Georgetown almost her entire life. Her dad, Chester, ran lobster factories in Georgetown and Boughtan Island, and her mum was the former Lauretta Blackette. Her grandfa-ther ran a mill and her grandmother was a dressmaker and seamstress. Two of Janie's aunts were milliners not far from Peter Morrison's tailor shop on Water Street in Georgetown:

Right next to the big house that my grandmother

had for a seamstress shop. Men's suits, with the vests and everything. I can see Peter yet sitting in the window where he seemed to do an awful lot of stitching by hand. Basting. I could tell you a comical story, but I better not tell you it... OK. Peter Morrison. I'd be about nine years old and I was going uptown, and he said, 'Come here, girlie. Come here, girlie.'

So I went over, and he said, 'Now will you go to the drugstore for me.'

I said, 'Yes.'

He said, 'I'll give you ten cents if you go up to the drugstore and get me a bottle of Beef, Iron and Wine.'

Prohibition was in force in 1926. Georgetown did have one of the half dozen provincial liquor vendors, but you needed a doctor's prescription or a "script" for bad nerves to buy any liquor. Beef, Iron and Wine was made by McKesson and Robbins of New York City, who touted it as "a nutritious tonic." It was 20 percent ethyl alcohol, plus a percentage of sherry, advertised as a pick-me-up, a remedy for loss of appetite, and to treat the myriad of diseases people were subject to before inoculations: smallpox, diphtheria, polio, scarlet fever, and perhaps worst of all, tuberculosis − TB − the wasting disease.

Well, I didn't know the difference. I thought it was tonic. That's what people took in those days. In a sense it was a tonic, I guess, if it was used properly. And he said, 'If they ask you who it's for, you say it's for your mother.'

I pondered that quite a bit as I walked along. I was scared of getting into trouble. Why say it's for my mum? Seymour Knight was the druggist, and he was a pretty stern old fella, and he had bushy eyebrows. His glasses were at the end of his nose, and he squinted, and he gave me a hard look, and he asked, 'Who's it for?'

I said, 'Peter Morrison.'

And he said, 'You go back and tell him he'll get no beef, iron and wine up here.'

So I go back and said, 'He wouldn't give it to me.'

And Peter shouted, 'You didn't say it was for your mother. And you won't get any ten cents.'

Like I said, even at the age of nine, no romancin' from Janie. When she grew up, she married a minister.

Uncle Ben's Converted Blueberries

Murray River Wharf

"I remember the first time I went to Murray River.

I had a lard bucket full of blueberries."

From pies to wine, one of the Maritimes oldest and sweetest crops is the versatile blueberry. Blueberries are a double-whammy super-food: they not only taste good but also are good for us. But in 1917, Milton Buell wasn't thinking about any of this when he ventured three miles/five kilometres down the road from his boyhood home in Abney to the booming metropolis of Murray River:

> We'd be lugging blueberries - they used to buy blueberries in season. It's great blueberry country through there and we'd pick buckets of them. Heck, yes. You know, I had never been to Murray River before. And all those wires overhead, the telephone wires, and the big buildings so close together, I felt quite nervous. And all those wires were singing, kind of humming, you know, I thought it was quite

a thing. I remember I got a couple of scribblers and some slate pencils, and I guess I must have got some candy, all for this bucket of blueberries. I'd be about 10 then, I suppose.

Don't laugh. I did at first, but then I checked out Murray River 90 years ago: CNR railway station, and next door, the railway hotel run by the White family; a livery stable; several general stores, including D.A. McLeod's with schooners tied up at its wharf; a blacksmith shop; a lobster cannery; a sawmill; a movie theatre and bowling alley; and a sleigh-and-carriage-maker. Plus, the legendary Dr. Lester Brehaut lived there, not to mention all those telephones making the wires hum like sirens, luring young fruit-pickers into the urban squalor.

Blueberries lower blood sugar levels and are one of Mother Nature's antioxidants. When I told my brother that, he demanded to know why Mom Nature didn't like oxen. He works in the woods and eats a lot of blueberries, so obviously they're not a brain food, like fish, according to my mother. Thinking back, she may have been pushing fried smelts on us so she could have all the blueberries. So maybe they are a brain food.

Many general stores bought blueberries and shipped them either off-Island or to Mount Stewart for processing. Father and son Russell and Keir Clark also ran a big general store in Mount Stewart and had blueberries shipped in by train from villages up and down the line. Getting the delicate blueberries to market was a challenge in the days of horse and wagon. I found this entry in a diary written in 1900: "The roads weren't paved and the truck wagons didn't have springs. You could follow the path of a wagon-load of blueberries by the trail of juice left behind on especially rough roads." To paraphrase Dorothy, in *The Wizard of Oz*, the route to fame and riches is to follow the blue-clay road.

Back in the 1910s, Andrew Murnaghan worked in a general

store that bought blueberries. Andrew was from Donagh back when the Fort Augustus area had two wharves, a flour mill, a woolen mill, and two blacksmiths. There was a beautiful brick church and rectory, adjacent to a large graveyard in case anyone kicked the bucket:

> There was an old woman named Bridgette Cumminsky down here. They used to burn the fields around here every five years to make the berries grow. And this one year, there was a helluva crop and she came out one night with two big buckets, five or six gallons of blueberries. She came in the back way and set the berries out in the warehouse. I was tending to somebody and I needed something out in the warehouse. There was no electricity, and all I had was a lantern, and it wasn't lit. I ran out and I tripped over the two buckets of berries. They went flying everywhere. Says she, 'Ya did it now!' She was sitting near the stove and she heard the buckets go. 'Ya did it now,' she says. Her and I gathered them up afterwards. The floor wasn't that dirty. See, they'd be washed anyway wherever they went.

Washed or unwashed, Bridgette was paid three cents a pound for berries whereas Johnny Chuck MacAdam further east in Canavoy, was only paid a-cent-and-a-half a pound. In August 1932, Walter O'Brien wrote in his "Bristol Notes" column of the Charlottetown *Evening Patriot:*

> Blueberries are reported to be very scarce here and the price paid the pickers is 1 cent cash per pound or 1 ½ cents per pound in exchange for goods. Pickers are discouraged as an ordinary water pail full of blueberries is only worth about 15 cents. Three years ago, blueberries were worth 5-6 cents per pound and pickers could make a few dollars each day and lay in a supply of flour for the winter.

◆

In 1904, my old pal Robbie Robertson was born on the Snake Road in Kingsboro. His mother Lydia had 14 children, and when Robbie was only two years old, she died suddenly. Robbie's father, Johnny Jim the Bear Killer, so-named for his bear-shooting skills, was primarily a fisher. Cod prices back then mirrored blueberry prices: a cent to a cent and a half per pound. The family didn't even own a cow. However, they did make their own cod liver oil by rendering cod and hake livers in a 20-gallon wooden barrel, and the children picked potatoes for neighbouring farmers for 50 cents a day. And, when in season, everyone headed to the blueberry patch.

> We went pickin', my brother and I, and one fella, we had to pass by his house coming home. We had a bucket of blueberries and he came out and looked at them: 'Oh, lovely blueberries,' and offered us a fairly good price for them, but he didn't have the money just then. When we got home, we told everyone we'd sold our blueberries to this fella who didn't have the money. They laughed. They knew he never paid for too much. We're still owed, plus a good lot of interest on those blueberries now. I believe it was 50 cents he offered for the bucket. It was a good price anyway. He could have offered a dollar just the same, because he wasn't going to pay.

Live and learn. Blueberries don't mend broken promises, but they were credited with some medicinal qualities. The Mi'kmaq pressed blueberries into a round "biscuit" that they dried in the sun and stored in birch-bark boxes for the long winter ahead, and used the berries to treat tuberculosis. The leaves and roots were boiled up into a tonic used to treat rheumatism, a treatment apparently still practised. In September 2008 on CBC's *Maritime Noon* radio show, one call-in topic was rheumatism. A Nova Scotia woman called in to report that six years earlier, a 90-year-old friend of hers started steeping fall-picked blueberry leaves into a tea. Her friend drank half a cup every day, claimed it tasted great, and the 96-year-old had no rheumatism at all.

♦

> I love blueberries and, on our road, you could pull them down like you'd milk a cow: just hanging.

Notwithstanding her unusual metaphor, Roma Curley Mulligan from Freetown loved her blueberries and knew the best places to pick them.

> This lady from Emerald had a big family, and they used to come and fill a factory milk can full of berries. Now you can't find blueberries to pick, and you pay an awful price in the store. They're not the blueberries we used to pick along the railway track. And when you got enough for yourself, you'd sell them for a dollar a bucket. A milk bucket. And a dollar-a-bucket for strawberries or raspberries too.

Roma mentioned the "factory milk can," a reference to the 80- and 100-pound cans used to ship milk and cream to the butter and cheese factories that once dotted the Island. Roma was born in 1917. She told me that when she was a young girl, she could go to a hayfield and pick a bucket of *wild* strawberries in no time. I emphasize the word "wild," those tiny succulent strawberries, which, as she proclaimed, "made the jam of jams." Now the jam of jams is the 8:00 am traffic on North River Road.

The western end of Prince Edward Island is also prime blueberry country. Stompin' Tom Connors, who grew up in Nail Pond, included in his album *Stompin' Tom: Unreleased Songs from the Vault Collection,* a cover version of "Blueberry Hill," the song made famous by rock and roll legend Fats Domino. If you call it up on YouTube, make sure you first cram a blueberry in each ear. It's terrible. On the other hand, we can be thankful Fats didn't sing a cover version of "Bud the Spud."

Now where were we... oh yes, up west. Ralph Cooke was born in Cape Wolfe, and had 10 siblings. Their father took the adage "idle hands are the devil's playthings" seriously, and insisted the children should always be busy, especially on Sundays.

> On Sunday, when the blueberries were on, we'd walk from our place at the shore a way back into the woods – it'd be about three miles – and we picked blueberries all day. We'd take cardboard boxes, and put them under a tree, and we had dishes to fill them, and we'd pick hundreds and hundreds of pounds of berries. I don't know if any of them ever came out of the woods. Left there to rot. We'd carry what we could out, but the reason for picking them? Working. Working. He didn't believe in us just laying around. We were glad when we got old enough to get out of that.

No doubt. I remarked to Ralph it was an odd philosophy, counter-intuitive to how many Presbyterian families observed the Sabbath. Work and play of any kind was prohibited at least until sunset on Sunday: the stove wasn't lit, water wasn't hauled, and only the livestock was fed. And blueberries remained unpicked.

◆

Ben Clow would have put those abandoned blueberries to work, "work" as in ferment. At the turn of the last century, Ben ran a big general store in Murray Harbour North and, in his spare time, crafted his own wine. Roy Clow loved to visit his favorite uncle:

> Oh, God, yes. He was a big, big man, square-built man, about six-foot-four, and he'd weigh about 300 pounds. He was good on his feet too, light on his feet, and he loved his booze... In blueberry time, he bought blueberries from all the ladies out in the

country and he shipped them to Charlottetown. Even when he was getting to be an old man, he had one of those whisky kegs, a 45-gallon keg – a hogshead they called it – and he'd buy 30 pounds of blueberries. He'd dump them in the keg, and he'd add 20 pounds of sugar in on top of them, scatter it around, and put in a box of yeast cakes.

Here's where lightness of foot and liking of booze coincide:

He'd take his boots and socks off, and get a bucket of water and he'd wash his feet right clean, and he'd get in the barrel and he'd walk around and around and around in the barrel. He'd smash the blueberries all to pieces with his bare feet. I'd seen him doing that, around and around, and he was laughing to kill himself. He'd cover that up with a piece of rubber oilcloth, and set it in the sun and leave that for 30 days. He wouldn't touch it, and then after 30 days he'd take a glass of it and HOLY OLD. You talk about strong. Blueberry wine. When I was only a little fella, he gave me a glass and it set me drunk. I was as drunk as hell when I went home. And Ben got drunk on that every day, and his wife used to threaten to dump it out, but she was a small little woman. He put it up in the old store where she couldn't get at it.

In hindsight, Ralph Cooke's father may have been right. But you never know, Uncle Ben's Converted Blueberries may have contributed to his long life. Some people claim blueberry pie is a cure for hangovers, so maybe you can have your wine and eat it too. A hair of the dog. Now, where's that box of yeast cakes?

Jim MacAuley 1st WW veteran

I remember the day the First World War was declared. We lived on a farm, and my father went to Charlottetown that particular day, horse and wagon. You didn't have a telephone. You didn't have a radio. There was no communication, and Mother and I were getting the cattle in the field, and my mother said, 'Here comes Chester down to meet us. There must be something wrong.' When he came down, he told Mother that war had been declared that day.

Ella Willis' memory of July 28, 1914. She was four years old at the time, living on the family farm in Hampshire, ten miles west of Charlottetown where telephones and the outside world rarely intruded. Yet, the war didn't take long to enter their lives in a very personal way. Her first cousin John Sanderson had signed up to fight overseas. After he'd completed his training, he shyly, yet proudly dropped by for a visit in his uniform.

I remember the day he went to war. He came up to say good-bye to my mother. He was dressed in khaki and was on horseback. That was in 1916, the last time anyone saw him.

John was 19 when he was shipped overseas.

He was killed two weeks before Armistice. That was quite a tragedy in our family. I remember that very clearly. I was in school at the time and, strange as it may seem, it was the practice of the day when they got the word of a death, they came to the school and took me home. He had been brought up with my grandparents and was sort of like an uncle to me.

That same year, 1918, Ella's neighbour bought a Model-T Ford and, after church one Sunday, offered to take her family for a tour. They packed a picnic and headed for Borden, a daunting 40-kilometre journey, with hopes of seeing the German prisoners of war rumoured to be working at the new ferry terminal. The men were German nationals whose ships had been seized at the outbreak of war. Hundreds worked on the mainland in the vast hay and vegetable farms in the Tantramar Marsh between Amherst and Sackville. Several hundred had been sent to PEI to reroute the rail line running between Cape Traverse and Summerside to Borden. The POWs marched out of Summerside every morning where they were bunked down in the ice rink. Another 40 or 50 were bivouacked in the rink at Borden. The day was a success, and Ella's Mum managed to get a photo of the prisoners as they worked on the ferry wharf at Borden, little knowing a German thousands of miles away would eventually kill her nephew.

◆

Josephine MacIsaac was born in Orwell in 1894, and was 20 when the war broke out. Her brother Walter marched off to war and, like other sisters across Canada, Josephine sent him letters and newspapers and little treats from home.

> We sent parcels. You'd send underwear, cookies and fruitcake. They used to love to get a parcel from home. There was always a crowd around ready to grab.

Four long years later, Walter returned, one of the lucky ones. However, war has a way of changing things, and nothing would ever be the same again.

> He was struck with shrapnel and he couldn't stay home on PEI because he was choked up and he'd smother, so he had to go out west. Mustard gas. He was a teacher; he taught school out west. There were a lot of boys from Orwell and Earnscliffe who went off. They all didn't come back, no. There was a young Praught man, a lovely looking fella. He wasn't away very long. They said he cried all the way over. He decided that was his last and he was killed. And there was a MacDonald fella from Cherry Valley, up at Cherry Valley corner. He was killed too. It's hard, those wars, isn't it?

Walter had been mustard-gassed, one of thousands of young men whose lungs were blistered and melted by the silent killer. Dozens of returning Island veterans, hoping they'd be able to breathe easier, headed for the drier climate of the prairies.

◆

William Stewart knew first-hand what being gassed was like. William was born on a Southport farm in 1898. At 17, he joined the 8th Canadian Siege battery, "The Happy Eighth," as a gunner. His memory faded in and out after a mustard gas attack overwhelmed his battalion.

> They hit us with mustard gas about the 29th of July

in '17. We were gassed during the night. The reason it was called mustard gas was because there was an odour of mustard from it. Wherever that hit and splashed on the walls, we found out afterward [that] it would take 48 hours before it deteriorated and evaporated into the air. Your eyes started to water; then we became blind. Then it hit your chest and then your stomach. You threw up even the lining of your stomach. There were trainloads. The French trains, instead of a whistle, had like a 'toot toot.' I can still hear in a semi-conscious state the 'toot toot toot' and then the rattle of the fast train. The tracks were all cleared for the ambulance trains. I don't know how many cars. It was a bad time. I can still remember an odd time becoming conscious and hearing the train passing over the switches and then the 'toot toot toot.' I can still hear that in my dreams now. I don't know how many thousands, but there were tremendous casualties.

William was one of at least a 1.5 million soldiers gassed with phosgene, chlorine, or mustard gas in the First World War. Over 90,000 soldiers died this way, even though the use of chemical weapons had been outlawed and was considered a war crime. Mustard gas blistered the moist parts of the body: armpits, eyes, skin, lungs.

William had been gassed immediately after the Third Battle of Ypres. His ambulance train reached the French coast and his next memory was being at sea on a boat.

I remember distinctly I was loaded on a beautiful yacht that some British millionaire owned, turned it over for the use of the armed forces, and it was turned into a hospital ship. I can remember an orderly asking me if I smoked. I said, 'Heck, man, not now.' He said, 'Do you smoke?' Well, I used to smoke a pipe once in a while. Every man that was a casualty on that boat, if he smoked a pipe was given a pipe; if it was cigarettes, he was given a carton of cigarettes by the man who owned that ship. So I really travelled back to England in style although I didn't realize it.

Doctors in England were stymied by this vicious new form of warfare. Soldiers filled the hospital wards, their heads wrapped in bandages, struggling with every breath.

> I went to a hospital in Southampton in the southern part of England. It was practically all gas casualties. For pretty near two weeks, I was semi-conscious and more or less blind. But I woke up one morning and the nurse was bending over me. I said, 'Good morning beautiful.' She said, 'Gunner, I don't believe you can see me, can you?' I said, 'Sure I can.' She disappeared and inside three or four minutes back came four or five doctors and two or three other nurses. I was the first one to get my eyes open. They thought we were all going to be blinded. So, I got one peep at that little nurse and she really did look beautiful.

You'd think William's war was over. Although he never took a breath without wheezing again, he recovered enough to be sent back into battle. He had already fought at Vimy Ridge, proudly quoting Canadian General Sir Arthur Currie, who supposedly said after the successful assault: "Canadians die. They do not retreat." William made it back to PEI, and eventually wrote his memoirs of the war.

Speaking about the French ambulance trains, William said he went looking for his wounded brother. He found him more dead than alive, buried under a mound of soldiers in one of the boxcars at the back of the train that was used to haul the dead from the front lines. His brother had been wounded in the spine by shrapnel. He suffered for five miserable years before finally succumbing to his wounds in a Charlottetown hospital. William was always haunted by the thought that his brother might have been better off if he'd left him to die in that boxcar.

The First World War was supposed to be, as U.S. President Woodrow Wilson proclaimed "the war to end all wars."

That quote is used ironically now, but after a four-year bloodbath for a few muddy acres in Flanders, with 20 million dead and 21 million more wounded, who would have thought that within 20 years, a generation, another world war would break out.

Jim MacAuley was a "century baby," born in 1900. His mother died in childbirth, and Jim was often left at the Catholic orphanage in Charlottetown while his father went off fishing cod and hake for weeks, sometimes months, at a time. He hated the orphanage where twice a week the children went from door-to-door asking for pennies or bread. Jim never knew when or if his father would return to reclaim him, so when the First World War broke out young Jim seized the chance to see the world and leave his old life behind. He was turned down by the medical officer in 1914, but returned wearing his first pair of dungarees the next year and joined the army. He spent three years fighting Germans in trenches across Belgium, hiding in bombed-out cellars, wrapping his arms and legs at night to ward off the rats. The soldiers were almost feral, living on rabbits and bully beef with brief excursions behind the lines to rest up and drink cheap French wine. Quite an experience for a teenager.

He also survived mustard gas, and said the first airplane he ever saw flew low to drop bombs on him. However, an airplane he saw in 1918, on the 11th of November, was different.

> We were guarding this big house and a white plane came over, a German plane, white, at twelve o'clock. It landed and they walked into this place we were guarding and they stayed in it for three or four hours. They came out in the evening shouting, 'The war is over! The war is over!' Well, I guess we cried. God, I was excited. Going to go home some day. The eleventh day of the eleventh month. Yep. Nice day over there, yeah. We got all excited when they came out and shouted, 'War is over everybody! The

war is over!' And bugles, big bugles! We just settled down then. We were out of sleep so we just slept and washed our clothes. We had a great time then. They said, 'You're going home, you're going home.'

And home, it was, back to Stanhope, back to early mornings on the water hauling cod lines. The silence must have been overwhelming after years of pandemonium and endless bombardment. Jim and his father sold their fish at the old market square in downtown Charlottetown where the Confederation Centre now squats. On that first Armistice Day, while Jim was washing the mud from his uniform, the world was celebrating peace at last.

♦

I remember them burning the Kaiser up in market square... a dummy Kaiser they burned at the end of the war, and the big celebration they had with the big bonfire. A big stuffed dummy they had hanging on a rope, and they set him on fire.

Gordon Stewart was five years old when he saw the Kaiser go up in smoke, a few feet from where, a few months later, Jim MacAuley would be selling his fresh cod for three cents a pound. Gordon said he never forgot that day. Interestingly, he later joined the Charlottetown fire department and was fire chief for over 20 years.

Across the Island, ships in harbours blasted their horns and steam engines blew their whistles. A few miles up the Hillsborough River, Mildred Thompson was busy in the fields on the family farm in Marshfield.

The final day of the First World War was the most beautiful day in the fall. The turnips had to come in and you loaded them in a cart in those days. And we heard the whistles all the way from Charlottetown following the river. Oh, the sounds. So, it wasn't long until our own factory, the butter factory, started. He didn't have enough steam on, but boy, was he whistling his pipe.

Mildred and her Grammie had been sending care packages to cousins and nephews fighting overseas. The soldiers returned. Life went back to normal. For men like Jim MacAuley and William Stewart, the memories never faded.

"Back Again From Hell": Spanish Flu

Evelyn Shaw MacFarlane,
born 1906 Desable PEI

I'm back again from hell...
secrets of death to tell;
and horrors from the abyss."

—Siegfried Sassoon, "To the War-Mongers"

With the signing of the Armistice on November 11, 1918, the First World War was supposed to be the end of the dying. Instead, returning soldiers inadvertently helped spread an incredibly contagious flu.

The Spanish flu: that was when the first bunches of soldiers came back from France. Vimy Ridge and Passchendaele, the epidemic broke out there. And that was the winter the Spanish Flu broke out here in Pictou County.

Flo Arbuckle from Ponds in eastern Pictou County was 18 when her family was struck by the Spanish Flu. Across the Strait in DeSable, PEI, Evelyn MacFarlane, born in 1906, was a 'flu survivor who also noticed the correlation between the returned men and the arrival of the flu.

We had the flu. All of us. They were coming home from the war, and my uncle and my cousin came home. Mother and Dad were both in bed. My cousin,

61

who'd come home from the war, came up to look after the horses and cows in the stable, and my uncle, who lived over the road, came at night to see if we were all right. But he wouldn't come in the house. He'd just come to the window.

At least three people in French River died of the Spanish Flu. Yet, every day for months, Mary Lisa Duggan put her life on the line attending to the sick and bedridden. She cooked food, washed bedclothes, and emptied her neighbour's chamber pots. She never caught the flu. Across the Island farmers milked and fed their neighbour's cows twice a day. Crops in danger of rotting in the fields were harvested, while the afflicted lay propped up in bed, propped up to drain the fluid from sodden lungs threatening to drown them.

Ada Arbuckle, my cousin, she took the flu. She was about 19 years old and she didn't walk for a year even after she got better. It was that bad, it just withered your muscles. It was terrible. Three or four young people I knew around here died. The schools were closed, and the doctors in New Glasgow were busy going to houses. And the hospital was full, and the doctors were that busy, they couldn't come out to the country. They hadn't time. They had patients there to attend to, going from one to the other. People were dying. Oh, it was awful.

It's now more than 100 years since the world's worst pandemic to date came roaring in hard on the heels of the First World War. The Spanish Influenza outbreak began in 1918 as the war, which had claimed millions of lives was grinding to a halt, and continued claiming lives into the winter and spring of 1919. Not all countries kept records of citizens who had died from the flu, which was estimated at 60 million world-wide. It became known as the Spanish Flu, because Spain did keep records, so it appeared, on paper, at least, that the 'flu had originated there.

But it spread like wildfire, even to tiny hamlets like Ponds in rural Pictou County.

> My brother Edison took it, but he survived. I was 18 and I took the 'flu in the old farmhouse on the hill. Edison and Papa put me to bed in a little bedroom off the kitchen, and they kept the fires going with hardwood all night long to keep the house warm. I had such a fever I didn't know nothing. I must have had pneumonia. No antibiotics then. They were giving me all manner of hot drinks, hot lemon, and rubbed me with Rawleigh's Liniment. They would put Vaseline on me first, then put the liniment on and put a hot flannel on top. I was all choked up and I could spit the stuff up. I had no appetite to eat; they had to feed me with a spoon I was so helpless.

Young people like Flo Turner seemed especially susceptible to the ravages of the flu. People developed pneumonia, their lungs filled with phlegm and fluid, and they literally drowned. Newspapers advertised various cures, and one, Vicks VapoRub was originally a home remedy, but was now in mass production and in such demand that supplies had to be rationed. People were so desperate to treat Spanish Flu's raging fever, they dusted off the old home remedies: mustard plasters, salt-herring on the feet and neck, a drop of kerosene on a sugar cube. Evelyn MacFarlane grew up believing the adage "feed a cold, starve a fever."

> The rest of them all had it before I did. You weren't to eat anything, any solid food, that's what the doctor said. But they thought that I was getting better and Mother gave me a biscuit to eat. In no time, I was just blazing, my face was so red. My father got the 'flu when he went to a cattle sale, and he stood in the door to ask if he could put the horse in the barn. They say it was the worst place to be, in the doorway, just asking if he could put the horse in the barn.

> The doctor used to smoke when he'd come in.

Smoked a pipe all the time he'd be in the house. I guess that was to keep the germs away.

Other 'flu survivors told similar stories about doctors furiously puffing away on their pipes as they tended to their patients. Other home remedies were unique, like the one practised by Cora Ferguson's Hampton, PEI, neighbours.

One family – the man grew garlic and they all chewed up on garlic. And none of them in that family died with the flu. They say there was nothing better than the garlic.

Kathryn MacQuarrie's father, further along the Hampton shore, had an unusual and perhaps tastier method than chewing garlic to keep the Spanish Flu germs at bay.

He liked what they used to call a 'snort.' At that time, you couldn't get alcohol – rum or whisky or anything – without a doctor's script. My father and the doctor were very good friends so he could get a script. If you couldn't get scripts, of course, moonshine was available. I can remember one fellow who thought he was taking the 'flu – that deadly flu, the Spanish 'flu – and he went and got a bottle of moonshine and he drank it, and came in the house and flopped on the floor, and the next day he was fine. So, the moonshine cured his flu. That's right, it did. I think Robbie Burns said something about how good a drink was for certain things.

In fact, he did. Here's a few lines from "Tam O 'Shanter":

Inspiring bold John Barleycorn!

What dangers thou can'st make us scorn!

Wi' tippeny, we fear nae evil;

Wi' *usquabae,* we'll face the devil![3]

"John Barleycorn," according to Webster's dictionary, is

---

3   www.poetryfoundation.org/poems/43815/tam-o-shanter

"alcoholic liquor personified" and "*usquabae*" is Gaelic for "water of life," better known now as whisky.

Living in a teetotal house, 18-year-old Flo Turner wasn't counting on a shot of shine to cut her fever.

> I got out of bed as far as the first door and I fell on the floor. My brother Edison picked me up and took me back and put me to bed. [He] covered me up and just as he was going out the door, he looked back at me and my nose was bleeding. He turned around and grabbed a towel, and my nose bled, and it bled, and it bled, until it soaked the towel. I bled until I was pale.

Perhaps as many as 400 Islanders died of the Spanish flu. In 1918, the Charlottetown Patriot reported that Dr. Stewart in Georgetown caught the 'flu while attending to the sick. He was dead in three days. In Toronto, a thousand people died of the 'flu in one month; in Philadelphia, 711 died in one day. Gravediggers couldn't keep pace. In November 1918, Arnold McGrath's father who was the sexton at St. Peters Roman Catholic church in Seven Mile Bay, PEI, dug a grave for a Canadian soldier who had died of the 'flu while guarding German prisoners of war in Borden. However, before he could be interred, the soldier's family had the body sent home for burial, but, as Arnold noted, "Luckily a woman died of the 'flu that night so the grave wasn't wasted."

The Spanish Flu knew no borders: India, China, Russia. A quarter of the population in Britain caught the 'flu and hundreds of thousands died. Vincente Elordieta who was born in Liverpool, England, in 1908, was ten years old when the 'flu struck his end of town, the Merseyside docks, an area still reeling from four long years of the First World War.

> They called it the Spanish Flu but we Spanish Basques called it the English Flu. Oh gosh, there were lots of people dying all over the place with it. My aunt died of the flu, and why we never caught

the flu, I'll never know. She used to cough and spit into a spittoon. The city wouldn't allow us to keep her in the house, because there was so many of us. But that's where my aunt died. It was awful.

"Pauper" is an uncommon word these days. When Vincente was growing up in the Liverpool docks, people's lives were cut short by the double-edged sword of poverty and the onslaught of disease.

TB was another bad thing. It was a terrible thing to be buried as a pauper. This Basque woman from up Park Lane was collecting money to buy a coffin for her ten-year-old daughter who'd died. We had some money, so we gave her half of it to buy this coffin to bury her child in. The Delaneys, Henry, he died, and they had him laid out in the corner of the room. The rest of the family was sitting and cooking and eating and so on. They couldn't bury him, no money and the city corporation said if you don't bury him by tomorrow, they'd take him and bury him. So, his mother and his sister and others went up to the cemetery, Anfield Cemetery, in a streetcar. Cost a penny to get there. They put his coffin in a cart, and put him in a pauper's grave. Henry Delaney. Oh, the poverty! It was nothing to see three or four kids pushing an old baby carriage with a casket on top down the streets. A coffin, a plain wooden coffin.

Dehumanizing misery lurked around every corner. Peters Road, PEI, was hit hard especially by the Spanish Flu. Jim MacLean remembered how the 'flu tore apart the social fabric of the community. Mourners followed behind the horse-drawn hearse from a safe distance and didn't enter the church, but stood outside and sang hymns from there. One man refused to talk to his neighbours and boarded up his doors. He climbed a ladder to enter and exit his house. He was dead three days later.

It may be he shall take my hand

And lead me into his dark land

And close my eyes and quench my breath—

It may be I shall pass him still.

I have a rendezvous with death.[4]

We left Flo Turner with a nose bleed saturating a towel.

They called the doctor, Michael MacDonald in New Glasgow, and asked what could they do, and he said to put cold cloths across her face and on the back of her neck. Ice-cold cloths. He said the nosebleed might save her life. And it must have, because I got better. The fever went down when my nose bled, and I knew everything that was going on. Before, there were times when I didn't know nothing. It was the high fever I had. So, I must have been tough.

That's an understatement. I interviewed Flo several times; the last time was when she was 95. She had just recovered from a bout with the 'flu that had dragged on for days. Her daughter had taken her to outpatients at the Aberdeen Hospital in New Glasgow. Flo was dehydrated and very weak, so they kept her in overnight. It was her first time in a hospital. Ever. She was feeling much better and complained, "I had the Spanish Flu when I was 18, and here we are all these years later, and I caught that damn 'flu again!"

Just as she had in 1918, Flo bounced back. When I drove by a week later, she was up on her porch roof repairing the shingles.

---

4   Alan Seeger, "I Have a Rendezvous with Death," Poems, New York: Charles Scribner's Sons (1917).

Frank Woodside, Summerside

The name of the man was Phil the Barber and he had electric lights strung up over the ice, a big patch of ice that he kept clean and flooded, and that's where we played hockey and skated. It cost ten cents.

Frank Woodside was born in 1910 and grew up in Summerside. His father Albert had a blacksmith shop on Queen's Wharf next to Phil the Barber Gallant's harbour rink:

When I was about eight or nine, my father made me a pair of skates in the blacksmith shop. He was always busy because he was a good blacksmith. People who knew him in the country, they'd land there and he could shoe a horse in 13 minutes. Take off the shoes and point them, and nail them on and clinch them up in 13 minutes.

Four shoes, one dollar, 25 cents a hoof. Beside skates for kids and shoes for horses, Albert also made anchors and sleighs in his shop.

At one time, strapping on the blades and going for a skate was one way to find a boyfriend or girlfriend, hooking up at the hockey rink, the Tinder of its time, teen-age love and triple Lutzes. Another son of Summerside, was my old pal Herb Schurman, born in 1911, one year after Frank:

We played hockey on the ice between Read's wharf and Holman's wharf and the Railway wharf. They'd have a big barrel out in the centre that tar used to come in. They'd give us the barrels, and there'd still be tar sticking to the inside and they'd let us burn them on the ice. That would keep us warm, and at night it would light the harbour up. We used to play hockey. Then in the evening, it was mostly skating.

And there was another way for the youngsters to keep warm:

There was an old fella down at the railway crossing. There were three or four railway tracks where Schurmans is now, the retail branch where the mill used to be.

Back in the 1910s and '20s, Summerside harbour didn't have as much landfill as it does now. The present-day Schurmans' lumber yard and parking lot is now closer to the water. Nearby was a little wooden shack where a gentleman by the name of Heckbert always had a fire burning:

This old fella would let us go in the shack, nice little shack, lots of heat in it and he'd let us put on our skates and leave our shoes there. Martin Heckbert, great old guy. There were four tracks there, and he'd have to come out with a sign and hold it up much like the school crossing people do now. When the trains were coming, he'd hold his sign up to stop the horses because that's what it was then, mostly horses. Lots of horses ran away, scared of the steam
. engines.

Herb and his pals would skate all afternoon and, when the sun was getting low in the sky and their bellies started to rumble, they'd head back to Martin's shanty to retrieve their warm boots. It was near the end of Martin's shift, and sometimes a friend of Martin's had dropped by for a visit:

They'd be talking and we'd be putting our shoes back on, sitting around listening to what was going on. There was a latch on the door, you know, the kind of latch you put your thumb on, and Martin would go to the latch and make a clicking sound by making the latch go up and down. And he'd point to us and say, 'Your mother wants you right home.' He didn't want to put us out, but the fella visiting him had a bottle and they wanted to have a drink. They didn't want to have it in front of us kids. So, we thought he was getting a telegram message because all the telegraph wires ran right over the railway tracks. 'Your mother wants you right home.' Oh, Martin Heckbert. He was a great old guy.

Herb said Martin also wrote poetry while waiting for a train to rumble past, poems about everyday people and life in Summerside. Herb said he loved "the old fella," and said everyone who knew him did too. Imagine still being remembered that way 100 years later. We should all be so lucky, and we probably would be if we were as kind-hearted as Martin Heckbert.

◆

In Charlottetown, there was once a caretaker's cottage, a small building between Fanningbank, the residence of the Lieutenant-Governor, and Government Pond. The pond is long gone, infilled to park cars; but before cars took precedence, it was a playground for students like Russell Stewart and Garfield Creamer who, back in the 1930s, attended the old West Kent School. Russell lived near the school:

A big-four-storey red brick building and, when I was going there, it had about 600 students. The place was run by the principal, the secretary, and the janitor. And his name was Ward, and he lived on the premises. He doled out the most discipline of all. He was the most feared of anybody. The Government Pond used to run all the way along West Street. It was all black mud. We'd go stumping ice cakes in the winter, jumping from one ice cake to another, and, of course, we'd get into trouble doing that if we got caught. Many's a days, they'd pull people out, up to their heads all black from falling in the mud. It was soft, just like tar. A lot of fond memories.

Not for the Mums, I'll bet.

Garfield shared Russell's memories:

We used to have ice sports every winter, and all the classes would get together and go up to the Forum, and have races and relay races to see who was the best.

Russell:

West Kent and Queen Square schools were always competing with each other. In those days, they called West Kent the Protestant school, and Queen Square was the Catholic school for boys. West Kent was mixed, girls and boys. There was a competition every year between the cadet corps, and we'd have a bugle band and there many trophies in the old West Kent School.

But none in Queen Square, right, Russell? "Right!"

Competition was so fierce between the arch rivals that former West Kent students who lived in the east end of Charlottetown told me that to avoid passing anywhere near Queen Square school – next to St. Dunstan's Basilica – they'd detour for 10 minutes to avoid a confrontation. Thus, they never saw the Queen Square trophy case either.

In 1951, a West Kent student looked out a classroom window and saw a strange sight on the ice in the middle of the harbour: a deer slipping and sliding along, its thin legs struggling to get a grip on the ice. Although Garfield had graduated from West Kent years earlier, he still saw deer on more than one occasion:

The deer were brought to PEI and they were roaming around Charlottetown. I've seen them in our back yard. They came into Charlottetown from the outlying areas where the woods were, and came across the ice and went on their merry way.

Those deer skating across the ice always brought classes to a halt. They weren't native to the Island and had been brought over from the mainland by Premier J. Walter Jones. The deer were mostly tame by the time they arrived from New Brunswick, and some had escaped from holding pens on the Jones farm in Bunbury. Sadly, the 100 or so white-tailed immigrants didn't last long: the deer got into people's gardens and orchards, and were shot as pests. The last deer was seen in the 1960s in the western end of the Island, not skating, but merely walking through a farmer's field.

◆

I used to go to the rink although I couldn't skate very well. The boys would sit me up on the promenade, and then they'd come along and take me for a skate. Hib Saunders was a hockey player, and he used to take me. I could never get anyone to go fast enough, but don't let me go.

Eileen Hickox was another alumnus of the old West Kent School. She was born in 1912 and grew up on Spring Street. Bands played live music, and the skaters went round and round, reversing direction every three or four big band tunes.

The Recce [PEI Regiment] band used to play quite a bit. They used to have band concerts where the fountain is now on Grafton Street, near the three soldiers' monument. On Friday nights, they used to have band concerts. There was no other entertainment. No radios back then.

Sometimes Eileen's hankering for skating fast didn't work out. When she was a teenager, she was courted by her future husband, Lester, who took her for a skate:

> There was 50 cents on the ice this night, which was a lot of money at that time. Somebody had dropped 50 cents on the ice, and when we were coming around the corner I saw it, but we couldn't get stopped for me to stoop and pick it up. We had to leave it there.

That 50 cents would have come in handy because after the skate Lester went all out and took Eileen for a treat at White's Restaurant just up the street: "We used to get banana splits for a quarter. Them were the days, what?"

◆

One of the largest covered rinks on the Island was in Victoria-by-the-Sea, the home of the Victoria Unions and Union Sisters champion hockey teams. For 15 years, the huge rink with its roof and natural ice was run by H.B. and his dynamic wife, Kathryn Wood:

> We had a lot of fun in it. There were all kinds of things going on. We had a Rink-a-Phone, which supplied the music. It worked perfectly and, on a calm night, the older people in the village said they could hear it plain as day. It was like a phonograph, and our favorite tune was the "Skaters' Waltz" and "Mockingbird Hill" was another. I think I still have those records stowed away, and the Rink-a-Phone too. We used to have carnivals, and that's where our local premier [Walter Lea] skated with his girlfriend Maude Rogerson. And he married her, so there were a lot of romances made during those skating days.

After parking their horses and sleighs in the Wood's barn across the street from the rink, would-be Sonya Henies and Barbara Ann Scotts flocked to the rink especially when there was a "costume carnival." Some women preferred hockey to costume carnivals. Victoria Union Sister Cora Ferguson told me that she was happiest when she accomplished what was known in hockey circles as a "Gordie Howe hat-trick": a goal, an assist, and a fight. Cora was proud of her "sharp elbows."

Frank Woodside probably had a couple of Gordie Howe specials to his credit. He both skated and was a renowned hockey player, even into his 80s, skills he honed in his youth on Summerside harbour:

> Phil the Barber was the man. He had a little shack there. It was an oyster bar actually and he might have been bootlegging at the time, I don't know. But anyway, he had this little shack. And, of course, he was pretty smart too, because he hooked up a set of lights over the ice. They called him "Phil the Barber," so he must have cut hair too. There was a song about him on a record:

> *Where do we go from here, boys, where do we go from here?*

> *Down to Phil the Barber's to get a drink of beer.*

> *If Pat walks by a pretty girl, he'd whisper in her ear,*

> *Oh Joy, Oh Boy, where do we go from here?*

> *See? I never forgot that.*

The day I interviewed him, Second-World-War-veteran Frank had just finished forging a pair of eel spears:

> I'm 85 and I still skate. As long as you think you can do something, why not do it? But you have to watch out what you're doing. I fell twice. I took a header, but anyway, I'm always on the move.

An understatement for sure. When the ice melted, Frank went fishing. Said one of Frank's many admirers, "Lovely man. When you were out driving around, you'd see a man alone fishing off a bridge, and we'd say, 'I bet that's Frank.' And it always was."

Three Men and their Boats
(Not to Mention the Pig)

Tom Trenholm and Dad Capt Wm Trenholm 1924
on Marine in Barbados

Captain Thomas Trenholm was one of Canada's last schooner captains. Captain Tom was born in 1910, the son of Captain William Trenholm, and the brother of three more sea captains. He had uncles and cousins who were sea captains, better than "a life with the pick and shovel," Captain William's take on the "miserable existence" of a landlubber. Captain William Trenholm was related to the Port Elgin, New Brunswick, Trenholms, and, as Tom said, "He loved schooners," and to prove it, once owned seven of them at the same time.

And I can remember their names: the *Minnie*, the *Freddie A. Higgins*, the *Rayburn* was one he owned here on PEI at one time; he had the *Victoria*, that's four. He had the *Telephone*, a schooner he bought in Charlottetown. He always bragged that he never set foot, never went aboard, and then he sold her; that's five. Then he had a little one called the *Happy Go Lucky*, and the last one, the *Urania* that he sold to Captain George Allen, an old fella in Montague, a cousin of my father's.

Tom said, there was "a story attached to all of them": In 1919, Captain William bought a Model-T Ford and sailed around the Maritimes with the car lashed to the deck of the *Rayburn;* The *Freddie A. Higgins* hauled "solar" salt, sun-evaporated salt, from a Caribbean island called Salt Cay in the Turks and Caicos. Not knowing their father was going to sell the Telephone immediately after buying it, Tom and his brother hid two kegs of rum in the hold. The new owner kept one and let Tom and his brother retrieve the other. And the *Urania:*

We got into a hurricane with the *Urania* out here about 150 miles west of Bermuda on her way back with a big cargo of molasses. The old fella said, 'My God we're going to get something. I don't know where it's coming from. There's clear sky everywhere.' There was a little bit of an undertow and a groundswell coming from the southwest. She was just rolling, rolling, not enough wind to fill her sails. The Old Fella said, 'Take the sail off her and furl everything up, but leave the jumbo up.'

In the nor' east clouds like cotton batting began to come over the water, coming in rolls, the clouds tearing overhead like the devil, big black clouds tearing and ripping, and the Old Fella said, 'We're going to get it!' It bore down on us right fast and struck the vessel on her starboard side. Leaving the jumbo up is what saved the vessel from washing to pieces. When it struck on the starboard beam, the jumbo went to ribbons. I stuck my head up to have a look and there was nothing anybody could do except keep from going overboard. We were flying with this force of wind

– I'd say 150 miles an hour – only God knows. There was a loud bang, like a gun went off, and tore that jumbo sail off. Away it went. I wouldn't doubt it's still going, to tell you the truth. And that's 70-odd years ago.

"Pine down and molasses back," went the old refrain; in fact, they had taken a load of Gaspé pine lumber and shingles down. Their load of Barbados molasses was destined for a sugar refinery in Maine. Captain William's entire family was aboard the *Urania*. Mrs. Trenholm was born on the tiny Dutch Caribbean Island of Saba, and was a school-teacher. She "schooner-schooled" the four children as they sailed the Atlantic seaboard, Captain William contributing to their education by conducting strict violin and piano lessons at night in the main cabin.

On another trip south, heading to British Guyana, a hurricane swamped the Trenholms who were saved by the RMS *Aquitania,* a Cunard liner and sister-ship of the *Lusitania* and *Mauretania*. As Tom loved to point out, it was always an adventure on a sailing ship. When he turned 17, Tom was given command of the schooner *Douglas E. Parks.* One day, she started "taking on water," sailor talk for what a landlubber like me would call "sinking." Captain Tom and his crew were five miles off the rugged coastline of Louisbourg, Cape Breton.

There was a lot of confusion, you know, a vessel sinking under your feet. There was only three of us – my brother Russell, myself, and this Newfoundland fella. Well, alright, we couldn't stay aboard. The thing to do was find out how much she was leaking, you know. If she was leaking more than you could keep out, well, you know the answer to that. You know what you would do? Get in the dory there with the other two fellas. Or stay onboard and go down. You're not going to do that. I'm telling you, she wasn't going to be afloat very long.

Alright, we left her and, by God, we put in an awful night in that dory. Five miles off and the wind blowing off the land, late November, and the spray that blew into the dory froze in the bottom of her. If we weren't busy trying to row, we'd have froze to death. The three of us kept that up, we had to keep going, two oars pulling on one side and one on the other. That's all that kept us from swamping when that sea hit. There was a lot of frightful misery to it, with every chance of losing your life. It didn't look good. This was all at night, and this Newfoundlander said, 'Skipper, why don't we land?'

I said, 'On this coast? Yeah, and get drowned. It's all breakers and high cliffs. If we attempt it, we'll drown!' When you see death facing you like that you smarten right up, you know what I mean? I was kind of scared myself, but I never lost my cool. We were in her until 8:00 the next morning before we got our feet on the land.

Right. I think I'll opt for the pick and shovel.

Throughout the Second World War, Captain Tom and his wife, partner and First Mate, the former Mary MacGillivray from Louisbourg, hauled coal from Cape Breton to Newfoundland. They were still sailing schooners into their 70s. Tom then took up boat-building, and built 64 fishing boats and several yachts in his shop overlooking Murray Harbour. In their 90s after years of debate and delay, both Tom and Mary finally received their wartime backpay and recognition as merchant mariners during the Second World War.

♦

A few miles up the coast, Roy Clow from Murray Harbour North sailed, fished, and built thirteen fishing boats. Roy was born in 1917 and, as a boy, fished lobster, cod, mackerel, and herring. In 1939 when the war broke out, Roy sold his boat and fleet. Lobster prices were five cents a pound. When he came home after the war, lobster prices were 25 cents a pound, good enough to get married. So, Roy and his Nova Scotian bride Margaret laid the foundation for a new house in Montague. Roy framed and sheathed the three exterior walls and shingled the roof. But before he installed the missing end wall and the windows and doors, Roy decided to go fishing so they could pay for the house in cash. He built some traps, bought some rope, and anchors, but he needed a boat:

I built the boat in the house. Margaret helped me. The neighbours didn't know what in the hell to make of it. They thought I was crazy. Three hundred dollars to build the boat, finished. I didn't have too many tools and I borrowed quite a few from Garth Johnston – he was building boats down in Peters Road. He didn't mind sharing: he was glad to be able to give some instruction and tools. And after I built the boat, I built a Lunenburg dory, a popular dory in the Maritimes. The Lunenburg schooners that fished on the Grand Banks all used these dories. They all had a dozen dories on the ship. I built three of them and sold two.

The fishing boat didn't quite fit in the house, its prow poking out into the driveway. Roy put in a six-cylinder car engine and went fishing, leaving the shell of the house to finish later.

The last day of the fishing season I went to work on the house again, and we put up the inside partitions and finished it all. George Clow down in Murray Harbour North cut 157 panes of glass for me. I worked at night puttying them in. One hundred and fifty-seven panes. My God, I was awful disgusted, I'll tell you! We'd work until 12:00 at night, puttying windows.

The pain of windows. Months later, Roy's hands still smelled like turpentine.

> The house cost $350 to build. We had 100 acres of lumber down in Murray Harbour North, and I cut all my own lumber, and got it sawed at Jim Finlayson's mill. I had an old truck and I hauled it all to Montague. I did the work myself. And that's what it cost me.

Roy carried Margaret over the threshold and they moved in.

> I didn't have a well. We had an outside toilet. I was getting the water from my sister next door.

So, Roy had a well drilled — $500 — and the interior walls plastered — tack on another $72. Now we're up to $922, not counting the gas to haul the lumber to and from Jim Finlayson's mill. They could afford to splurge on water and walls, because the car engine Roy had put in his boat made it the fastest boat around. It attracted a lot of attention and he wound up building 12 more boats.

Those wooden boats are long gone, but the house that Roy and Margaret built is still standing in Montague, 26 feet by 36 feet, one and a half storeys. The first time I went down to interview Roy, Margaret kicked us out of the house because we were making too much noise having fun. She couldn't hear *Coro9nation Street*. So, we did the interview sitting in the driveway in Roy's car, looking at the side of the house that 50 years earlier had the bow of a fishing boat sticking out of it.

◆

Like Roy, Tommy Gallant's father Henry was a fisherman who ran a little rum, and like Captain Tom, Henry was a schoonerman. The Gallants lived in Bayview in sight of the Cavendish sandspit. Henry was also a carpenter... of sorts.

He had a dory, perhaps of the Lunenburg variety, but the dory got old and Henry recycled it into a pig pen.

> He had a pig. Ah, God, I have to laugh. Terrible. He had this small old boat, and it rotted, so he sawed it in two and he got the wise idea it would make a pig pen for the winter. It was quite high, and he turned it over, and he put a fence around it, and put some straw in it, and in the summer, he got a little pig from somewhere. So, the pig kept getting bigger and bigger all the time. He was going to kill it in the fall so we'd have something to eat besides fish. It was a good idea, really.
>
> Now, the road went right past our house and the farmers used to love to talk to my father because he was full of jokes. So, this one winter morning there came a hell of a snowstorm and my father couldn't find his pig. A neighbour came in and said, 'Henry, you used to have a pig out there.'
>
> My father said, 'I've still got him. I just can't find him.' The snow had drifted in and the pig had moved up to the front of the boat as far as he could get. The pig was there. My father finally found him and dug him out.

Sailors considered it bad luck to transport or even say the word "pig" on a boat, supposedly because pigs can't swim – they can – and even living in an upside-down boat was pushing the poor porker's – and Henry's – luck.

Tommy was born in 1922, and he and Henry were familiar sights to the New London lighthouse keeper Maisie Adams. She'd shake her head as she saw them heading out into stormy waters while every other fisherman was heading the other way for safe harbours. She said Tommy always made up for her fretting by throwing her a big codfish as he sailed past on his way back to port. Henry took young Tommy to sea for the first time on his 47-foot schooner:

I was coming nine years of age when I went out with my father on my first trip in the Gulf. And I was so sick. We left around four o'clock in the morning and we sailed for two hours. We were out about five miles beyond the Cavendish sand dunes and there was quite a big swell, and I took sick. I laid on the floor of that big sailboat, all day. All we had to eat was a slice of bread with molasses on it. Probably two or three slices, I don't know, I couldn't eat anyway. I coaxed my dad to throw me overboard. Many, many times. And all he'd say was, 'Eat!'

Oh my God, when he'd mention 'eat,' I'd throw up worse than ever. Oh, I was so sick. I'd ask him to throw me over because I figured I was going to die anyway so it didn't make any difference. But I hung on until five o'clock in the evening, and we sailed into New London harbour, and I never was sick since and that's a long time ago. Never.

I could write a book about Tommy Gallant. When he was young, his life was hard, but Tommy never lost his sense of humour. He taught himself to play the mouth organ out behind the barn and could drink a glass of water standing on his head when he was 80.

If you added up the years Tom, Roy, and Tommy spent at sea, you wouldn't get much change from 200 years. Anyone who dropped by for a visit and a cup of tea – just don't show up when *Coronation Street* is on – got a few laughs and some insight into a way of life that's long sailed into the sunset: schooners tied up at every wharf; an 80-pound gaff cod; a walk on the deck of a rumrunner. They lived long lives, but not long enough to tell all their stories.

♦

Here's one more from Roy: In 1936, when Roy was 18, he and George Millar and a few other pals decided to take

Roy's fancy new lobster boat with the $75-engine across the Northumberland Strait to Pictou where the Lobster Carnival and the boat races beckoned.

> Four or five of us went over to Pictou and we stayed all night. There was a bunch of schooners in there from Murray Harbour South, and they had the holds cleaned out and laid with straw. The schooners were full of people: girls and women and men and everything. They slept in the schooners. So that's how we slept that night.

Pictou had lots to offer besides girls in schooners, including elephants and a dancing bear.

> There was a circus there and a fella was going to jump off a 90-foot pole into a tank of water. George and I were about three-parts-full and we thought we'd get a good close look. It was fenced all around, back about 30 feet from the tank. So, we went under the fence and started over to the tank, and this guy up the pole – you could hardly see him – hollered, 'Don't come in here, you fellas! You'll get soaking wet.'
>
> We said, 'Ahhh, go on and jump. Go ahead and jump.' He jumped alright. When he hit the water a bunch of water came out over top of the tank and we got soaked to the skin. The tank was only about six feet deep.

You might wonder how Roy and George were "three-parts-full," when in 1936, PEI was still in the grips of prohibition. However, in Nova Scotia, liquor, like teen-aged boys, was footloose and fancy-free, hence Roy and George being "three-parts-full" but not, as it turned out, as full as some of their shipmates.

> My brother Ed and Ivan Henderson – Ivan was never off the Island in his life and he wanted to go to

Pictou, so he came too. They were awful anxious to know where the liquor store was.

Young lads, first time away from home in a town where no one knew them, and cheap liquor. What could go wrong?

Soon as we got to Pictou, they were asking people, 'Where's the liquor store?' 'Right up there, just go around the corner, you can't miss it.'

'Have they wine up there? They say you've got good cheap wine here.' 'Yeah, you can get a gallon for two dollars.'

Two-dollar-gallon-of-wine. Then it's possible something MIGHT go wrong.

So away went Ivan and Ed up to the liquor store, and the wine was cheap, but just trash. They got a gallon each and wondered where they were going to go to drink it. So, they got looking around and saw a lovely big house with a nice lawn. They were sitting on this man's lawn and turns out he was the mayor. He came out and he put the run on them and he called the cops. Ed and Ivan were both in jail inside of an hour after we got to Pictou. They kept them in all day and all night, and they never saw the boat races or the circus and got nothing to eat. All they got was their gallon of wine. My God, it was funny.

Sins paid for in full. End of story. Not quite.

We were going home the next day and we had to get them out of jail. The cops didn't fine them; they just let them go. They missed everything! Never [saw] a damn thing because they were down in the basement in jail.

Travel broadens the mind and the two-dollar-gallon-of-wine drinkers learned a few things on their odyssey. They were hungover and seasick all the way back to Murray Harbour. As they neared the Island, Ivan Henderson looked up blearily and said the red soil of PEI never looked so good.

Not sure if he ever left again. Or drank wine that came in gallon jugs. Like Ed and Ivan, lessons most of us have also learned the hard way.

Six Degrees of Separation

Joe & son Ivan Cunningham hauling firewood 1941

We're all connected. Let's see, my grandparents Thompson had a coal furnace, with a three-foot-square black, ornate, cast-iron grate in the main hallway. Grandad clanged away down below, while upstairs next to the big heat-breathing grate, Nanny fiddled with a handful of mysterious chains hanging just out of my reach.

On the other hand, grandparents Cunningham had a problem: Grandfather Joe Cunningham. Joe fought modern plumbing, furnaces, electricity, telephones, and anything to do with the 20th century. He managed to stave off most, but lost on a technicality with plumbing. Ivan, his son, dug a quarter mile trench and buried a one-inch pipe running into the kitchen from a spring in Duncan's Hill back of the orchard. No electric pump, totally gravity fed, one brass tap and a battered sink and it took three minutes to fill the same little green glass, which for the previous 500 years had sat next to the water supply being replaced: a dipper and galvanized bucket of water.

So, Joe and Grammie heated with the kitchen wood range, with a coal-based burner in the living room. Not that any-one ever went into the living room, unless it was to steal the candy, chicken bones and coconut bonbons Grammie had hidden where she was sure her grandsons *would* find them. She cooked Joe's porridge on top of the woodstove, the pot up to its neck down a front burner hole, next to the slab wood's hot flames, boiling up a froth. It was a special "porridge pot," the bottom black with soot which came off when your rubbed it, as soft to the touch as velour.

◆

Lulu Thomson, sad to say, is not a relative. But there's a connection: firewood. Lulu was a great woman who learned the virtue of kindness and the reward of hard work from her parents and grandparents. She was born in 1909 on a farm on the Dock Road near Elmsdale, PEI. Her dad had six horses with names like Bess and Phil, Jack and Bill. They pulled plows and harrows; the driving mare drove them to church every Sunday; two others hauled milk to the creamery and delivered the mail. The horses snigged logs out of the woods, then Lulu's father would hook two horses up to treadmill, sawing the wood into stove-length blocks. The treadmill was called a horsepower: the horses walked steadily on the slanted treadmill, much like a Stairmaster you'd see in a gym, powering the saw blade.

> A lot of wood. We had two stoves going, one stove upstairs and one stove down. Mum and Dad would get up two or three times through the night. Us kid would be upstairs sleeping. We didn't have to get up, but Mum and Dad looked out for the woodstoves. It took an awful lot of wood. I split and helped saw hundreds and hundreds of cords of wood.

I bet you burned 15 or 20 cords a year.

> That's for darn sure. And then poor old Bert Ward... we'd be coming out through his place with the team of horses loaded with wood, with chains across so the sleigh wouldn't tip, driving the horses out through that road in Miminegash. We stopped at Bert Ward's and took some lovely fire wood into him, but he said, 'Girls, don't leave any more wood. I don't want it. I'm going to die.'

> So anyway, we left the wood and went home, and told Mum and Dad he wasn't all that good. So they went through and Mum gave him medicine and everything, but he died. So I don't know what they did with the wood. They took it to some neighbour.

They say firewood heats more than once. Let's go from firewood to Kathryn MacQuarrie Wood. Kay Wood, as she was known to everyone, and Kay knew everyone. She was special and smart in so many ways. She bubbled like a mountain stream, always fresh and full of ideas. She ran one of the first tourism business on the Island, lived on a heritage farm, wrote a newspaper column, recorded her beloved Victoria-by-the-Sea's history, and, along with her husband H.B. Wood, ran an indoor hockey rink, a huge building with a wooden roof, artificial ice, and a rink-a-phone, a contraption that played big band music to skate to. Kay said a lot of courtin' and sparkin' went on in that rink... but not all of it:

> I'd like to be travelling with the horse and sleigh right now. I loved the sound of the bells. In the wintertime, everyone had a different sounding bell. You would know who was going past by the bell. Some people had three big bells on the top of the harness and some of them had the bells all around. After a while, you'd get to

> know the different sounds. Ours were very sweet, three high bells on the top of the harness.

Everyone knew the MacQuarries were coming.

Oh yes. The was a jaunting sleigh and, of course, a wood sleigh to go to the woods to cut firewood for the stoves in the wintertime. My older brothers would want to go see the girls and wanted the special sleigh. At our house, my father had a deadline, which was ten o'clock. Be in the house at ten o'clock or be grounded.

Same for both boys and girls?

No. The boys didn't have to. Whatever boyfriends we had, had to be out at 10:00. And they knew that. I think that was a good strategy for my father who had five daughters.

Five daughters. No wonder the man had a "strategy." Having raised only one daughter, I agree with a 10:00-sharp curfew; boyfriends out, drawbridge up, the 'gators go in the moat, and the hounds are released.

Our next connection... Kay Wood to Wood Islands. Mary Stuart Sage was born in Wood Islands on New Year's Day in 1923, "The Year of the Big Snow." In the middle of a blizzard, Mary arrived on the scene unexpectedly: her mother was alone, so Mary's grandfather stumped through the drifts to "midwife" Mary into the world. Mary's father Hector Stuart ran a sawmill, built boats, and ran a general store. Christmas was an especially busy time of year. So Hector and Maud-the-mare were hauling extra groceries and the mail weighed down with Eaton's and Simpson's catalogues from the train station. The store was the local hangout: milking done, men gathered in the evening around the pot-bellied stove:

He liked talking to the guys and playing cards. I swept the store, put the fire on in the mornings. At Christmas, we always got mitts and candy and gum. When I got a little older, I used to count the gum before Christmas and then count it after, so I knew it came from the store. I was reaching that age where I was starting to figure things out.

But one of the weirdest things: we used to have a pipe that went up through the ceiling into our bedroom. We did away with that and had an outside chimney. But I looked down the hole that was left one night, and I saw Santa Claus warming his hands and that vision is so clear. Yeah, I was positive I saw Santa Claus.

The stuff that dreams are made of... Mary did have a great imagination. It might have been Mary who told me that, instead of mailing her letter to Santa, she put it in the woodstove thinking the smoke would take her requests up to the North Pole. That's when Mary was a little girl, before she put the gum supply in the store under surveillance.

◆

The next connection: Mary Sage. Sage is an herb: Herb Schurman was born in Summerside in 1911. When Herb was a lad, his father, a teamster, died young, leaving his widow with a large family. But Herb's mum was a strong, determined woman, and Herb and his 12 brothers and sisters grew up in a house full of love and music:

> We had an awful lot of fun back then. We had more fun in a week than the kids do today in a month. Some of the grandchildren couldn't say her name – Emma Jane – so they nicknamed her 'Schurmie.' She got Schurmie until the day she died. She was noted for being kind to kids and a great cook, and gave kids the old-fashioned fat ginger snaps and sugar cookies. After school, couple of cookies and a glass of milk. She was a great lady and she lived to be 94.

Herb grew up in downtown Summerside, skated on the harbour, rowed to Holman's Island to smoke his first cigarette, worked in the old post office, became a town councillor, and later the deputy mayor.

I was born in a little house on the corner of Cambridge and Euston Street, and it's still standing there. It wasn't very big, but it was home. I was just as proud of that little house as if I was living up on Beaver Street in one of the Holman houses. We had more fun in that little house and had an awful lot of good neighbours. In those days, there were two services on Sundays, one in the morning and one in the evening.

My sister sang in the choir and after the morning service, she'd bring somebody home from church. A lot of the people from the Christian Church came from the Linkletter Road: the Linkletters and the Murrays and the Rogers. She never missed a Sunday bringing a girlfriend back home to have dinner with us. Then go to church Sunday night again, get out about 8:00, and they'd all arrive back at our place. We had a piano and all the neighbours – the Brehauts, the DesRoches, the Gaudets, the Simmons, the Crossmans, and the Phillips – would gather around Sunday night and we'd have a singsong. It was all the old hymns like "Onward Christian Soldiers," and "Will Your Anchor Hold," and "The Old Rugged Cross," and "Softly and Tenderly."

Sing until 10:30 or so and then they'd have a lunch, pot luck, sandwiches, and cookies or a cake. Have something to eat and then about 11:30, they'd all go home. Mother loved it. She had a lovely alto voice, but she wasn't one to sing. When I was a little fella, when she was baking, she'd be humming. I'd catch on to the tune and I'd hum along with her, but when the gang would be singing, you'd hear her alto voice. Ah, that was living in those days. You made your own fun, you made your own music, you had lots of friends, and nobody was any better off than you were.

No wonder Herb grew up to be the man he was. He acted and sang in amateur theatricals, played Santa Claus, and if anyone needed a helping hand or a kind word, Herb was there with bells on. Sometimes literally.

♦

One more degree of separation: Kay Wood talked about sleigh bells. Dougald Dunkie MacDonald will complete the circle. Dougald Dunkie lived all his life in the hills of eastern Pictou County where the old Highland Scottish traditions endure to this day. When he was a boy, Mum and Dad switched to Gaelic when discussing anything to do with Christmas. They raised fat turkeys and geese to sell in New Glasgow in December.

It was really nice at Christmas time to go to town Christmas week. Winter would be set in then good and solid, and the sleighs would start out at Ardness, coming and coming. Then we'd start out here in Baileys Brook, all horses and sleighs. Everybody had bells and ribbons on their horses. It was pretty nice. Frosty night going to Avondale to catch the first train in the morning at 10:00, go to New Glasgow, sell all this stuff, and come home on the late train. The train would be that loaded you couldn't get a seat.

The horses were all tied at the Avondale station, side-by-side, blankets on them. Boy, a frosty night coming home. It was really, really Christmas week. All the bells ringing, the horses one behind the other going through Avondale. The Ardness bunch keeping over that way and we'd come home our way. Everybody'd be drinking, happy as Hal. Some of the fellas singing Gaelic songs coming through the woods.

You remember that do you?

Oh heavens. I was a part of it.

We're all connected. And if you hear anyone speaking the Gaelic, you know they're probably talking about your presents.

A Good Horse was Precious

Dutch & horse -Emily of New Moon

They say a horse is a good judge of character. I've only had to deal with horses a few times, and every time, the horse took an immediate dislike to me. One tried to knock me off by running under a tree branch and then into the stable through a low door. Another time, I was an extra in the *Emily of New Moon* TV series. I had a small re-occurring role as the sheriff, and in one scene had to ride a horse. Fast. The horse knew how to gallop. I didn't. We shot the scene over and over and over. The sheriff fell off a horse and got trampled. By the producers. I was written out of the show.

Hard-working horses were the order of the day when Roma Curley Mulligan was a young girl. Roma was born in Freetown in 1917 into a family with Irish blood on all sides, and where the first generation of immigrants shared their one horse from farm-to-farm.

My grandfather, I'd say, he lived a good four or five miles from his other two brothers, and they shared the horse. One horse between three people. Imagine. I don't know what kind of crops they put in but they did awfully well. They came to be well-off guys at the end of it.

Roma loved horses as did her parents, and like most farmers in the Freetown and Shamrock and Thistle area, they were especially keen to show how they had prospered. There was no better way than by driving fast horses.

We had lovely horses. We had this mare named Min. She could pretty near talk. I shouldn't tell this story. My father and mother gave me a little ring with three stones in it. I don't know where in the name of God they'd ever get the money to buy me this ring. I wasn't scared of the horses, even when I was little, but anyway I used to take my ring off and go out to the stable, lift Min's foot — she'd lift her foot for me — and bury my ring in her foot. In the frog part of the horse's foot.

From crossword puzzles, I know that the frog is the soft bottom part of a horse's hoof. The frogs of horses I have known flash through my nightmares.

So, this one day my mother couldn't find me. I guess I was three or four at the time. I wasn't going to school yet anyway. And when she came out to the stable, wasn't I sleeping under the mare's belly. She wouldn't hurt me. Oh no, she wouldn't hurt me. Minnie was her name, and good horses were priceless. A good horse was precious.

If I had tried that, I'm sure I would have croaked. Think about it.

Roma's dad sometimes treated his horses to a taste of beer. Apparently, horses like beer. To confirm her story is Vincente Elordiata, a Basque who grew up in the docks of

Liverpool, England, where huge shire horses were used to haul freight up from the Mersey.

There used to be over 4000 local horses, big heavy Belgian and Clydesdale horses. They would put five or six horses in tandem, one after the other, all chained together. It was really something to see. The horses knew their job and there was no cruelty with those horses. They were looked after wonderfully. The teamster would call, 'Ayyyyy up,' and you'd see every horse dig into his collar, pull the chain tight. Then, 'Hyyyup,' and then they'd head off, pull the load right up! Right up! Right up! Five, six, seven horses, and this was happening four and five times an hour. To catch the tides.

Beautiful horses, well looked after, well fed, and so on. And horses love beer. In Liverpool, when you bought a pint of beer, the barman put the glass on the slop-stand and he had to overflow it. To get it full. And the overflow went into this slop bucket. He wasn't permitted to sell that, but a carter could go into the pub with his horse's bucket, and the barman would put in two or three pints of slops for a penny or a tuppence. And the carter would take it out to the horse. I've seen those horses sucking down that beer. You'd hear the suction. The horses loved beer. I saw that morning, noon, and night.

Work hard... drink hard. Makes me wonder if those famous Carlsberg horses, the beautiful four-horse team pulling around wagon-loads of beer, weren't delivering those kegs of beer to a bar but were heading home to play cards and watch the football game. Bet they were Colts fans.

♦

My father got the name for being a great conversationalist because he used to sit and listen to people talk. He could recite everything they ever said to him, right back. Oh, yeah.

Father Francis Corcoran grew up on a farm in Baldwin Road, the Irish enclave near Cardigan, PEI. The horses on the Corcoran farm might have gone beer-less, but to compensate, they were chatted up and serenaded by Father Francis' father, Martin.

He used to keep talking all the time when he was out in the field, talk to the horses, and sing, and all the rest of it. People used to do that, talk to themselves and tell stories. I'd hear him out in the barn currying the horses and doing the work around, those monotonous jobs. That's the way they lived. Things that would be boring. Take cutting the hay. The horse would be going round and round. Or ploughing. That was boring work, but see they covered it up by singing all the time.

The fields are alive with the sound of music. I never heard my grandfather sing to the horses. Curse maybe.

His favorite horses were Diamond and Ned and Jim. Ned was the chestnut, a good trotter and a beautiful horse. And Diamond was a little bigger. Dad used to talk to them all the time and, Diamond, she would follow him. He wouldn't need any reins.

Obviously, Martin Corcoran and his horses were coordinated, right down to a fraction of an inch.

He'd be cleaning out the stable, throwing the manure, and some would catch on the step and he'd say, 'fifteen-sixteenths,' and she'd take a short step ahead with the cart so he could reach down with the fork and pick up the manure that had fallen. You know, there was that much rapport with the horse that she knew exactly what he was saying. Yeah, 'fifteen-sixteenths,' that was a short step.

The horse-whisperer who taught his horse fractions. Amazing.

◆

Island folklorist and author John Cousins says there's a horse sub-culture on PEI, right down to a litany of horsey superstitions. If you heard a horse but didn't see it, it was believed to be a sign of impending death, a forerunner. At one time, farmers considered a white horse bad luck, and even avoided buying a horse with white feet; the whiter the socks, the worse the luck. Arson was once known as "a visit from the red horse," and in "Revelation" 6:3-4, the red horse of war is the most feared of the Four Horsemen of the Apocalypse.

However, ancient superstitions and the Bible aside, farmers like Martin Corcoran considered the horse a friend, and many family photos included the horse.

◆

I'd have to do blood tests when I worked for the government and when I'd get to O'Leary, I'd have to go out to West Point. So, I'd rent a horse and sleigh, and it'd take an hour and half to get there, and I'd near freeze to death. Get the blood samples taken, be careful they didn't freeze, and head back to O'Leary.

Charlie Scranton was an egg-grader and a government poultry inspector. He spent many hours in a horse and sleigh travelling from farm-to-farm across the Island.

I'd get back to O'Leary and, in January, it would be way after dark. Every road went through the fields, all over. And a lot of the horses you'd get would be pretty slow. Touch them with a whip and they wouldn't go any faster; they'd just wiggle their tail a little bit faster.

The horse probably knew the roads and fields better than Charlie, and it just took getting caught in a blizzard once in unfamiliar territory for the plodding horse to redeem itself.

Definitely! The horse would find its way home.

I experienced that as a young lad. We had a party at our house, and there were three people there by the name of Kant, [one was] married to a distant cousin of mine, and they lived two miles from where we lived. The three of them played the bagpipes. I remember them standing in the middle of the kitchen floor all facing one another, playing the bagpipes.

What, no banjos?

So afterwards, I took them home with the horse and when we nearly got to their place, a storm came up, a nor'easter. Coming home, I couldn't see anything. I put the reins over the dash and let the horse go. After an hour and a half, here we were beside my barn in Southport. The horse took us home by himself. I'd heard a horse could do that. I couldn't see where I was going, and there were lots of places we had to go over an open field. The horse knew where he was going.

The Kants, their bagpipes, and Charlie were all safely delivered home thanks to a smart horse with its innate GPS. Sadly, after the Second World War, the days of the horse were numbered. Factories went from building tanks to tractors and cars, and, with the economic boom, people traded in their Percherons for a Pontiac. In 1956, Malcolm Irving traded some of his horses in on a new tractor. He still kept a horse "for snigging logs and jiggin' around"; more out of love than necessity. And 85 years after, he memorized this ode to the horse, he was able to recite it perfectly, word for word.

The Horse

O Horse you are a wonderful thing:
No buttons to push, no horn to honk,
You start yourself, no clutch to slip,
No spark to miss, no gears to strip.
No licence-buying every year
With plates to bolt on front and rear.
No gas bills climbing up each day
Stealing the joy of life away.

No speed cops chugging in your rear
Yelling summons in your ear.
Your inner tubes are all ok
And thank the Lord they stay that way.

Your sparkplugs never miss and fuss
Your motor never makes us cuss.
Your frame is good for many a mile
Your body never changes style.

Your wants are few and easily met
You've something on the tractor yet.

After everyone switched from horses to tractors, Mac said
you could buy a horse for $40 or $50. Most though, he said,
wound up being sold for $20, cut up, and fed to silver foxes.
A sad end to an old pal.

Steam threshing near Portage La Prairie, 1900.
(Courtesy Provincial Archives of Manitoba)

Harvest excursion 1900 prairies - steam threshing.

In 1922, Milton Buell bought a government-subsidized return railway ticket for $15, and, along with 899 other Islanders, was crammed into one of 27 railcars, and headed west.

> We went to Winnipeg and then we went to a place called Antler, Saskatchewan. A farmer hired us there for that season, stooking and threshing. Four dollars-a-day for stooking, and seven dollars for threshing. Of course, that was good money. That's why we went out.

Milton was born in 1907 in Abney, PEI, and was one of thousands of Islanders who made the long journey by train in hopes of finding work on a prairie wheat farm. It was his first time off the Island, not quite 14, no bigger than a whisper. He made his first trip to Murray River, five miles down the road from Abney, when he was 12. He sold a bucket of blueberries for 25 cents, and was in awe by "all the big buildings" he saw in Murray River.

Maritimers have a long history of travelling far from home to seek work. For many men in the late 19th century, continuing right up until the stock market crash in 1929, the yearly cycle was: plant the crops on the home farm in the spring; fish cod and lobster in May and June; make the hay and fill the wood box; and, in early August, head out west on the harvest excursion train. Spend a couple of months working in the wheat fields, saving as much money as possible. Then catch the train home in time to harvest the oats and potatoes on the home farm. In November, it was time to butcher the winter's meat supply, salt some fish, and hitch up the mare and head to the woods for the next winter's firewood. If you were lucky, you spent Christmas with the family, got drunk on New Year's Eve, then took off again, this time to a New Brunswick or Nova Scotia lumber camp for the winter. When May rolled around, repeat the cycle.

Thanks to his father, Milton was good with horses. The farmer in Antler entrusted him with a team of heavy draft horses, which meant Milton got up at 4:00 in the morning, an hour before everyone else, sorted out the team's harness and fodder, and was hauling his first load of stooked grain before sunrise. That's when Milton had his breakfast, hot and hasty from the chuckwagon. Work on the farm was a joy compared to the trip out on the train.

> They used to do some stupid things. You'd hear the story that women would hear the train coming and they'd holler to her kids, 'Come on into the house everybody and shut the door. And bring the cow in with ya.' I noticed when we passed through the country, there wouldn't be anybody around. So, I guess everybody went into the house to be safe, keep out of harm's way. But we didn't do any mischief.

Right. Not the Prince Edward Islanders like Milton. It was

those rowdy Cape Breton Islanders. And they weren't kidding about safe-guarding the cow either. A popular stunt was tying a cow to the back of the train, where the poor animal was dragged to its death until there was nothing left but the horns. An editorial in a 1909 Edmonton newspaper warned: "The harvest excursions are running-time for the people of northern Ontario to hide in the woods."

Donald Nicholson wasn't disappointed when he went looking for new adventures on the harvest excursion train, leaving the family farm sprawled below the Hartsville Presbyterian church. Like Milton, it was Donald's first time away from home and off PEI.

> In 1922, I left home when I was 16. It was quite an experience. It was quite a wild outfit on the train. Crazy. I think Cape Bretoners were the worst. At every station we came to, if the train stopped, they'd run out and if there were stores, they fairly took over. I remember up through northern New Brunswick, the train stopped, and a dozen young fellas went into this store, and they stole two boxes of Derby hats. You remember the Derby hat? Never paid a cent and made for the train. Every once in a while, they'd prance through the car where we were seated, the tallest fella was in the lead back to the shortest fella at the end, all wearing Derby hats. They used to make an awful racket.

The outward-bound excursion train was a mile long by the time it reached Ontario, augmented by hundreds more Bluenosers and Herring Chokers. Pat Hennessey from northeastern PEI went out on the 1924 harvest excursion.

> On the way out, some of them would be ram-shagging the stores, go in and take stuff, and run and not pay. I saw that up in Quebec. It was a damn shame. A little store, a man and a woman and their daughter; the men would duck out without paying and they couldn't do a damn thing.

While with good reason, Maritimers were not always welcomed with open arms, but they were tolerated at least. Around the same time the First World War ended, wooden shipbuilding in the Maritimes gave up the ghost. The shortage of work here proved a boon for the labour-hungry prairies. Maritimers were rough around the edges, but as a farmer in Indian Head, Saskatchewan, commented, "Maritimers are miserable toughs and worse, but I never saw one that wouldn't work."

They had to be tough just to get there, crammed into old worn-out third-class rail cars. Louis Hall went west in 1926 and said:

> It was bad enough sitting on them hard-assed seats all day in a car with no springs, but I had to share an overhead wooden shelf at night with another skinny young fella. I can tell you we were well-acquainted by morning.

The men were so rough that the railway provided women with separate cars. Muriel Boulter MacKay was born in 1895 in Albany near Borden, PEI. She didn't make the ten-mile trip into Summerside until she was 12. Muriel was an outstanding student. She had her grade ten by the age of ten, and had passed the college entrance exams. Her parents thought her too young for Prince of Wales College and the bright lights of Charlottetown, so Muriel was kept home on the farm for two years. She earned a first-class teaching certificate in the next two years, and, by the time she was 16, she was back home in Albany teaching at the one-room school she had attended. She moved to Halifax in 1915 to be close to her father who was teaching basic training to soldiers destined for Flanders and the horrors of the First World War. The Boulters survived the Halifax Explosion in 1917, and when the First World War ended, Muriel decided to take her teaching credentials further west to Saskatchewan.

I had a well-equipped school. Had a piano in it, had dishes in it, and you could get a meal or do anything you wished. Quite often, I used to make soup for the youngsters. Where I boarded was three miles from the school and I used to walk to school quite a lot. And I rode horseback to school. When it came cool weather, the family next door let me drive their horse and wagon, and take two of their youngsters to school with me. We had a building at the school to put the horses in and tie them up. A lot of children came on horseback.

Muriel was an accomplished rider thanks to the two years she'd spent at home between her schooling. She helped her father snig logs in the woods and rode Tom, her favorite horse, bareback all over the farm. Muriel loved teaching, and loved learning; she enjoyed the mix of nationalities that made up her little schoolhouse on the prairie.

They were everything: Hungarians, French, Americans, English, and Scotch. I don't know if there was any Irish or not. It was a one-room school and I had about 30 youngsters.

Was there any difference between the students she'd taught in Albany and the ones out west?

Oh, yes. Different altogether. I think they were more willing to learn out there. More obliging. Easier to handle than they were here. I don't think I ever used the strap out there. I did here on the Island. Oh, yes.

While out west, Muriel met and married George MacKay in 1918. Ironically, George also came from Albany, from a farm just a jaunt down the road from the Boulter's. A year before Muriel, he'd gone out west to seek his fortune. They set up house in Saskatoon, but eventually came home. Years later, as Lieutenant Governor and wife, they entertained Queen Elizabeth II and Prince Philip at Fanningbank while they were on their royal visit in 1973.

Milton Buell went west several times, and most enjoyed working on a farm in Alberta owned by a man originally from England.

> We only be there five or six weeks altogether. We saved some money, but we got caught in Winnipeg, young and foolish, always looking for something to buy. I think each one of us bought a watch at a second-hand store.

Money was a much-discussed topic for the harvest excursioners. Another topic that always cropped up, almost as important as the wages, was food and water. The grub. They tried to steer clear of farms where the water had a sulphurous taste and smell: "what you'd expect the water in Hell to taste like," one disgusted man told me. Often the food on the farms wasn't much better, certainly not to the standard of the food left behind: Mum's home cooking. In the farmhouse that Donald Nicholson grew up in, three generations shared the kitchen, and there was always something tasty bubbling away on the woodstove. Not so much on the prairies:

> There was a man there, oh, he was just a no-good cook. He was always chewing tobacco. They claimed he'd be spitting in the bread. At any rate, the workers got sick. I think he was leaving too much soap on the dishes and people got diarrhea. So, the men stopped working and said they'd have to fire him. So, they did. And then they got this man who had been a cook on a passenger steamer out of Glasgow, Scotland. And he was a top cook. His only weakness was he'd go on a binge. He'd save up the vanilla extract and lemon extract, and go on a binge. So, they'd fire him and get somebody else who was no good, and he'd be hired back again until he'd go on another binge. But he was a top cook.

Jim MacLean from Peters Road in eastern PEI went out on five harvest excursions. He was always blessed with decent food. His beef was with the clouds of black flies that swarmed man and beast alike, whether out in the fields or sitting down to supper in the bunkhouse.

> You couldn't be fussy about the flies. We'd have big bowls of apricots on the table and there'd be these little black specks in it. You'd think it was spices or something, but it was those little black flies. It was no good trying to pick them out – there was too damn many. You'd get a fly in your biscuit and you'd dig it out. Big black fellas. You wouldn't eat them but you'd have to eat the little black ones.

On some days, Jim ran a team of horses hauling stooks to the thresher and had to put bandanas over the horses' noses so they wouldn't choke on the flies.

Donald Nicholson was fed mustard sandwiches on one farm. Two unbuttered slabs of bread with a swipe of mustard in between. He could have used some of Jim's flies for a bit a protein. Instead, he quickly moved on to another farm where mustard sandwiches hadn't been invented yet. After the wheat was harvested, Donald stayed out west and landed a job along with 200 other men, cutting railway ties for the Canadian Pacific Railway in a lumber camp near Sioux Lookout on the northern Manitoba-Ontario border.

On a good day, Donald and his partner produced 30 ties. They felled the trees using crosscut saws, limbed them with axes, then sawed the tree into five-foot lengths. They had to square three sides with an adze and then haul the ties out to the rail-side for pickup. They made 14 ½ cents per tie, $4.35 a day, split two ways. But the bunkhouse bed was free, as was the grub. Lots of deer and moose, some bear, and those two mainstays of lumber and mining camps across the country: beans and...

> Prunes. Do you know what they called prunes in the lumber camp? C.P.R. strawberries. Yeah, C.P.R. strawberries.

Donald feasted on C.P.R. strawberries, cut railway ties for five months, then headed to the States. He turned 17 while working in a granite quarry in Quincy, Massachusetts, then spent a year lay-preaching in New York City soup kitchens. He finally came home to attend Divinity school and to his life as a Presbyterian minister, at one time serving four churches in rural PEI at the same time.

Yet, most Islanders conceded the good money out west was worth suffering homesickness, black flies, and water from hell. Back home a farm labourer on PEI was making a $1.00-a-day, assuming there was work available in the first place. Pat Hennessey was one of many Maritimers who considered the 1920s as tough as the Great Depression of the "dirty '30s."

> There was nothing doing here on the Island. You wouldn't get a $1.00-a-day. It cost me $31.15 to Winnipeg, return, and half-a-cent-a-mile from then on.

Pat was born in St. Catherines east of Souris in 1902, the son of a hard-working, poorly-paid blacksmith. He packed up and went west on the 1924 harvest excursion, stooking wheat in Manitoba for $3.50 to $4.50 a day.

> I cleared $200, clear of the little stuff you'd buy. A plug of tobacco. That was a lot of money back then. A helluva lot of money.

In Winnipeg and Montreal, if the harvesters could avoid the pickpockets and the touts, who were as numerous and irritating as the prairie flies, then they might return home with some much-welcomed money. Pat already had his return ticket, so for safekeeping on the journey home, he asked the farmwife to sew all but $10 of his cash into the lining of his coat.

> After I got home, I gave the money to my father. He had a big family and expenses, so that's what I did with it. Yeah.

Milton Buell, Donald Nicholson, Muriel and George MacKay, and Pat Hennessey all came home. Pat went to work at his father's forge, happy to once again be smelling the comforting mix of red-hot metal inside and the salt air outside.

> I didn't think of staying out there. I didn't like it at all. Not a place to live. You'd see a light about every mile or so. The houses were so thin, I'd say it'd be an awful dreary place in the winter. Oh, I wouldn't like it.

Be it ever so humble...

Snow deep & horse 1910 PEI

I remember my father trying to get us to school. There was no such thing as closing the school, no matter what happened, and him driving us with the horse and sleigh from our farm to the school, which was not very far. He had to drive on the side of the road because the middle was all filled in. I remember the horse getting all tangled up in the telephone wires. He [Father] had to get out and take care of the situation.

Ella Willis, R.N., was born in Hampshire in 1910. She was 13 years old in the Year of The Big Snow as 1923 became known. Many Islanders ran out of firewood that winter – the Island was deathly cold as well as snow-bound. One farmer told me that after running out of wood, they burned all the barn stalls, and after digging up fence posts to burn, they finally went to the woods and cut green wood to burn. In the spring, the stumps were ten feet high.

Gerald Best, born in Crapaud in 1911, laughed:

> 1923. I remember it quite well. My father went to his brother's in Tracadie. The route in them days didn't follow the main road in the winter. It wasn't plowed.

Go into this field, cross the road into another field all the way from here to Charlottetown. So, he went to Tracadie and while he was down there the weather moderated. Coming back, he was crossing the telephone lines in Bonshaw and the horse broke through the snow and got tangled up in the electric wires fifteen feet off the ground. And that's the truth.

Electric wires in 1923? Surely, he meant telephone wires, but Gerald was right. The Crapaud/Tryon/Victoria area along with places like Freetown and Breadalbane had electricity much earlier than most of PEI because of enterprising mill owners who generated power at their dams. Mind you, only for a few hours a day, usually in the evenings except for Monday mornings. Wash day, a breeze if you had one of those new-fangled wringer washing machines.

Gerald knew all about snow. In the 1930s, he drove a school "bus" called a van: horse and wagon in summer, horse and sleigh in winter. Big money – $1.50 a day, $7.50 a week – and he supplied the wagon and sleigh and fed the horses. He said it was "hell on earth" breaking through the drifts. Not sure what the horse thought.

Milton Buell was born in Abney, a hamlet halfway between the Murrays – River and Harbour. In the winter of 1923, Milton was 16. He remembers the train not always making it to the Murray Harbour station for the night where the ash and clinkers would be cleared, the water topped up, and the train was loaded up with coal for the early morning run to Charlottetown.

One year, it took the train a whole month to get from Charlottetown to Murray Harbour. It was the narrow-gauge line, before they widened it out. One month. Of course, there was no rotary plow then. The engine would push as far as it could and then the shovelers would have to get out and shovel and shovel. It was so darn deep that the men were up on the snowbank looking down at the telegraph poles.

They were three storeys up. One fella would throw the snow as high as he could, and the next fella would throw it up again so they were three lifts up before they got it over the top. Then, when the engine was freed up, it would back up and take another run, and, of course, get stuck again. It took them a month.

John MacEachern appreciated the break from farm chores when he was growing up in Hermitage near the Vernon River loop. Water to keep the steam up to keep the pipes from freezing wasn't an issue. He recalled:

If the train ran out of water, they shovelled snow into it to keep her going. They had to bring coal in by horse and sleigh to fire the engine. It didn't have enough aboard for a month, of course. Those were the days of snow! When the steam trains were on the go, on a frosty evening, gor, it was pretty to see the smoke rolling up from the engines.

Like many young men in rural PEI, John appreciated the winter storms and blizzards. It meant cash in hand for shovelling out trains stuck in railway cuttings.

Your pay wasn't very big. I think 40 cents an hour. I remember them being stuck down in Bunbury, handy Walter Jones' one night. You'd shovel her out and she'd get stuck again, and she'd go ahead and back up and get stuck again.

The winter of 1923 was especially lucrative for the shovelers.

One time, we went to Murray Harbour and the train got stuck in Iona first. We shovelled her out there and then she got stuck again, and a new bunch of men come on to shovel. We got into Murray Harbour at 1:00 in the afternoon – we'd left Hermitage at 5:00 the previous evening. Everybody was getting hungry. We just had cheese and crackers that we got at a store in Uigg. We got to Murray Harbour, and they took us to the hotel [Prowse's] for dinner. I can see the woman cutting bread. She couldn't slice it fast enough for everybody we were so hungry.

John mentioned Walter Jones, later the Premier of PEI. Before that, Walter had been principal at the Hillsborough Consolidated School or the Macdonald Consolidated School in Mount Herbert. Some of the students travelled by train – the station was next to the school. Others were picked up in vans, similar to the one Gerald Best operated in Crapaud. The school was one of only four in Canada and was funded initially by William Macdonald, from Tracadie, who had made millions selling tobacco. Besides regular lessons, students learned home economics, blacksmithing, and each grew a vegetable garden. Macdonald also funded Macdonald College at McGill in Montreal, and was credited with the progress in agricultural research, not only in Canada but around the world.

◆

Of course, with all the snow and cold, the winter of 1923 had its share of tragedies.

> I think we were really too young to realize what was happening, but I remember the evening he died. I must have known there was something badly wrong because his sisters were there with my mother.

Bertha Ross was 12 when her dad died in the winter of the Big Snow. The eldest of four children, she was traumatized when a tree fell on him while he was cutting firewood at their farm in Durrell near Spry Point on PEI's eastern shore.

> I started to tremble and they couldn't get me stopped. I knew there was something wrong but I didn't know how to express it. They had brandy in the house for my father and one of my father's sisters said, 'I'm going to give her a little bit of brandy.' That's the only drop of drink I ever had in my life. But, anyway, it

was a bad time, no doubt about it. Very bad. A big funeral. He was well-thought of. There was a verandah
on the house and the snow was up above the verandah roof. They had to cut in through it to get into the
house to get the casket out. Cut a tunnel. It certainly
was the winter of the Big Snow. That was the 29th of
March in 1923. It was a bad time.

Bertha's Mum took over the farm and ran it with only the
help of her children. Bertha said they learned a great deal
over the next decade about self-sufficiency and determination, thanks to her mother whom she said "was as tough
as boot leather."

Herb Schurman had happier memories of 1923. Herb was
born in 1911 and lived his life in downtown Summerside.
His father died young too, and his mum raised their eight
children on her own, keeping a few hens in the back yard
for eggs and Sunday dinners. Neighbours like the Deighans
had a cow, and the priest down the street kept pigs. Many
people had a horse shed. Herb recalled the winter of 1923
being especially hard on working horses:

> We didn't know what it was to have a street plowed.
> The streets weren't plowed at all until the 1960s.
> The sidewalks were plowed with an old wooden plow
> with a galvanized front on it. A lot of the time, they
> were wooden sidewalks. They had a horse to pull the
> plow, sometimes two horses one in front of the oth-
> er, and I remember the old fella who plowed, Bob
> Phillips. Every second house had a horse and a cow.
> But they couldn't keep the sidewalks clear because
> the horses would get stuck and he'd have to get his
> shovel and shovel out the plow.

> There was an awful lot of snow. I know one time –
> 1923 I think it was – when we lived in that little
> house on Cambridge Street, both doors were snowed
> in, and there was a snowbank right up to the top of
> the dormer on the back side of the house. They got

my brother dressed up for outside, and took him up and dropped him out the upstairs window. He slid down the snowbank and he shovelled out the doors. But we had lots of fun in the snowbanks, and we made lots of snowmen and snow forts. We used to have fights – neighbours would build a fort in their yard and we'd build one in our yard, and we'd make snowballs and throw them at one another. That's how we had fun. And sleds. We'd coast especially on Saturday and Sundays. Not too much on Sunday. They weren't too fussy about letting you do too much on Sunday.

The trains didn't run on Sunday either. No doubt the shovellers, like everyone else, appreciated the break.

Addie Hamm told me the train that took a month to get from Charlottetown to Murray Harbour first got stranded in front of their farm in Bunbury. Her mother fed and boarded the trainmen for six days before they were able to inch their way to the next snow-blocked cutting. No money changed hands. I interviewed Addie 80 years later, and she was still fuming, not because her mum hadn't been paid, but because the conductor had kept his stash of peppermints to himself the whole time. And Addie liked peppermints.

Rum and Salt Water

Vivian (White) & Austin Graham

We've all heard the expression "the days of wooden ships and iron men," an era of prosperity in the Maritimes, when the great Samuel Cunard in Nova Scotia, and the Peakes and Cambridges on PEI, built and sailed barques and schooners. Sleepy little Murray Harbour in southeastern PEI was one of the last schooner ports on the Atlantic, a village of sea captains and sailors like the Whites, the Dunns, and the Chapmans.

Vivian White Graham was born in "the Harbour" in 1921. Her grandfather was one of those sea captains:

> My grandfather was George Dunn. He was a captain and, when he was 13, him and his brother ran away from home, because his father had been hired to go to Boston to go to war, fight for somebody. Those times, you could hire somebody to fight in your place, and so his father went up there to fight and he never came back home. He married a lady up there, 'up in Boston,' and he had another family.
>
> So, my grandfather's mother, when she found out he wasn't comin' home, she remarried and she married

a Catholic man. At that time, a Catholic marrying a Protestant, you know, that never happened. Anyway, he wasn't a very good father to my grandfather and his brother, so they jumped on a ship, one of the vessels that came from Murray Harbour. One fella got off at Murray Harbour and one went to the Magdalene Islands and settled there. He was quite musical and he would sing all the songs that had real good stories to them. How we wish we wrote some of those words down. Captain George Dunn, he lived to be about 99, and he drank more rum and smoked more tobacco. If there was a storm and he run out of tobacco, he'd smoke tea: put tea in the pipe.

♦

Boat rum was about the same price we now pay for gasoline – $5 a gallon. Milton Buell from Abney, halfway between Murray Harbour and Murray River, told me that during the Spanish Flu epidemic in 1918-19, he drove an overworked and exhausted Dr Lester Brehaut on his rounds in the doctor's Model-T Ford. One time, they ran out of gas in the middle of nowhere. Milton hated to, but shook the doctor awake. The old doc rubbed his eyes and jumped out of the car and disappeared down the road to a farm they'd passed a half mile back. He returned with a gallon jug of moonshine, and poured it into the gas tank. Milton said the Model-T purred; said it never worked better.

Many people were involved in the rum business, some like Roy Clow buying two five-gallon kegs at a time, one to sell for $10 a gallon, paying for the other, which made the long winter nights on a farm in Murray Harbour North a bit more tolerable for Roy and his brothers.

Other people were running illegal liquor on a larger scale. Lorne Francis was born in Bay Fortune in 1925. Lorne was the last to run the family business making wagons and the famous Francis cutters – one of the best horse-drawn sleighs in eastern Canada. Lorne grew up in relative luxury; in fact, he's the only person of the hundreds I interviewed over the years who didn't notice a decline in the family's fortunes during the Great Depression. One reason was because his father knew how to make money. Lorne was driving his dad's cars by the time he was 14, and hauling loads of coal in two-ton trucks around eastern PEI. Lorne kept his eyes-and ears open:

> You know John F. Kennedy's father, Joseph, he was in to Souris in a boat. Load of rum. Selling it. He was in the rum business. Sure. I can remember when I was going to school, a cousin of mine and I used to go to the back of our farm that ran down to Rollo Bay shore. Couple of weeks or a month before that somebody – nobody knew for sure – brought in this load of rum. Hundreds of kegs all buried in the sand in Rollo Bay and the tide came the wrong way and washed the tops clear. The farmers down there all got some out of it.

Ironically, besides Lorne's father selling wagons and sleighs, he also sold tractors. Maybe he was prescient. Lorne talks about one local who bought a tractor, not to plow furrows, but to haul away some of those kegs of rum that kept washing up along the shore.

Rum running ran longer on PEI than the rest of the Maritimes, mainly because prohibition lasted considerably longer: until 1948. Fishers couldn't pay the bills with cent-and-a-half-a-pound cod and hake, so they ran a few kegs, selling them to local bootleggers. Lorne Francis laughed:

> They used to joke about them lighting their pipe with two-dollar bills. Ha. They got rich all of a sudden.

"The Automobile is... a Fad"

Model-T Ford

"The car that put America on the road." The Flivver. The Tin Lizzie. In September 1908, the Model-T Ford rolled out of a Detroit factory and into the heart of any North American who had the thousand dollars to buy one. By 1913, after Henry Ford had incorporated the assembly line into his massive car factory, the price of a Model-T dropped to under $500.

By 1923, the same car cost less than $300. Ford had achieved his goal: to produce a car that even his own factory workers could afford to buy, and road-builders have been scrambling ever since to keep up to an increasingly mobile world.

In a tasty bit of irony, the same year the Model-T premiered, cars were banned on Prince Edward Island, thereby living up to its reputation as the Kentucky of the North. No doubt every one of the 40,000 horses on PEI in 1908 was afraid of the noisy, smelly automobile. Farmers didn't like cars either. Stella MacDougall was born in 1910 in Bedford, 15 kilometres east of Charlottetown. Her uncle M. J. McIvor came home to PEI from the Boston States every summer.

He had one of the first cars on the Island. He used to come visit us in Bedford. His wife and my mother were sisters. But when he got to the York Road, they wouldn't let him come any further on St. Peters Road, so he had to go down through Grand Tracadie. He got as far as the Duggan Road. We lived beyond that. Well, when he got to the Duggan Road, the farmers were there with pitchforks and shovels, and I don't know what all. Two or three men wouldn't let him go any further so they had to abandon the car, leave it there, and walk the rest of the way to our place. He didn't say too much. I guess he thought he was lucky to get that far. And then one of those men was the first man to have a car in our area.

Two-faced? Or simply a case of putting the car before the horse.

Stella's first job was behind the counter at Court's General Store, next to the Bedford railway station. She always equated the first canned goods in the store with people who had enough money to drive a car. She said the only people buying canned peaches owned Model-Ts.

By 1913, the ban on cars on Island roads was partially lifted. You could drive a car on specified roads but only on certain days. I suspect M. J. McIvor, who was from Kinkora and who incidentally is credited with jump-starting the seed potato industry, was driving on a restricted road. Or as Stella pointed out, maybe on the wrong day.

They couldn't go on the road on market days – Tuesdays and Fridays – and on Sundays they couldn't be on the road during church hours. The cars scared the horses.

Lester Hickox was born in 1909. He remembered when both cars and horses drove on the left-hand side of the road:

They changed from one side over to the other, from the left-hand side to the right-hand side, and they had quite a problem with it too. People meeting on the road would take the wrong side, a real fuss. Two old farmers would meet on the road and the horses were used to going their own way, and they'd get into a big argument as to who was on the right side of the road.

We had one incident that I well remember: my grandmother lived in Clyde River and we were down there – this was on a Sunday – and we saw a car coming. Now the driver was supposed to stop if you put your hand up. The wagon that we had was a buggy with a top on it, and there was some doubt whether the driver of the car had seen my father putting his hand up. But anyway, he didn't stop. He kept coming and there were two men in the front seat and two women in the back seat. And our horse was a big heavy horse. He got in reverse, and he started backing up and he pushed the wagon up onto the bank on the side of the road. So now we were sitting up looking down at the car. My father was kind of short on the fuse and he let a roar of him, 'You get that car out of there or I'll put this horse into that car!' And these two women in the back pretty-near went out the other side of the car.

Chalk up one victory for the horse... one battle, but not the war. In fact, Lester's father, Spurgeon Hickox, must have figured if he couldn't beat them, he should join them, because he swapped his horse and buggy for a 1914 Model-T Ford with a brass radiator.

Not everyone who bought a car got rid of their horses. Richie Smith, whose farm was at the bottom of Mount Thom in New Glasgow, PEI, across from Campbell's Pond, told me, "I always keep a horse around just to look at." Islanders loved their horses, even the wild and woolly western horses imported from Alberta by horse and cattle traders like Wellington MacNeill from Tea Hill. The western horses were big and cheap, but also had a well-deserved reputation for kicking, as did the Model-Ts.

The Model-T was barebones. No extras were included in the base price, so buyers paid extra for windshield wipers and electric starters. Most people opted to hand-crank the car to get it started. If they weren't paying attention, the crank would suddenly snap back and give their arm a nasty twist. Charlie Bell, born in 1913 in Lower Tryon, was driving his dad's car when he was only 14.

> A 1917, right-hand-drive Model-T. You had to crank it. Mother also learned to drive, one of the few women drivers on the Island. And when going to the store she had to make sure there'd be a man there who could crank it and start it for her. It was a treacherous thing. Unless you set the spark right, and sometimes even if you did what you thought was right, the crank would kick back. I had a brother, Kenneth, he went to start the car one day at church, and broke his arm. So, we had to send for the doctor. He came up and put Kenneth under ether and set the arm. Had to get one of the neighbours in to help him pull the arm back in place, then he put a splint on it.

Broken arms and sprained wrists went hand in hand with the Model-T until 1928 when Ford replaced it with the Model-A. It had an electric starter.

Keith Mutch grew up on a dairy farm in Keppoch and his first Model-T didn't come with many extras, like windshield wipers, speedometers or headlights. It wasn't fancy but the price was right.

> I bought a Model-T up where Mills' Meat Market used to be on Hillsboro Street in Charlottetown. It had a connecting rod burnt out, a failing they had, but I bought it for $5.

The Tin Lizzie had interchangeable parts, was easy to repair, and, as Ford advertised, came in any colour you wanted as long as it was black.

> We had an old car and were in with the milk this Sunday morning. I got my father to pull it home. He

wasn't too happy about the idea, an old pile of junk coming home. That following winter, I got working on it when I wasn't busy on the farm. I put in another connecting rod and fixed up a few other things. I had to spend $5 on it. I thought twice before I'd spend that kind of money. Then in the spring, I sold it and got $15 for it and I thought I had the world by the tail. Tripled my money, not counting the labour. You didn't count labour in those days.

Keith was 17 at the time, and he owned a car until he died. The Model-T was like a loss leader: Ford figured once you felt the wind blowing through your hair, you'd always want a car. That philosophy changed the world and, in hindsight, maybe not for the best. By 1913, Ford had more than halved the sticker price and thousands of Model-Ts were charging down city streets and country lanes. The world's not been the same since.

Keith's Model-T wasn't the first one in his family. Years earlier, his uncle Thorley Mutch had abandoned the family farm for the bright lights of the Big Shamrock.

My uncle was working up in Boston. He went up about 1920, and my father wanted to get hold of a car. So, my uncle said he could buy a Model-T up there and drive it back home down to the Island for him. So, he bought the car and he started down but he only got about halfway when a connecting rod burnt out. So that was as far as he got that year.

There's a pattern emerging here: all we have to do is connect the rods.

I don't know if he took the car back to Boston or if he just left it there, but the next year he got the car going and drove it the rest of the way to PEI. We used that Model-T a good many years on the farm, used it to saw wood too. Put a belt on the hind wheel and sawed the winter's supply of wood with it.

That's not all. Ford sold a "tractor conversion kit," a special attachment for a set of gears that went on the back axle, plus big wheels with iron spikes, so you could plough and harrow. Roy Clow grew up on a farm in Murray Harbour North where neighbours had bought conversion kits, transforming their Model-Ts into tractoroids. Dr. G. Inman went a step further, cruising over the snowdrifts in a machine unique to eastern PEI.

> He had an old snowmobile made out of a Model-T Ford. Dr. Inman'd go out in all kinds of weather. They put tracks on it like a bulldozer, and it was an awful crude-looking thing. When he couldn't go out with his car, he'd try to make it with that thing. He'd go over fences and everything else in the way.

Yet another tradition still practised by some snowmobilers. To be fair, the Model-T was advertised as the car that could go anywhere, even on a schooner as Captain William Trenholm proved. Captain William once owned seven schooners at the same time, including one named *The Telephone.* I'm sure there's a tech millionaire out there somewhere with a yacht named Dot Com, but I digress.

Captain William's three sons became sea captains, and in 1920, when Thomas was ten years old, the Trenholms were sailing two schooners loaded with bricks from Pugwash, NS, to Souris, PEI.

> The *Freddie A. Higgins* carried about a hundred tonnes and the *Rayburn* carried about 120 tonnes. She was owned here in Murray Harbour one time by a Captain Davey. The two schooners had a load of brick and a fella from Sussex NB, J.D. Fryer, who was an agent for cars and engines and he sold my father a Ford car, a Model T Ford that they put aboard the *Rayburn.*

Tom and his mother and sister were sailing on the *Freddie A. Higgins* with his father, and the *Rayburn* was captained by Tom's older brother.

We got into Souris before he did. My brother Russell had just come back from the First World War. That was 1920, so he'd been back a couple of years. In any case, we were landed there on a Sunday morning. My father said, 'We'll put the car ashore and we'll go to Montague to visit the Allens, and show them a bit of style.' After all, he was the owner of an automobile, you know what I mean. A lovely automobile.

So early Sunday morning they piled into the Model-T and headed south from Souris to Montague to visit Captain George Allen, a relative, and his family.

Oh, everybody felt great about the trip. An automobile, by God, we owned an automobile. We're really up in G, you know what I mean.

Ah, not really. "Up in G": had to look that one up myself. It's a lyric from the 1880s song "The Sidewalks of New York" and either refers to jail (gaol) or more likely Gramercy, an upscale area of New York City. "Some are up in G, some are on the hog..." I take it to mean livin' high on the hog, that is, doing well. Where were we? Right, haven't left Souris yet.

Well, we got her ashore, and the Old Fella cranked her up and got her going. Oh boys, we felt some darn good about it. Got aboard and headed for Montague. At that time, we had to cross on the Newport ferry, a paddle-wheel or some darn thing. I think there were paddle wheels on it, across the river.

The village of Newport is near the mouth of the Cardigan River. It was probably a cable ferry, although there were paddle-wheelers on PEI at one time.

But before we got to Newport, ah God, things started to go wrong. The roads were the worst in these back places. It was all horse and wagon, pretty well, and wagon wheel ruts. The road was rough you know, and if there was a big rock you just drove over it the best way you could, but the base of the engine struck something.

Ford boasted that the Model-T could be repaired with a half-dozen wrenches that came with the car. Thusly, the Trenholms tightened the leaking oil pan and continued on their way.

We got to Montague but it wasn't by the route they take now from Souris. Not at all. We went into Captain George's house in Montague, but he wasn't there at the time. As far as they could figure out, Captain George Allen was a half uncle of my father. At that time George would be about 60 or 65, but in any case, he wasn't as big a man as my father.

Not many people were. Captain William was six feet tall and weighed 300 pounds.

Captain George was a man, if he had anything to say, he'd say it. He was scared of no man. He gave the impression he was scared of nothing or nobody.

Ditto for Captain William, in spades: he had a monkey for a pet, liked to drink rum, and he always carried a gun.

Captain George had two daughters there, and Russell took the girls out for a run in the car. He was a little on the show-off side, a great fella. But finally, it was time to go back to Souris. So, we started back around three o'clock. You couldn't drive very fast — there were only two gears in the thing. We got part of the way back, church was out, and the people were on their way home.

This was back in the days of both morning and evening church services with Sunday school in between.

We met a horse and wagon with I don't know how many in it. As the horse got closer, the sound of the engine made the horse jittery. They were terrified at the sound of a car. So, alright, Russell pulled the car over to the side in order to let them go by. And the engine stopped. If the engine hadn't stalled I guess they wouldn't have gone by. They were terrified and when they got abreast of us, good God, the horse took off. You talk about running. Russell started to get the car going again and gave the engine a race to get her out from the side of the road, and he burnt the lights out.

It got dark after that, he could only drive in low gear, my father sitting beside him hollering and bawling, 'You're going too fast. You can't see where you're going.' And Russell hollering back, 'I know I don't know where I'm going. If I slow down much more it'll stall.' Russell had a dog's life the rest of that trip. He'll never forget that!

Finally, in the pitch dark, no lights except for a few isolated farmhouses giving off a yellow kerosene glow, Russell went to one of the farms, and came back with a barn lantern crowned with a filthy globe.

He hung that over the bow — we called the front of the car the bow — on the radiator cap and hoped the light would shine out ahead. That was worse than no light at all. Most of the light was shining back, and Russell was pretty near out of his mind. The Old Fella was giving it to him, telling him what to do.

In the end, young Tom leaned out over the front fender with the lantern, scratched and jostled by every passing branch, something he never forgot either.

Well, anyway, we finally got back at eleven o'clock that night. We got her down to the wharf and the Old Fella said, 'If that's automobile driving, I've had enough. Give me the old horse and wagon.'

Captain William loaded his Model-T back onto the deck of the *Rayburn*, and sailed to Louisbourg to pick up a load of Sydney coal. While there, he decided he wanted to drive the car himself. The family gathered to watch. The first time Captain William tried to stop the car, instead of hitting the brakes, he yelled, *"Whoa!"* and crashed. And that, as they say, ended that.

Captain William might well have taken the advice of the president of the Michigan Savings Bank who, in 1903, advised Henry Ford's lawyer, Horace Rackham, not to invest in Henry Ford's fledgling motor car company, telling him, "The horse is here to stay but the automobile is only a novelty, a fad." Instead, Horace Rackham ignored the banker, invested $5,000 in Ford stock, and several years, later sold the stock for $12.5 million, about half a billion dollars in today's money.

In 1999, the Model-T Ford was voted The Car of the Century. Horses – and Captain William – didn't get a vote.

Mary MacPhee Malone at the MacPhee homestead.

I'm not sure if there's a certain date for it, but after shearing the sheep in the spring, you'd be careful
not to shear them too early, because you always got a
'sheep storm' around the first of May.

Robbie Robertson, born in 1904 in King sboro, was a fisherman, as were Robbie's father and Robbie's sons.

Cold and wet and windy. Could be snow too. If you
put the sheared sheep out too soon, you'd get the
sheep storm. Some farmers wouldn't shear their
sheep until after a certain date.

I hadn't heard of a sheep storm before. I Googled it, and up
popped an almost identical explanation from the Nantucket
Historical Association. Nantucket is a small island off the
coast of Cape Cod. Robbie fished out of Basin Head as did
his good friend and fellow fisher, Clive Bruce. They were

instrumental in getting the wharf that's there now so they wouldn't have to haul their boats up onto the white sand every night.

Clive Bruce was born in 1910 in Red Point east of Souris, PEI . Like Robbie, Clive fished for over 60 years and was a noted weather forecaster:

> There was always a storm that came in May when I was young. A nor'easter with snow and rain for two or three days. The farmers would have their sheep all sheared and the young lambs out in the commons, and this sheep storm would come. If people didn't get their sheep gathered in somewhere warm, some of the lambs died. The fishermen always called that the sheep storm.

♦

Mary MacPhee Malone was born 1925 in Big Pond near Rock Barra on PEI's north side, not far from where Clive and Robbie fished. Mary had 13 brothers and sisters, and her mother Cecilia Hennessey and father Michael MacPhee raised sheep:

> My mother made salve out lamb suet, alder bark and alder peelings. It was good for burns. She'd take the bark off the alder, then steep it. It was a brown liquid. Then she'd add this lamb suet from a lamb roast, you know that nice soft clear suet. She'd put that in little cans, this off-white salve, and it was good for burns. She must have learned it from the Irish side, her mother and them over there in St. Catherines, near the Mooneys. Her father was a blacksmith.

No doubt him working at the forge every day gave his wife plenty of opportunity to try out her lamb salve. A few years ago, BBC radio ran a story about a breed of sheep named for the Orkney island of North Ronaldsay where it originated.

This hardy breed lived entirely on beaches, feeding on kelp and seaweed. This unusual diet led to scientists testing the mutton for natural antibiotics. A case of having your salve and eating it too.

♦

At one time, the lowly herring was the most common cure, if common is the right word, for pneumonia or a high fever. Amy Bryanton was born in 1904 and lived to 104.

> I had the cold. Now, I'd be four or five years old. We had neighbours who lived across the field from us, Jake Duggan and the wife Ellen. They heard I was sick with a cold, so Mrs. Duggan told Mum to take a salt herring, split it, and put one half on each foot. Tie it on each foot to take the fever down. So, Mum did that. I got better, yeah. Well, that was alright but every time I went to the table to eat, they had to carry me because I wouldn't walk on the herring.

I was surprised they used herring and not sole. The salt herring cure starts off a litany of more exotic home remedies involving animals in some form or another:

> Raw chicken. That came from my grandmother Johnston. That would take the fever down.

Charlie Deighan didn't scarf the raw chicken down KFC-style. I'll let his wife Rose explain:

> They used to get a chicken and put their feet in a dead chicken. For high fevers. Charlie's grandmother told him that they'd slit the chicken, one [side] for each foot and it'd take the fever out.

Charlie was born in 1921, and had 19 siblings. He served in the Second World War with the special forces unit dubbed The Devil's Brigade, and The Black Devils by the Germans. His father Ernest was a train driver and taught Charlie, who used to fire for him, how to drive a steam engine. Charlie was a C.N.R. railwayman for 40 years. He also played hockey for the Summerside Crystals. Some days, he'd fire all day on the western freight to Tignish, come home, grab his hockey gear and fire the "hockey special" to Charlottetown, play the game, and then fire the engine back to Summerside. Incredible stamina.

The Deighans lived in downtown Summerside and, not far away, Margaret Townsend Crozier was born in Grangemount, now called Sherbrooke, in 1916:

> He had a terrible fever, and they took a hen, split it, opened it, and put it at his feet. Now, I'm not sure how long they left it there, but it reduced his fever and the flesh of the hen turned black. That was my brother Frank.

Their father was Major Townsend, his name, not his rank, and their mother Margaret Brown, who was one of eight children. Margaret was one of the "angels of mercy" in the 1918-19 Spanish Flu epidemic, bringing food and clean bed linen to sick neighbours, cleaning dishes, and emptying chamber pots. She somehow avoided the flu.

A few miles east of Sherbrooke, Harry Heffell and Marjorie Heffell Somers shared the family farm in Travellers Rest in their sunset years. Harry was the eldest of nine children, born in 1904, and Marjorie was the baby, born in 1923. Their father William was a farmer and a cattle and horse trader. Their mother Maude, née Raynor, worked in both the house and in the fields. The Heffells loved birds of any size and description. Their house was a cacophony of chirping budgies, and Harry had a barn full of exotic geese and ducks.

Marjorie remembered one unusual home remedy involving poultry:

> This young girl lived up the road, a young Blanchard girl, and she was very sick, in her lungs, pneumonia,

and the doctors gave her up. They came and came to the house, did all they could, and said that was it. So, my mother's Aunt Amy Raynor lived down at the creek here, and she was sort of a midwife and used to go when there was sickness, and she said, 'Well, Doctor, if you're all through and have given this girl up for death, I'll take over.'

So, she went home and she killed a hen. And then she took the hatchet and cut the hen right in half, feathers and all, and all the insides in it. And she went up with it and she put one half of the hen on the child's breast, the other on her back and strapped it on with a cotton cloth. She left it on there and I would say within twenty-four hours she took it off and it was cooked. It drew out all that inflammation. It would be called infection today. It was something like the salt herring [cure], see, that would draw out the infection and cook the meat.

I was the one who had salt herring on my feet, and it took my temperature down and the fish was cooked. As was the chicken, you see. The girl got better and she lived to be an old lady. Josephine Blanchard was her name. I often heard my mother tell the story. It's strange how those old remedies worked, but if you tell a lot of doctors that today they laugh. And druggists, because they want to sell their drugs. There's no money in chickens and salt herring today.

And if salt herring on the feet or a sacrificial hen didn't bring the fever down, Aunt Amy had another cure: "Fry up goose grease and onions to make a poultice if you had an awful chest cold or pneumonia."

Likewise in Georgetown, where Frances Lavers Llewellyn was born in 1913, the middle child of seven born to Harry Lavers and Mabel Stewart. Mabel was a midwife who had her own version of the salt herring cure:

They would put the salt herring in a sock and put it

around your throat. That was for a sore throat; a bad, inflamed throat. I heard my mother say, 'You better get the salt herring in the sock.' And onion plaster to break up a cold in the chest. And everybody had a bottle of liquor in the house for home remedies. Mostly brandy. I remember one time the doctor came down because Mum had pneumonia. I was in bed with her. I can remember him saying, 'What's wrong with the little one?'

'Oh,' Mum said, 'She's not feeling very well. She has a bellyache.'

'Give her some whisky,' he said, 'in warm water and sugar.'

Well, I liked it so much, I had the bellyache for over a month.

♦

Up on Munn's Road, Boswell Robertson would have been surprised a doctor was even summoned:

You never went to a doctor. I remember threshing in the wintertime, you'd take the chills and they'd give you Rawleigh's Red Liniment, and put you to bed. And if that didn't cure you, I don't know what would.

Rawleigh's Red Internal Liniment was sold by the Rawleigh man who went door-to-door selling his kitchen and barn products: vanilla extract, pie fillings, salves, ointments, and the Internal Liniment, which promised to relieve aches and pains, stomach cramps, 'flu, coughs, and "various gastrointestinal tract conditions." It contained, among other things, oil of spearmint plus *capsicum Annum,* a variety of chili pepper related to cayenne peppers... as Boswell found out:

Did you ever drink it? Oh, it would burn the stomach out of you. A few drops in hot water and drink that. A half hour after drinking that, you'd be sweating; the water would be running off you in bed. You could use the liniment on the outside of your body too, but, boys, this was hot stuff. This would knock the chills out of you, and the 'flu too.

Rose O'Keefe Deighan, born 1927 in the paper-making town of Grand Falls, was proud of her Newfoundland heritage. Rose wound up moving from one island to another after she met and fell in love with her future husband Charlie Deighan, who briefly served in Newfoundland during the Second World War before going overseas. Rose's mum was Mary Griffin from Harbour Grace, and her father, Charlie O'Keefe, was a stationary engineer who, as a young man, went off killing seals on a big vessel in the annual spring hunt.

March was called the 'hungry month' because no matter how good a season they had fishing, it all went to the merchants in St. John's. People would go in and get their supplies for the following winter: a barrel of flour, a barrel of molasses, whatever, and they'd bring that home so by the time winter was over and March was coming, they were hungry. There was no more food. They all ran out. That's what my mother always said, 'This is the hungry month of March.' Then, you see, the only thing they had left was to go 'swiling,' go to the seal hunt. So, that's what they used to do in order to get some money to get some food. My father used to go on the seal hunt. They used to call it 'going swiling.' He said they'd get out on the ice and when their feet got cold, they'd take the seal and they'd slit them down the centre of their belly, take the guts out, and then put their feet in so their feet wouldn't freeze.

Rose had a relative from Carbonnear, Richard McCarthey, who survived the 1914 sealing tragedy when, during a blizzard, 78 men died alone, or huddled for warmth in twos or threes, abandoned on the ice. Therefore, in what seemed like good fortune initially, the outbreak of the First World War in 1914 gave Rose's father a chance to quit swiling. He first joined the Navy, then the Army while overseas. He was wounded twice, and, like most First World War veterans, he wouldn't discuss the war except to say he hated the British.

> It was terrible. He wouldn't talk about. If he was having a few drinks, he would talk about the war, and cry about it. One time he was out on patrol and the Germans were coming, and there were dead bodies all around. So, to save himself from the Germans, he had to pile the dead bodies up and hide behind them so he wouldn't be caught. Another time, he had real good friend, and they were out and his friend got shot. Dad carried him on his back for miles and miles and miles to the Red Cross Station. When he got there, his friend was dead on his back. He hated the British with a passion. Anyone who wasn't British, hated the British. He was Irish, so it goes back. [Newfoundland was] a British colony then. It stayed with him all his life. Hard tack and bully beef, that's what they ate. Newfoundlanders never got over the war. So many of their young men were gone. They never recovered really.

On July 1st when the rest of Canada is celebrating Canada Day, it's a day of mourning in Newfoundland and Labrador. The Royal Newfoundland Regiment, also known as the Blue Puttees - when they ran out of khaki leggings, they issued blue ones to the Newfoundlanders - suffered huge losses at Gallipoli. Then, on 1 July 1916, in the first Battle of the Somme at Beaumont Hamel, the RNR was almost wiped out. Of the 780 Newfoundlanders who went "over the top," 110 survived; 68 were available for roll call the following day. However, less than a year later, on 23 April 1917 at Monchy-le-Preux during the Battle of Arras, fortified with reinforcements, the Royal Newfoundland Regiment lost 485 men in one day. They stopped the German advance, but, as Rose's father said, "We were nothing more than cannon fodder." That's why July 1st is Memorial Day in Newfoundland and Labrador.

♦

Back to unusual home remedies.

> Take a half teaspoon of sulphur and molasses every day, and it'll clean your blood. Years ago, that's why people never had cancer. You can still buy sulphur. Mix it yourself with molasses to make a good paste. The old people always did that, every day, yeah.

Amy Bryanton learned her vast array of cures from her grandmothers Caseley and Adams, who lived in the Spring Valley/Kensington area. As a little girl, she followed them to the woods to pick cherry bark and spruce tips to make spring tonics and cough syrup.

Notwithstanding sulphur and molasses, one disease we still don't have a cure for is the dreaded cancer. Cancer patients around the world use the anti-cancer compound Taxol, which is produced by yew trees. Interestingly, the yew is sacred in places like Wales and can be found in every kirkyard. Ironically, yews grow sinewy branches perfect for making the best bows and arrows, instruments of death.

While interviewing Peter Whitty about delivering coal and groceries with a horse and wagon for Matthew and MacLean's big general store in Souris, his friend Mary mentioned a local man:

> Alex Paquet was the seventh son of a seventh son or something, and he had this cancer cure.

Mary Dunphy O'Hanley was born in Souris in 1921.

> I was at his house — I never had the cure — but I know people who got it. He made some kind of an ointment. I don't know what he made it out of. I don't know where it ever went. Or if anybody's got it now. I knew of people that took it and they said they got cured. People used to go to his house to get it. He lived down along Chapel Street, right in Souris. I don't believe that, do you? I never did believe it. By God, cancer's not that easily cured.

After that intriguing bit of news, whenever I was interviewing someone from northeastern PEI, I asked about the "cancer cure." Here's what I heard:

> When he was around 60, he got skin cancer in his ear and he heard about a Paquet man in Souris who had a cure that had been passed down through the Catholic Church.

Here's Gordon Dockendorff, born in 1925 in Mount Hope. Gordon's father was Vine Hall Dockendorff, born in 1871, a teetotaler who chewed tobacco only once in his life.

> When one person who knew the cure died, they'd pass it on to another person, not   necessarily the same family. So, Dad went to the Paquet man and got this cure. It consisted of a little bottle of ointment or salve, white salve, which he rubbed on the cancer and then he covered it with a jelly substance from another bottle. And after a couple of weeks, the cancer started to get drawn out from his ear, and he had to put a bandage over that to hold it in place so the tentacles of the tumour wouldn't break off before they were all out of his ear. The tumour just raised right out of the ear. That cured his cancer.

Vine Hall's brother was also cured:

> His brother George was cured by the same method. He had cancer on his lip from smoking a pipe. I think when Mr. Paquet died, the secret died with him. He didn't have a chance to pass it on. Some people used to
>
> say it was made of spider web, but I've never been able to verify this.

Potato farmer Boswell Robertson was born in Munn's Road in 1924. When he was a boy, his mother kept a boarding house, and Boswell drove the commercial travellers around to the many general stores in the Souris area.

There's another settlement north of here about the size of this one, but there's no one living in it now. I can remember one of the women living there, she had cancer, and she had a plaster on her neck that drew it out.

She lived?

Yes. I can remember her quite well. Different ones had it done. Some had lip cancer too, that I'm sure of. It was something Paquet mixed up. But it done the job. Years ago, it was surprising the people that had that plaster on.

Robbie Robertson lived nearby on the Snake Road in Kingsboro:

When I was a boy, I'd hear them talking about it. It was a patch they put on the tumour. I don't know if Paquet ever revealed the secret of it or not.

Rose Grady had relatives cured by Paquet's salve plus, as she said, a lot of "faith prayers." Rose's husband Reg Grady told me he thought Paquet travelled around with his cure, to New Brunswick and Nova Scotia, down to the New England States and even to France. No one else mentioned this but Robbie did know this story:

A McInnis woman – Anastasia – came home from the States to have it out on her foot. She had the cancer in the foot, had this plaster put on, and it drew the cancer out.

And Robbie had heard that one time the cure didn't work for a local man:

The little fella sat on his knee. His son Arthur, sat on his knee, and touched the thing – the plaster – and it came off before all the roots had been drawn out. And the cancer got him at the last of it. This cancer cure: only one person was supposed to have it, and he died and it wasn't passed on.

Clive Bruce, born in 1910 in Red Point tells a similar story:

I know all about that cure. Well, alright then: Paquet made a plaster, and put it on you and you were not to touch it or take it off. Wallace Murphy in Elmira had cancer and had the plaster on, and it was just hanging there. If he'd left it three or four more days, it would have dropped off, but he got tired of it dangling there and he gave it a pull and the cancer went crazy. Killed him in no time. Paquet was supposed to give that cure to one of his nephews, but he died in bed before they got somebody there to take down the cure. Nobody's ever come across that cure since. We're talking in the 1920s because Angus Strang in the [East] Baltic had lip cancer and he was going to get the cure but Paquet died before he got it.

Everyone I talked to was convinced the cure died when Alex Paquet, who was born in 1874, passed away in 1947. Clive tells this macabre story about one of his neighbours:

He just walked up and down the road all day and all night, suffering his heart out. You'd hear him roaring with the pain. They used to kill a chicken every night, put it on his face in the morning. and there'd be nothing left but the bones. It was an "eating" cancer. He'd put a chicken on his face – the only way he could get any rest. When it, the tumour, was eating that chicken, the pain eased up. It ate the chicken, not him. Going to school, we used to see him and the poor man's face was half gone, all red and his tongue hanging out. And I'd feel sorry for him.

Paquet was going to make a plaster for him, but he died before Angus [Strang] got down to him. I never saw what it was. They called it a plaster. He cured a lot of people. Angus Stewart from the Baltic had cancer. They called it 'pipe cancer': he used to smoke those clay pipes. He got a plaster put on his lip or mouth, and it drew it out and he lived to a good old age.

Clive had one of many theories about how Paquet died and where the cure originated in the first place: "Old age, I guess. According to [Indigenous] tradition, he wasn't to tell anybody."

Other people insisted the cure was passed down through the Catholic Church, but most agreed that only one person was allowed to have the recipe at any one time. Camilla Paquet thought the cure was passed on to Alex's wife Annie MacDonald. Years after I first heard about the cancer cure, Louis MacDonald, born 1911 in Cornwall, was talking about home remedies, and surprised me with this:

> If you had cancer of the lip or anything like that, there was supposed to be a remedy that, if you put it on, it would draw the cancer thread out from way down. Terrible painful remedy. It was an old-fashioned remedy.

Louis didn't recognize Alex Paquet's name, but did say you had to be careful not to disturb anything after applying the salve and bandage. Coincidence? Louis' dad George was originally from Glenfinnan, east of Charlottetown, and was the manager of a general store and a lobster cannery. Had he picked up the story in his travels?

Reg Grady thought Alex was a relative of a Souris icon, Fidèle Paquet, the man who donated land for St. Mary's Roman Catholic Church graveyard high on the hill overlooking Souris. Alex was Fidèle's grandson. There's a miracle associated with Fidèle: when he died in 1863, the bells of the church suddenly started ringing even though there was no one in the church at the time.

Grey Mitts Bring Grey Skies

Jane Harris Fraser, Murray Harbour

Jane Harris Fraser was born in Cape Bear in 1912, the year the Titanic sank. Her father, William Fletcher Harris fished – two cents a pound for lobster – and was a prohibition officer. Jane's mother, Jessie Fergusson, had an arsenal of old home remedies.

Dad wasn't superstitious. Not a bit in the world. Well, the only thing he was superstitious over was, and we always laughed about it, for some unknown reason his mother would never allow them to cut their toenails or fingernails on a Sunday. And I'm sure he never did that in all his lifetime. I don't know why.

It was believed that, if you cut your nails on Sunday, the devil would follow you around for a week. The Harris family must have had excellent karma then, because good luck seemed to follow them. From their home in Murray Harbour, the entire Harris family heard the 1917 Halifax Explosion. Twelve years later, they heard the dishes rattle in the cupboard and watched a ten-foot tidal wave, or *tsunami*, roll in after the 1929 earthquake in the Gulf of St Lawrence between PEI and Newfoundland and Labrador.

My father Billy fished and went on the cutters after the rumrunners when fishing was over. A few years later, he bought a vessel, the *Arizona*, but she was lost one night in November. Came up a storm and I think 14 vessels were lost that night going from Georgetown to Charlottetown. 1921 or somewhere around there. The sails blew off his vessel near Point Prim and he drifted right across the Strait down to Pugwash. They didn't think they had a chance in the world; they were helpless with the sails gone.

There was an Andrew Cain and a Wilson Arnold with him on the boat. They managed to get ashore in an old dory. He said they could see a little faint light way, way off in the distance, and they climbed up a desperately steep hill, and people by the name of McIvor took them in and kept them. He came and he brought one of the boys, Wilson, here to the Island, because he was an orphan. Some years later, Wilson went out fishing and he was lost overboard and was never seen since. Lost at sea somewhere out on Fisherman's Bank.

If you were superstitious, you'd almost think that was Wilson's destiny. Maybe the Arizona was launched on a Friday, which was considered bad luck. Or maybe they were fishing on a Sunday – bad religion.

We went to the United church in Malpeque." Keir MacKay was born in 1913 in Darnley, delivered by Dr. Keir after whom he was named. The United church in Malpeque was Presbyterian until Church Union in 1925. Some Presbyterians refused to join the United Church and, in 1927, consecrated a new church across the road, now the Malpeque Museum.

We were allowed to play around the house on Sunday, but Uncle Herb wouldn't shave or clean his shoes or anything on Sunday. He wouldn't even clean the stables out on Sunday. He wouldn't do anything except milk the cows and feed them.

Keir's dad Frank was a farmer who died in 1943 of spinal meningitis, which Keir says he contracted while splitting firewood. His mum, Lucy Abbott, was left with nine children. So at the age of 14, Keir went to work as a labourer on a nearby farm for $7.00 a month. The farmer was not only cruel to Keir and his brother, but also was cheap. He once charged them 50 cents for a ride into Summerside even though he was going there anyway. The work was hard, the hours long, and the brothers had only one day a week free to themselves – Sunday – hours that they spent in church. Probably praying for higher wages and a kinder boss.

"Oak eats iron." It may have been Vincente Elordieta who first mentioned this shipbuilding adage. Vincente was a marine engineer who designed ice breakers, and he knew his lumber. Oak is one of several varieties of wood, along with red cedar and Douglas fir, commonly associated with the corrosion of iron and steel because of the volatile compounds like acetic acid released under damp conditions. I thought "oak eats iron" was just another salt water superstition like "never bring an umbrella up on deck because it invites rain." Or one from Captain Tom Trenholm: "Don't cut a loaf of bread upside down or the ship will sink."

Maritimers have grown up with superstitions like these, and more: no whistling, no grey mitts, or women allowed on a boat for various "reasons": whistling summoned the wind; grey mitts brought grey skies; and women were just plain bad luck. Tell that last one to my sister-in-law Lois Ross who's fished with my brother Kevin for 30 years. Better wait until she's hauled and baited that last lobster trap.

♦

The old fellas wouldn't leave a bucket upside down and you couldn't wear grey mittens. No women allowed on boats. We women could go out after the fishing season was over. If the fishermen only had a cent or two and it wasn't blowing, they'd fire the money overboard to get that much worth of wind. One day, an old fella didn't have anything but a quarter, and he threw that over and it blew the sails right off his vessel. A quarter's worth of wind!

Ada Baker MacKenzie was born in Beach Point on 11 November 1918. It was an auspicious day all around, because that was the day the First World War ended. Vincente Elordieta was born into a seafaring family 2,000 miles east of Beach Point, in Liverpool, England. Like Ada, he knew whistling was considered laying down a challenge to the wind:

> You shouldn't whistle on a vessel. They used to whistle for wind [in the days of sail], but when the steamships came in, anybody caught whistling got a clap on the ear because we didn't require wind on steamships. They were self-propelled.

The Bakers, who were German immigrants originally named Becker, settled in the fishing community of Jeddore on Nova Scotia's Eastern Shore in the 1770s. Ada's father was Stanley Baker, and her mother Phoebe Penny from eastern PEI also came from a long line of sailors. Phoebe had nine children, made bread twice a day, and recycled the empty 98-pound flour bags into clothes for the children. In 1936, Ada married fisher Chester MacKenzie who went to sea at the age of 11. Ada and Chester fished cod, hake, and lobster together. At the time, it was unusual for a woman to be a "cork" or helper.

> That was the best years we spent when we went fishing. When Chester turned 65, he retired and I went with him. We fished for a lot of years. They used to fish all night back then if the fishing was good, the hake. It was a hard old life. It was good. I caught as many as Chester. I skinned hundreds and hundreds of pounds of fish. Cod and hake off Toby's Bank. I used to bleed every one whenever we caught them,

when they were alive, and they were as white as the snow. Skin them all, bone them, and dry them, and put them up in pound packages.

People came to the house and bought them, and we sold them to the stores. We got eight cents a pound for them in trade. He'd get the lend of Nathan Irving's horse and sleigh to take them up to Hughes' store in Murray Harbour. Some of those codfish were as long as this table, four feet long, big codfish, loveliest fish you ever saw. One day Chester caught one, before the war [1939], and his brother couldn't hold the fish up to get its tail off the ground. Now that was a big fish. There's no fish left now.

Ada also worked as the head cook at the local lobster factory, long hours for $100 a month:

Lem, my uncle, used to fish with Chester and one day, Chester made enough money to buy our cow, the first cow we had. I think we paid $59 for her. That was a cheap cow. In the winter, Chester would be up before daylight milking the cow before he went smelting. That was all done with the lantern. One year, the hay was so scarce, well, there was no hay to get really, other people would cut hay on the marsh, but Chester and I went over to those islands, Gordons Island.[5] There was hay in the back of that and he cut, I don't know how much, with the scythe and that wasn't easy work. I'd be there keeping the mosquitos off him. They're terrible over there. And we made a stack of hay, enough for the cow for the winter, and in the fall, he got some of it home. He took the punt and towed a dory, and would fill the dory full of hay and bring it home. We used to have a barrack out here, and you'd lift the top, put the hay in it, and then put the roof down on the hay.

---

5   The Murray Islands in Murray Harbour: Reynolds, Herring, Cherry, Thomas, and Gordon.

A few miles down the coast, Frances Lavers Llewellyn was born in Georgetown in 1913. Frances was the middle child of seven, born to Mabel Stewart Lavers, a midwife. Frances helped her mother deliver babies, over 400, and says her Mum never lost a mother nor a baby. She was rarely paid, "$2.00 maybe." Frances' father Harry Lavers died young, aged 42, and her determined mum carried on raising the family on her own. In the 1930s in the middle of the

Great Depression, Frances married local fisher and mechanic, Emerson Llewellyn. They had lots of love, but little money, and, like their neighbours, they raised farm animals in their back yard just as her mum had done:

> You had your beef and you had your pork and there was always fish. Everybody had a pig, everybody had cows, everybody had hens, right downtown. We had a pig every year and we had pork, and it wasn't like the pork you get today. When it was cooking, you could smell it out in the yard, and it would make you hungry. It was fed with potatoes and grain. Then in the fall, we'd gather apples to feed the pig and that would sweeten up the meat. Oh my, I can smell that coming in from school. We're having roast pork today!

If the preferred pork ran low, there was always salt cod and mackerel:

> We didn't eat much lobster growing up. Then we would go over to Poole's [general store] in Lower Montague and, if you could scrounge up $15, you could get enough sugar and beans and butter, a quarter of beef. $4.50 for a quarter of beef. We didn't have a cow, our next door neighbour, Peter's [Llewellyn] grandfather did. People rented land out by the pulp yard. One of the lots was right across by the graveyard. That wasn't my job, but my two sisters wouldn't go unless I went. They'd say 'If you won't come, we won't go.' So I had to go in the morning to get the cows and milk them. So, I was herding cows.

Georgetown is arguably the Island's finest harbour and still has a thriving fishing industry.

> We always had fresh fish. You could buy a codfish three-feet-long for a quarter. They'd be longer than a wheelbarrow. They'd go out fishing in the morning, and they'd come in and peddle them around in a wheelbarrow, and the cod would hang over the end of the wheelbarrow. So we had lots of fresh fish.

For good health and luck, another old superstition recommended that when eating a fish you start at the tail and work up to the head. And, as Mabel Stewart, who was born in the early 1880s, said, avoid lobster for social reasons.

> When my mother was young, lobster was a poor person's food. She lived in Gaspereaux, and when the big storms would come, the farmers would go down and gather lobsters up off the shore, and put them on the fields for manure. They'd be dead then. There was that many lobster.

♦

There's an old saying that "salt water cures all." On a 1998 BBC radio programme extolling the virtues of salt water, an 88-year-old woman, who had lived her life near the English Channel, was cited:

> My father always used to say if you don't feel well or if you're worried, get yourself to the promenade especially when the tide's going out, and you'll lose all your fears and all your little bits of coughs and colds. It goes out with the water. At 12 o'clock at night when the moon was full, we'd all go out with torches and lanterns to get in the water. It was like a street party in the water.

No chance she'd call that "skinny-dipping." Any midnight swims I experienced swept away my cares and my bathing suit.

"You won't get a cold if you get a dip in salt water in frigid weather." Andrew Murnaghan, born 1915 in Donagh, was the last man on PEI to dig mussel mud, right into the 1980s, more for the fun of it in the latter years. He'd cut a 10-foot diameter hole in the thick ice, set up his digger, a capstan and a big scoop, and walk his horse in circles around the capstan lifting big scoops of mussel mud off the bottom of the Hillsboro River. Before the convenience of limestone, brought to the Island from mainland quarries, every February when the ice was thick over bays and rivers, farmers went "muddin." Where the muddin' was good on the bottom of Bedeque and St Peters Bay and in the Hillsboro and Mill Rivers – the mussel mud was 10-to-20-feet thick. Several diggers were set up. The rich mixture of crushed oyster, clam, and mussel shells in a matrix of silt and seaweed, fertilized crops such as hay and grain to grow like Jack's beanstalk.

It was a cold, miserable job, heading out long before dawn with horse and sleigh to try and get a couple of loads before the early winter nights closed in. Occasionally, a heavily-loaded sleigh went through the ice, but horse and sleigh usually were recovered.

> One fella fell in beside one digger and the other digger was 20 feet away, and he went under the ice and came up in that hole. See, the tide would push him.

Whack-a-mole muddin' style.

One belief, I won't go as far as call it a superstition, was that you couldn't catch a cold if you fell into salt water, not even in winter.

> Yeah, that's right. Yeah. Oh, there was different ones fell in out here. There was an old Brazel fella out here fell in one day at my digger, and we got him out and put him into his horse and sleigh, and he went home. His clothes were all froze solid by the time he got home. He never caught a cold.

149

Mr. Brazel's wife and son wondered why he didn't get off the sleigh. His clothes had frozen solid and he couldn't move even his arms so they had to lift him off. It sounds like an early experiment in cryogenics. Walt Disney might have been interested: After Disney's death in 1966, rumours spread that his body was frozen cryogenically to be re-animated with future medical advances, and that his frozen corpse was stored beneath the Pirates of the Caribbean ride at Disneyland. Actually, he was cremated. By Puff the Magic Dragon... kidding about the Puff bit.

Whether muddin' on frozen rivers or travelling the bushed trail across bays and harbours, falling through soft spots in the ice was always on the radar.

> Some people went through the ice. The ice was bushed from this shore across to Sherbrooke. And that was used a lot. That was a life-saver. You could see from one bush to another.

Eddie Easter was born in 1905 in Hamilton, PEI, on a farm that ran down to Malpeque Bay. He said his father had a bad habit of running out of firewood every winter, so they'd have to hitch up the horse and sleigh, and head over the frozen bay to Summerside to get a load of coal. They religiously followed the spruce tree trail stuck into the ice by a brave soul earlier when the ice was forming. Some considered it an honour to be asked since it reflected their arcane knowledge of hidden springs and currents, which was one reason they were often paid a nominal $5 or $10 fee for such a dangerous job. Yet people still plunged through the ice even when bushed, folks such as the appropriately-named Eddie Easter, who fell through but survived to rise again.

> I had an experience in late March one year. We had been digging mussel mud not long before that, but the ice was getting a little bad and we had to get the digger ashore, but I thought I could still walk across. Recently, there had been a thaw and a snow-storm, and snow drifted in ridges all across the bay.

Between the ridges was water up to your ankles, but I walked pretty well across. I had my carpenter's tools and a hand sleigh, and I had a 'slice,' a flat bar that was Uncle George's for stripping wooden shingles. And that's what saved me.

The ice broke. I could swim a bit. Once I had to let the slice go, but I caught it between my knees. I broke the ice ahead of me until it held, and I reached back and got the bar, and put that across the ice, and pulled myself up and got out of the water. Harry, my brother, was watching from home. I disappeared a couple of times, and he thought I was a goner. But after quite an effort, I got out. Not long after, Harry arrived on the scene. I was soaking wet and cold, but I never got a cold out of it. I kept active you see. If that had been fresh water but salt water's different, more buoyant, easier to swim in. Harry took me home by the road, about four miles, mud to the axles. It was all the horse could do to haul the two of us and a light wagon. I saved my tools and the little sleigh.

Uncle George's "slice" was a flat steel bar about a yard/metre long with a sharpened, tempered end that was driven under shingles to break off the nails when stripping the wooden shingles off a roof. Eddie treasured those tools. He became a master carpenter, and dotted the Malpeque area with barns and houses that he had built.

Another man who knew his way around salt water, albeit usually in a vessel of some description, was Vincente Elordieta, born in 1909 in Liverpool, UK. His Basque parents had emigrated to England from the Basque country on the French/Spanish border. Vincente jokingly said, "Basques are either shepherds or sailors." His family worked on the fleets of Cunard and White Star ocean liners that called Liverpool home port. Both his father and grandfather sailed the seven seas, and, like many sailors, were shipwrecked several times. Eventually, both men were lost at sea. His father was only 37. His body was not recovered; therefore, there was no proof of death. Vincente's mother had to wait seven years to collect his insurance. To feed her family, she took up dress-making and embroidery.

> My grandmother, my mother's mother, lost her father and three of her brothers in one night, on two different vessels. Now she claimed that she saw both of those ships going down, in a dream, vividly.

A few years later, 14-year-old Vincente was crewing on one of the Cunard liners. He started at the bottom as a scaler, scraping the soot and tar from the inside of the coal-burning boilers. He spent his 15th birthday working as a trimmer on the *Aquitania* in the so-called "black gang," the men in the engine room shoveling coal and stoking the huge boilers. Vincente worked his way up the ladder, and by the Second World War, he was an officer in the Merchant Navy. Inevitably, Vincente too was lost at sea when a German U-Boat sank his ship that was carrying the components of an entire hospital, from operating tables to bed linen to medicines, as well as the bulldozers, and I-beams to construct the hospital.

On the 10th of May 1942, the S.S. *Kitty's Brook* was steaming from Hoboken, New Jersey, to an American airbase near Argentia, Newfoundland, when she was torpedoed by U-boat 588. The freighter sank in minutes and nine crew lost their lives. Vincente managed to scramble into a lifeboat where he and his mates spent over a week at sea. Finally, they were rescued by a fisher off Lockeport, Nova Scotia. Vincente was badly frost bitten but recovered and in a month, was back on the water as chief engineer on a new ship. Naturally, Vincente had grown up hearing superstitions of the sea, one being it was bad luck to have 13 letters in a ship's name. S.S. *Kitty's Brook*. Count them: letters only, not the apostrophe. Another was that a live albatross was considered good luck ... a dead one was bad luck.

"I've only seen one albatross. We were pretty well north on the South Atlantic." But he did see other birds, some far from land. Even with all the hardships of a life at sea, or maybe because of them, especially during wartime, Vincente and his fellow merchant sailors valued life no matter how insignificant or trivial:

> I've had pigeons land on the ship 1,500 miles from the coast, in the middle of the Atlantic. They got blown out in a storm. I've been in gales where you could do nothing, just keep the ship upright. They're exhausted, and we always picked them up and looked after them. They nearly always had rings [identification bands] on them. One pigeon, with bands, she landed on the deck, and one of the crew – they lived aft – he came off watch and he was going aft with a bucket of boiling water to get washed, get a shower. This pigeon attempted to get on the edge of the bucket of this boiling water. So, I dashed into the galley and the cook gave me a saucepan of cold water and I put it on the deck and the pigeon jumped on the edge of it and drank. It was ready to drink that boiling water it was so thirsty. Now we kept that pigeon, put it in a box, the carpenter made a cage and we put it ashore in Colon, in Panama. The first British ship going back to England took that pigeon, fed it, looked after it, and gave it to the Pigeon Society[6] in England. She was a racing pigeon or carrier pigeon. We always got a lovely letter and acknowledgement from the Society. Twice I've done that.

After the war, Vincente went back to Halifax, courted, then married the "little nurse" – Helen Soloman from Georgetown, PEI – who had "brought [him] back to life" while recovering from frostbite in Camp Hill hospital. The newlyweds moved to Montreal where Vincente became a marine engineer, designing ice breakers using some speci-

---

6   The Royal Racing Pigeon Association.

fications from Basque whalers that his ancestors had sailed a thousand years ago. Science trumped superstition in the end. In time, Vincente and Helen moved to PEI, surrounded by the ocean they both craved and loved. As the lady in England said, "Salt water cures all."

Handles and Monikers the Island Way

Margaret Matheson Shaw born 1908, lived to 109

Islanders have a creative genius with nicknames and they wear them proudly. Tex MacDonald was the mayor of Charlottetown; Tex and his brothers Fiddler, Sandy, Rabbit, Sock, and Sput were also well-known on the sporting side of Island life. Big Alec Matheson was a PEI premier. And one bombastic member of the legislature from the western end of the Island was known affectionately as The Great West Wind. My real name is Reginald, which should make me proud since I was named after my great uncle, a First World War hero. But I embraced the nickname "Dutch," so-called for my mixing bowl haircut.

A hundred years ago, two austere Island doctor brothers couldn't avoid being nicknamed. Margaret Matheson Shaw, born in 1908, knew them both:

> There was Little Doctor and Big Doctor Murchison. One was a doctor in Bonshaw and was a little short

man, and there was a brother down in Clyde River. He lived handy to the church there. He was a big man. I had an awful bad cold one time – I wasn't in my twenties – I guess they thought I had TB, but I guess God didn't want me just then. The doctor used to come. I had a sister who took a bad cold in December. It turned into rheumatic fever. Dr. Murchison came to see her 28 times. I forget whether it was 28 times he came to visit or $28 he charged for all the trips. It was either one, it doesn't make much difference. She passed away anyway. It affected her kidneys. Martha Euphemia... she got "Phemie."

I asked if she had a nickname. Margaret replied, "My father was married twice and both wives were named Margaret." Not so much a nickname as a namesake. Margaret was 103 years old when she told me that story. She was 109 when the good Lord called her up, smart as a cricket right to the end.

Two other doctor brothers, Harold and Ira Yeo had nicknames as well. Harold was known as a "script" doctor – during prohibition a doctor could prescribe liquor to "soothe bad nerves" – and Ira was wonderfully nicknamed "Iodine Yeo."

Doctors making house calls or prescribing a bottle of rum to treat a nervous condition seems quaint nowadays. So does the job title "caponizer." Strictly speaking, caponizing is a euphemism rather than a nickname, but Charlie Scranton threw that word at me when I asked about his career as a federal poultry inspector. Charlie must be the only "chicken sexer" and "caponizer" ever inducted into the Order of Canada.

All a capon is is a castrated male chicken. A rooster. You castrate them about five weeks of age. I got to be pretty proficient at it. One time, we set a record for it. Now, when I went to agricultural college, a fast caponizer would do 60 in an hour. One time at Cecil Ellis', out in Donaldston – man, I had excellent help

– and I got up to 440 an hour. You could hardly believe how fast I could do them. And I had to use three instruments on every bird. Sometimes, after he's caponized, he might lay over and die. But I caught on pretty quickly: after I started doing it wholesale: throw the bird into the pen and he'll flap his wings, get over the shock, and he's as happy as can be. He forgets all about the operation.

The capons I interviewed refused to confirm Charlie's observations, especially the last one. Down on the farm they say a capon NEVER forgets. Charlie claimed his family was descended from a pirate named Cranton. The "s" was added later perhaps to throw the law off track. Stories about the infamous pirate nicknamed Bluebeard were supposedly based on the French nobleman – and serial caponizer... I mean killer – Gilles de Rais.

♦

Often, nicknames are passed down in families. A friend of mine inherited his grandfather's nickname "Manny Blue," so-called because he worked in a Cape Breton coal mine and could never wash the coal stains from his hands and face, hence the "blue."

My wife is a redhead, an often misunderstood and, in our house, feared, breed of homo sapiens. In Britain, redheads are nicknamed "gingers," and they have a redhead celebration every November, which reportedly began back in 2009 and was intended to offset "Kick A Ginger Day." My advice: if you're picking sides, go with the gingers.

Lenie Bolger's uncle James Bolger managed to combine both colours into his nickname.

Ginger Blue, he was a carpenter. Gabriel was Ginger Blue's brother – he played the fiddle – and in the wintertime, they'd work in the woods in New

Brunswick and then come home in the summertime and work the farm.

Lenie was also a great fiddler and a harness-maker from Foxley River in western PEI. Lenie's father also had an intriguing nickname:

Earring Johnny. He had two gold earrings in his ears.

Lenie's wife Estelle (Soloman) piped up:

His eyes were bad and it was supposed to help his eyesight, they said. He had holes punched in his ears and once he got the earrings in, they stayed. He was right in style.

When they were in their 70s, Lenie taught Estelle, who was from Georgetown and PEI's first female barber, how to play the fiddle. Lenie, short for Cornelius, lived to be 98, and Estelle, who was a firecracker, lived to 105. They were married for 73 years.

◆

Nicknames are prevalent in sports. Daniel Joseph Staub was a baseball player with two nicknames, both celebrating his red hair: Rusty, and later, when he played for the Montreal Expos, he was nicknamed *Le Grand Orange*. The NHL had Rocket Richard and his little brother the Pocket Rocket. Both played alongside slapshot innovator Bernie "Boom Boom" Geoffrion. One step below the NHL, PEI had hard-nosed hockey player Irwin "Tiger" Mackie who played in the USA back in the 1940s with fellow Islander Johnny "Snags" Squarebriggs. Then there was Daniel Lloyd Mathieson, from Breadalbane.

The boys down there called him Denver Dan. The nickname came from his first trip to Denver.

Lloyd headed to Colorado when he was 18 to play professional hockey. Like his parents, his young sister Anna MacFadyen knew Lloyd was destined for great things.

> I know he got a little bit of help from my mother. He had only $10 in his pocket. Mother never said anything, but I have a feeling that's where most of the $10 came from. I have a picture of him in his three-piece suit the first year he came back from Denver. He brought us all gifts. I got a little white radio. He brought in a box and he said, 'This is for you, Nettie.' It looked like a hatbox. Mother took the hat out of the box and, oh, it was gorgeous. Even at five years old, I can remember it was wide, with satin and straw with a mother-of-pearl pin. Mother looked at it and the look that came over her face. She didn't have very much and worked hard for everything she got. She tried it on and it fit her like the skin on an onion. Oh, the look that came over her face was worth paying for. She said, 'Lloyd, dear, how did you ever get a hat to fit me like that?'

> 'Oh,' he said, 'I asked the salesgirl if I could try it on.' Imagine! Him 17 or 18 years old in a hat shop in Denver! 'I'll take it,' he said. He tried the hat on and it fit him perfect, and if it fit him, it fit Mother. He didn't ask how much it was or anything. Oh my goodness, she was pleased. It was special. It just went to church and no place else. It was well-blessed.

As the years passed, Anna looked forward to her brother's visits home. Denver Dan moved back east to play in the Eastern Hockey League, first with the Atlantic City Seagulls and later the Hershey Bears, the eponymous team owned by the chocolate company.

> He had an old car coming back home because he worked all day in the Hershey chocolate factory and played hockey on the weekends.

Denver Dan eventually rose to the top in Hershey and was able to afford to dress in the snappy style befitting a Denver

Dan. But he never stopped being the kind and generous person who loved to make people happy. When he died in 2017 at the age of 90, he bequeathed $418,000 to the Queen Elizabeth Hospital. "His heart," his daughter Heather said, "never left the Island."

◆

Mathieson is a Scottish name and the New World Scots kept genealogical track of their ancestors with nicknames like "Sandy Duncan Big Alex," aka Alexander MacDonald, son of Duncan and grandson of Big Alex. Taking the naming sequence to new heights was Francis John Joe Long Angus MacDonald from Pisquid not far from where the Maple Hill MacDonalds lived.

One of PEI's famous doctors – Dr. Roddie MacDonald – was a Maple Hiller. He practiced medicine until he was 94 and lived to be 104. Unusually, his father Ronald was known as Ronald Peggy after his mother because, as Dr Roddie's son Colin noted, "She was the strong one in the family." Then there was Hazel Malcolm Johnny Peggy MacPhee, an interesting mix of her husband's name – Malcolm – and his parents John and Margaret MacPhee. Truly a mixed marriage.

One of, if not *the* last person to speak fluent Gaelic on the Island was the Reverend Donald Nicholson, no stranger to Scottish nicknaming patterns.

> With me, for the people who had the Gaelic, they referred to me as Domhnull Iain Beag Domhnull Iain: Donald, John, Donald, John. Four generations. They always referred to my father as Iain Beag. 'Beag' means small – but he was as big a man as I am and as strong as a bear.

Speaking of bears, PEI had bears until 1927 when George "Geordie" Leslie shot the last one, near Souris. In 1937,

Geordie fought Billy Maich for the vacant Canadian heavy-weight title. He lost by a KO. Kayo, incidentally, was the nickname of Moon Mullins' brother from the comic strip of the same name. Kayo slept in a dresser drawer and Moon was a prize fighter whose full name was Moonshine. A possible PEI connection?

Back to bears. A man named John Robertson, also from Kingsboro, in the Souris area, was nicknamed Johnny Jim the Bear Killer because, according to his son Robbie, his dad shot at least 14 bears with a muzzle-loader. Bears were considered dangerous to both man and beast, and farmers paid Johnny Jim to protect their sheep and cattle. And the Reverend Donald remembers another bear-killer.

> There was a MacDonald man – his people were from Nine Mile Creek – whose family was called the Bear MacDonalds. Evidently, the grandfather met a bear in the woods and he killed the bear with a stick. Ever afterwards, he was referred to as Bear MacDonald and all his descendants, in order to clarify which family they belonged to, were the Bear MacDonalds.

If it worked that way with my family, we'd be known as the Fly Thompsons. In fact, no branch of my family followed the traditional naming patterns, except for my mum whose Christian name was Mercie, a name going back in every generation to the 1630-Cape-Cod-Pilgrim roots. Not so with Reverend Donald's family, who emigrated to PEI from the tiny Hebridean islands of Rona and Raasay off the Isle of Skye – "rocks and rocks and rocks" – where they had an unusual naming-tradition if a child died.

> My father had a brother – Little Johnny, they called him – who died the same year my father was born. A month or two later, my father was born and that's what he got: Little Johnny.

Reverend Donald was a big powerful man. At 16, he'd gone west on the harvest excursions to work in the wheat fields of Saskatchewan, and eventually worked his way back home to Hartsville, PEI, via a lumber camp in Sioux Lookout on the Ontario/Manitoba border, a granite quarry in New England, and as a street preacher in the slums of New York City, nicknamed The Big Apple. (There's more of his story in the chapter "Harvest Excursions.")

The Rock of Newfoundland

Elsie Bowdridge Collier

Hurrah for our own native isle Newfoundland

Not a stranger shall hold one inch of her strand

Her face turns to Britain, her back to the Gulf

Come near at your peril, Canadian wolf![7]

Judging by the lyrics to that popular anti-union song the from 19th century, Newfoundlanders weren't always keen on joining Canada. Yet, in March 1949, Britain's oldest colony and Canada were united. Some Newfoundlanders were persuaded to leave their Rock and move to sandy Prince Edward Island. One of those ex-pats was Elsie Bowdridge Collier, born in 1912. When she was 17, Elsie left Newfoundland and found work as a domestic in Halifax.

---

7   Gerald S. Doyle, "The Anti-Confederation Song." Old-Time Songs and Poetry of Newfoundland. St. John's (1940) 69.

There she met and married her husband Charlie Collier – also a Newfoundlander – and during the Second World War, they moved to PEI.

Elsie grew up in a tiny village called the Messieurs near Burgeo on Newfoundland's south coast. Unfortunately, you can't hear her voice, so please read this with a Newfoundland accent:

> There was an old lady down home by the name of Mrs. Reynolds and she brought into the world 200 babies. She was a midwife. Two hundred babies and, out of the 200 babies, she only lost four. Believe it or not, because we knew her right well. Oh, she was a beautiful woman. See, you understand, she brought those babies into the world before we had a doctor.

Midwives are the unsung heroes of Newfoundland. Canada. The world. And when the doctor did arrive, it was in idio-syncratic Newfoundland fashion:

> Every six months, the coastal boat would come up, and she'd only land in Burgeo, so everybody had to go from Messieurs down to Burgeo, you understand.

Before we go any further, Elsie wasn't repeatedly asking me if I understood because I look especially stunned. Well, maybe. I think that was how she spoke to everyone. Moving on:

> There was a doctor and a nurse aboard, and well, that's all there was to it, see. Everything was by boat, yeah. That's all we had. And in the winter time it was dog teams. 'Cause we had a dog team, and the doctor had a set of dogs, and the magistrate had a set of dogs, and the police had a set of dogs, yeah. At that time, there was plenty of codfish around to feed the dogs. You could go out in a boat and see them swimming around in the water. And we would jig those fish, you understand, and take those fish for our own self, and take the heads and throw them in a barrel. Put a little salt on them to keep them, and that was the dog food, yeah.

Elsie had 10 brothers and sisters, and their mum, Matilda Dicks Bowdridge, was known to one-and-all as Aunt Tillie. Aunt Tillie was a relation of Prince Edward Island's most famous rum runner, Edward Dicks, captain of the schooner *Nellie J. Banks*, and one-time owner of the Dalvay-by-the-Sea resort. She was also a midwife and a country nurse. Naturally, she wasn't paid for her services as a midwife and healer. Few were, but Aunt Tillie also had a cow, and having fresh milk meant Aunt Tillie often provided milk for some of those newborn babies. Cows were a rarity along that rugged stretch of coastline, ravaged, and then swept smooth by glaciers, similar to Nova Scotia's south shore. Even if you had the means to buy one, cleared pastureland to feed the cow was as rare as topsoil.

> The ground was so poor, you know what I mean. There wasn't much earth. Some people couldn't even grow a garden and brought earth from miles and miles away in a big yellow dory, and spread it over the rocks to grow a few potatoes, and whatever. Yeah. Just the opposite of PEI, my dear.

The big yellow dory was her grandfather's, who shared it around.

> We had cattle – three cows – and sheep, and I used to go up with Dad every summer to cut the grass for to bring it down in the dory, and put it in the barn for the cattle. Yeah, boys, hauling hay in a boat.

As we chatted, Elsie quilted a pillow case, her hands never still. She was incredulous that I was incredulous that everything was done by boat: "Everything was in a boat, my dear." She had stopped asking if I "understood" what she was saying, and was now undermining my intelligence by tacking "my dear" onto her answers. I didn't say or do anything, because I didn't want to sulk or weep in front of a 93-year-old:

> There were no cars, my dear. I left Burgeo in 1929, and there were no cars there. No. Everybody had

a lovely boat. My gosh, they had beautiful boats! I mean even if you died, the casket had to go in a boat. They would take you down in a boat.

One last sail into the sunset.

Go back 70-80 years, and Prince Edward Island had a traditional connection to Newfoundland. Schooners hauled everything from oats and eggs to sheep and cattle to The Rock. Horse trader, cattle buyer, and silver fox rancher Wellington MacNeill from Tea Hill regularly shipped Island-grown produce and live animals to Newfoundland. His favourite nephew was Bus Gay:

> Uncle Well started shipping livestock to Newfoundland and St. Pierre. Produce as well. Potatoes, strawberries, hay. You name it, he shipped it.

Wellington had an office and a corral down on Charlottetown's waterfront at the Buntain and Bell wharf just to the east of where the Delta Hotel is now. He brought in wild western horses from Alberta by the boxcar-load, and he travelled the Island's back roads in his Dodge car with a huge roll of cash in his back pocket and a spittoon on the floor, spitting tobacco juice and buying cattle and turnips from farmers.

> One year, he had three schooners and a steamship in. He'd load potatoes in the hold, and then what he used to do was build a superstructure over the schooner's deck with two-by-fours and two-by-sixes, and put tarps over that. He put the animals on the deck. Anything at all, he'd ship. I remember my father had 16 plum trees, and we picked all the plums off them and sold them to Well, and Well shipped them over to Newfoundland.

Sounds like a combination of Noah's Ark and Darwin's ship HMS *Beagle*. Here's a bit of Island trivia: The *Beagle* was commanded by British naval officer and scientist Robert Fitzroy whose half-brother was Sir Charles Augustus Fitzroy,

Amy Bryanton

Kathryn MacQuarrie Wood

ymond Patton, blacksmith, Pictou County

Lorne Francis

Royal White & whale tools

Johnnie Reid, entrepreneur

Frances Reid Clinton

Lona Carver Acorn age 100 playing
crib on an iPAD

Agnes Sheehan, Bear River

Jessie Nicholson MacKinnon
telephone operator

Dr Lester Brehaut, Murray River, PEI

Ada Baker Mackenzie, Beach Point

Keir Clark, age 100, storekeeper, Montague

Andrew Murnaghan, Donagh,
mussel mudder

Josephine MacDonald MacIsaac, born 189-
Orwell Cove

Charlottetown, Prince Edward Island; William M. Stewart - centre back row.

Gordon W. Stewart, fire chief

Survivors of Battery - Christmas 1919 Charlottetown, Prince Edward Island. Note: Replica Gun - foreground

8th Canadian Siege battery,
1st WW William Stewart top row centre

Maisie Lamont Adams

Arnold McGrath, 7 Mile Bay

Vicente Elordieta & his parents,
Liverpool England

Jean Jones and white-tailed deer in Bunbury PEI 1

West Kent Schoo

Herb Schurman holding Summerside's
founder Joseph Green's tea caddies

Eileen Young Hickox at Island Tel job early 1930s

Tommy Gallant with anchor chain
from the Marco Polo

Captain Tom & Mary Trenholm on
70th anniversary

Lulu MacArthur Thomson

Mary Stuart Sage

Fr. Francis Corcoran

Rev Donald Nicholson

Muriel Boulter MacKay

Jim MacLean

Hillsboro Consolidated School and vans

Pat Hennessey

North Tryon school van 1943

Bertha Dingwell Ross

Adelaide Addie Hamm, Bunbury

Stella McQuaid McDougall

Model T skidoo & Dr George Inman

Keith Mutch

Model T Ford convertible

Charlie & Rose Deighan

Frances Lavers Llewellyn

May O'Hanley & Peter Whitty, Souris PEI

Keir MacKay

Mussel mudding on Boughtan River

Lenie & Estelle (Soloman) Bolger

Tiger MacKie

Colin Doctor MacDonald from St Peters

Wellington MacNeill and silver fox kits

Alden Birt, blacksmith, Fanningbrook

SS ULNA RCMP CUTTER

SHOOTING AND RUM SEIZURES, MALPEQUE BAY

Officers Allege Self-defence In Using Guns—Large Liquor Seizure. Nov 1930

A skirmish between the Customs and Prohibition Officers and three men, two from Darnley and one from Summerside in a motor boat in Malpeque Bay about three o'clocy yesterday mornig, led to the seizure of 142 cases of Scotch Whiskey and five ten gallon drums of alcohol and the landing of one of the men in the hospital with a gun shot wound in his left leg.

Officers Platts and McDonald for the Customs Department and Prohibition Officers Miller and Mann, on certain suspicions, went out to Port Hill on Tuesday night. In the early hours of Wednesday morning they saw a motor boat coming towards the place. As soon as the men in the boat saw the officers they turned about and went down the bay towards Malpeque. The officers gave chase and called to the men to stop. They state that they fired several shots as warning but comin up with the boat about two miles down the Bay near Bird Island, they boarded the boat. The officers allege that the men came at them with their oars and they were obliged to shoot to defend themselves. They are alleged to have had guns on them but did not use them.

On board the officers found the liquor mentioned above. They arrested the men and commandeered the boat. Liquor and prisoners were brought into Summerside between seven and eight o'clock on Wednesday morning. The prisoners were lodged in the Prince County jail. One of them, who was shot in the skirmish was taken to the Prince County Hospital. He has a gun shot wound in the upper part of his left leg. It was found on examinaton that the bullet had passed right through his leg. His wound was dressed; Unless complications arise his condition is not considered as serious.

The liquor was lodged in the Customs Office pending instruction.

The wounded man's story to Guardian representative is the one he had not been used to assault the floers and that the shots had been fired without the provocation or attack by the arrested parties.

S'SIDE JAIL SITUATION IS SERIOUS

Jail Filled To Capacity While Convicted Bootleggers Walk The Streets. Nov 19

The Prince County Jail is at the present time filled to its full capacity.

On Tuesday there were 31 prisoners in the jail and one, who was sentenced to one month in jail by the Summerside Police Court, if fine was not paid, would, if taken to jail, make 32. All the cells are even three below stairs, generally kept for rowdy prisoners.

There are not enough beds to accommodate the overflow of prisoners and a good many are sleeping on the floors. The jailor has been ordered to send away for more beds.

The inmates of the jail are mostly bootleggers. There are also quite a number of young lads serving time for various crimes.

The jail is so over crowded that the jailor refused admittance to a man given a sentence of some months by the Prohibition Magistrate on Saturday last. The jailor said, as he had no committal paper he was not going to let him in.

There are a number of bootleggers walking around town sentenced to jail who are waiting their turn, as there is no room at present for them. One man, who was sentenced about three months ago to 11 months for bootlegging, has left the county. Apparently he got tired of waiting his turn for admittance. The present epidemic of crime, which is going on in Summerside and the surrounding country is no doubt due to the fact that there are many still at large who have been thus sentenced, for whom there is no available accommodation.

Rumrunning on PEI 1932 Patriot

Charlie Bell

Dr AA Gus MacDonald

Clayton Ballum

Grace MacEachern Ryan born 1935

6 Hughes sisters from Bedford PEI

Horse and sleigh PEI

Mac Irving

Gladys Walsh Bryan

Lucy (Gallant) and Leonard Leclair

Edison C. Nelson, service station owner

Angus Johnston the Meatman

Berni Hughes Campbell RN -
6 sisters who were nuns

Harold & Velma MacDonald Ross,
Bideford PEI

Jenny Dugas, husband Waldron and his brother Roy Dingwell, Souris

Mac Dixon, miller in South Melville

MacRae family, New London lighthouse

Ambrose Monaghan, Kellys Cross

Mary MacKinnon Cantelo midwife 1827-1916

Fred Dejonge, 2nd WW survivor

Lloyd Gates, 2nd WW veteran
with the Mayflower Mill

Sheldon & Florence (Leard) Dixon

Captain Hubert White, Murray Harbo

Vernon McCarville, Thistle & Shamrock

Helen Cudmore with Oyster Bed Brid
store account books & diaries

John and Lois (Mackay) Campbell
1955 wedding

Jumpin' Jack, brother Ralph & Mum Winnie
(MacLean) RN Proud

Sheriff Bob and Katherine Dewar, Read's Corner & 3 Studebakers

Lettie MacKinnon, midwife, receiving award for 43
years as telephone operator

Murray and Blanche (Landry) Bennett wedding day
June 1945

Manson Murchison, Pt Prim,
PEI lighthouse keeper

Greta MacLennan Grigg

Splittin' cod & saving the livers

Cockshutt 20

Ivan Kennedy, storekeeper, Breadalbane PEI

Neill MacNeill, Little Sands, PEI

Keith & Jean Pratt & author, Bloomfield Sta. PEI

san Jones Andrews, Hazelbrook, PEI

Ed Deveau, 2nd WW veteran,
at his Rollo Bay workshop.

Hilda Beaton Hilchey, Flat River, PEI

the 11th Governor of PEI, for whom streets in Charlottetown, Breadalbane, Georgetown, and Summerside are named. They were illegitimate descendants of King Charles II as indicated by the name, *Fitz* = son, *Roy* = king.

It's possible, according to stories I've collected from Islanders who crewed on those schooners, that Well MacNeill shipped dairy cattle to Joey Smallwood's family in Newfoundland. It makes sense, because there's a direct genealogical line from Captain Joseph Smallwood, born around 1750 in Norfolk, Virginia, who immigrated to PEI, probably as a Loyalist, and Premier Joseph (Joey) Smallwood born in 1900 in Gambo, Newfoundland. For over 250 years, Smallwood descendants have been living in Lot 48, PEI.

Regardless of who, what and where, Elsie made the point that, while farm animals were scarce, the codfish were so plentiful she could see them swimming under her father's dory. The heads fed the dogs, the cod tongues and fillets fed the people, and, as in the other three Atlantic provinces, the cod livers were converted to oil for use as a daily tonic and to heal the sick.

> They'd put the livers in a barrel and the sun would melt them out.

You mean render them, right?

> Yeah, well, you've got a name for it, anyway. That's what our neighbours used to do. But I'll tell you what Mother used to do. She had a big pan and she'd put the livers in the oven to brown them up.

I was going to suggest "broil" but didn't dare.

> She'd pour the oil off and we used to eat what we called the crusts, you know. Sprinkle a little bit of salt on the livers after the oil was out, and it was lovely.

I figured Elsie was talking about the Newfoundland delicacy called "scrunchions." There was a long silence and then a

long sigh from Elsie. No. That's pieces of pan-fried salt pork...
"My dear." Shame-faced, I steered us back to the cod livers.

> I saved a woman's life with that you know. This woman lived up the Messieurs. I couldn't tell you how many children she had. Oh, my dear, they were really poor. In fact, we took one of the big girls to look after by day, to feed her and teach her things, you know what I mean. Her mother was sick for a long time. She had lung trouble. I got a bottle and put all the cod liver oil in the bottle, and took it up to her. She drank it and she got better. Yeah, and when the doctor came up on the boat, he said there was nothing wrong with her. That's the truth.

Elsie wasn't sure of the woman's ailment, but if it was tuberculosis, we have a similar story in the Thompson family. Uncle Fen stole a ten-gallon keg of boat rum from a female rumrunner, mixed it half and half with cod liver oil, and drank it all that summer. He claimed it cured his TB. Unfortunately, he was drunk for three months, and the neighbours had to tend his animals and harvest his crops for him. And, it turned out that he never had TB in the first place.

One thing is certain, Uncle Fen survived the 1918-19 Spanish 'Flu epidemic that killed several neighbours. As did Elsie, and, since her family lived on the south coast of Newfoundland, they also survived the killer 1929 Grand Banks earthquake aka the South Shore Disaster. That quake triggered a three-part tsunami wave felt as far away as Portugal. Dozens of people in Newfoundland drowned after being dragged out to sea:

> I can still hear it coming in like a big whoosh! And then it went right out. I had to put the milk on the stove for the cream to make the butter. I was tending the pan and the milk shook up and down in the pan, the stove covers rattling. The earth was moving, it felt funny, you know, moving under your feet. And

Mother at the time was coming back home, and she thought she was getting funny because the earth was moving and she was shaking too. She didn't know what it was. And that night, the big tidal wave came in. Boats were washed ashore.

Elsie and her siblings survived unscathed. Her father lost his hat. In eastern PEI, dories were swept up into fields and roads were washed out. Captain Ernest "Ben" Pike of the old Abby car ferry, another Newfoundlander who had immigrated to PEI, was 10 years old, living on the Burin Peninsula where 27 people drowned. A neighbour's house was swept out to sea and a passing schooner towed the house back. A mother and her three children were found huddled together on the top floor, dead.

Bad as it was, it could have been worse. The earthquake registered 7.2 on the Richter Scale, still one of the biggest in Canadian history.

Did I tell you about the lady whose baby was coming? Oh my, this woman, the poor thing, I don't think the midwife got there. They were living right by the water and they had what was called shores on their house.

Like stilts?

Well, we'll call them stilts anyway. And the wave came in and took the house out, and in the meantime, the baby was born. Another wave came in and brought the house back, and they saved the mother and the baby. I heard the old people talking about that. They couldn't get over it, how this baby came back and was saved, you know.

The tsunami hit on the 18th of November, and a month later, Elsie and her father were cutting firewood 20 miles/30 kilometres down the shore and found his hat where it had washed up in a tree deep in the woods. Vessels were refloated, but wharves were decimated, underwater communication cables severed, and tons of salt cod lost.

Not long after, Elsie left Newfoundland and found work as a cook and maid for a Halifax family, earning 50 cents a day. She met Charlie, who was originally from Harbour Grace. In 1944, he travelled to PEI, liked what he saw, so they packed up and moved to a house overlooking Murray Harbour. Except for the lack of rocks and boulders, it could almost have been Newfoundland, because Murray Harbour was one of the last schooner ports in Atlantic Canada. Elsie soon connected with the captains who sailed to Newfoundland on a regular basis. She sent canned lobster — she worked in the local factory — and chickens to her family. In turn, they sent her treats she had enjoyed as a child, like cod tongues.

> Oh, yeah, they're good. Fry them in a pan. Mother used to just roll them in flour and fry them in a pan with salt pork.

Salt pork. Aha! Scrunchions. Long silence. Big sigh. Scrunchions. I guessed right. Finally. Moving on.

> My brothers used to kill seals, but that's all the people had. They'd eat everything you could think of, my dear. I remember the seal flippers right good. Mother used to put them in the pan and she'd let them come to a boil and then she'd put them in the oven with pepper and salt and a little bit of onion. We ate the meat and the heart and the liver. Everything, because that's all the people had to live on. We could afford to buy salt pork, you understand, but the poor people couldn't afford it. We fried pancakes and everything in seal oil. Yes. There's nothing wrong with seal oil. Did you ever have it?

I've never tasted seal oil, and neither had Elsie's co-workers at the Murray Harbour lobster factory. That was about to change. Her co-workers used to tease Elsie when a schooner landed back with a parcel of Newfoundland treats for her.

I had a friend at the factory and he had a bet on that you couldn't make donuts out of seal oil. I made the donuts in seal oil and they were as light as a feather. He took them up and everybody ate them.

And liked them?

Sure they did.

Later, everyone was surprised to discover they'd eaten donuts boiled in seal oil. So, I'm not the only one Elsie took the mickey out of.

Elsie died in 2007, not long after I interviewed her. She'd had a rough time previously, losing family members, including her daughter and son-in-law in quick succession, but she was the archetypical Newfoundlander to the end: independent, resilient, kind-hearted, great sense of humour, and deadly honest, especially about herself. Like her homeland, Elsie was The Rock.

Laura Gallant Whitty

I finished grade six and I went to work. A cousin of mine ran a store just down the road and he wanted help in the store. His wife was pregnant and had to look after the other kids, so I went on there for a while. The money wasn't very big, $5.00 a month, but I had to go. Money was hard to get back then.

Laura Gallant Whitty was born in St. Charles, PEI in 1918, the eldest girl of eight children, and was working full-time by the time she was 13.

Then when I was 17, I moved down to St. Peters to work, housework – cleaning and washing and baking. I didn't get much more then $5.00 a month. In those times, you got fed there and your night's lodging.

Room and board plus $5.00 a month probably seemed like a good deal in the Depression years of the 1930s when so many Islanders were out of work.

> When I look back, those days were good. I couldn't complain about any place I was working. You know, if I didn't like it there, I could move to another one. That was the way it was. I didn't feel exploited. Not a bit, no, even though it wasn't a 40-hour job. I was there all the time.

Laura was the first up and the last to go to bed. She cooked all the meals, baked bread and bannock, and did all the sewing and mending. She had a half-day off during the week and a "quiet" day on Sunday, after first attending church and, after church, managing to cook the family's main meal.

Farm labourers were paid similar wages. In the 1930s, farm commodity prices had dropped through the floor. Yet, farmers had to keep planting and harvesting, hoping potato and turnip prices would rebound from a penny or less a pound. Help still was needed, and farmhands often worked for just their room and board, and the odd chew of tobacco.

> I left school when I was 12. My father died when I was five. He was 41 and left six of us kids, so I left school when I turned 12, and worked with farmers out there.

Alden Birt was born in Fanningbrook near Mount Stewart in 1921. Growing up in poverty and being farmed out to earn a few dollars did not foster many fond memories.

> You just worked and got your board and $10.00 a month. A month. That was in the wintertime. I got $12.00 in the summertime.

Some farmers would offer reduced wages in return for keeping their men on over the winter. One man told me in the winter of 1931, his wages dropped by half, to $5.00 a month, yet he was thankful for a warm bed at night... until

January rolled around. The farmer had decided to build a new barn, high on a hill in Park Corner overlooking the frozen windblown Gulf of St. Lawrence. He said he "danced a little jig" when the barn finally fell in the 1990s. You'd think Alden Birt's boss – and neighbour – would have had some empathy for his family's plight, but instead:

> I was a big boy – I wish I could work as hard now as I could then – and the man I worked for when I was 12 and 13 paid me $10.00 a month for every 26 days it was fit for us to go to the woods. So, we'd work about two months before we'd get the $10.00. And we still had to do all the barn work, you know, milking five or six cows, feeding the pigs and chickens, cleaning out the stables, grading potatoes, filling the woodhouse. That was all free to pay for your board. Up at 5:00 in the morning to start milking and separating the milk, and when it was fit to go to the woods, I remember we'd just set the lantern on the snowbank and go the lane with the two horses, and blow the lantern out on the way by. It was still only 6:00 in the morning, and everything done in the barn. And that's the truth.

And "that's when the real work started": nine hours with a crosscut saw and an axe, then back home at dark, making sure to grab the lantern on the way by, because after supper, there were cows to milk and pigs to feed.

Alden managed to survive five years on that farm. When he was 17, he jumped at the chance to apprentice as a black-smith. A year later, he moved to Charlottetown to work in the best blacksmith shop in town, Proud and Moreside, their forge was off University Avenue where the Jean Canfield Building sits now. The wages were better, but the hours were just as long and Alden was paying for his room and board, so he still wasn't getting ahead of the game.

> I was working 60 hours a week. Making $8.00 a week. Don't say I was foolish. And paying $5.00 a week for

my board. I'd been working there in the blacksmith shop for a year and so many months, and still only getting $8.00 a week. So, I said if there's not some more money in the pay envelope, I'm leaving. And on Saturday I quit and went home to Fanningbrook.

So, on Sunday, Proud came out to hire me back. There had been a big rain and there was a great big hole in the road between Mount Stewart and Fanningbrook, and Proud got stuck in the hole. Percy Sentner – another blacksmith in town – had heard that I had left and he needed a man, so he came out to hire me too. He passed the hole in the road, and Proud's car was stuck in the hole and he couldn't get out. Proud and Sentner were always at loggerheads. They wouldn't speak to one another. Sentner turned around and went back to town and left Proud stuck there. Anyway, he got out somehow – a tractor pulled him out – and he went back to town. Sentner sent me a letter in the mail. I went in on Tuesday morning and hired on for $12.00 a week.

Alden was a quiet, easy-going man, one of PEI's last black-smiths. One day, he was cleaning out his shed and sold his two anvils to a man on the Lower Malpeque Road, not far from where, years earlier, he had apprenticed to be a blacksmith. The next day, he had second thoughts, and went back and asked to buy back one of the anvils. For old time's sake. The man refused, even when Alden offered him $50, double what he'd been paid for the anvil.

♦

As tough as it was working on a PEI farm in the 1930s, imagine the heartbreak every day for a farmer surrounded by the rocky, acidic soil of southeastern Nova Scotia.

My father was a fisherman. He farmed and fished, the worst jobs you could possibly do because you'd fish all morning, come home dead tired after doing a day's work on the water. If it was a windy day, you wouldn't get home until near dinnertime, and you'd have started about 3:00 in the morning, before daylight. Then he'd have to farm. Hook up the horses, and in the spring of the year, try to put a crop in. He was working day and night.

Islanders considered Charlie Scranton one of their own, but in fact, he moved to PEI in the 1940s from the family's hardscrabble farm in South Manchester, Guysborough County, where they'd farmed since the 1700s, and where Charlie had been born in 1916.

The soil wasn't one bit like PEI soil. It was very rocky, hard to clear a piece of land. I remember one time I thought I'd clear some land in the pasture. We ploughed it with a pair of horses, a good man and I, and it took us two weeks to plough the land. Then it took another two weeks to pick the rocks off it. And we only had about half an acre. It was almost impossible to clear it was so rocky. The best thing that ever happened to me was leaving Guysborough County and coming to PEI.

Guysborough County's loss was PEI's gain. Charlie flourished in PEI's fertile soil. After serving his country in the Second World War, he worked for the Department of Agriculture testing poultry, while developing one of the best Hereford beef herds in Canada. Charlie was famous for the big 10-gallon Stetson hat he wore as Master of Ceremonies at the Easter Beef Show. In 2007, he was awarded the Order of Canada for his years of dedicated charity work, which went along with his 2005 honorary Doctorate of Laws from UPEI.

◆

Ella Edwards knew all about the Island's fertile soil. Ella grew upon a Hampshire farm where she was born in the farmhouse parlour in 1910. She excelled at school and after graduating from Prince of Wales College, she became a psychiatric nurse after taking graduate courses at Yale University. In 1933, Ella returned to PEI, the middle of the Great Depression, and said she was lucky to make even a bare living as an R.N.

> Times were very hard in those days. I was getting $3.00-a-day for my nursing. I do remember after I trained, going to a neighbour's house for 10 days, and he didn't have the $30.00 I was owed when I was through. He gave me what he had. That was just the way it was.

There was no Medicare or health insurance back then. People paid doctors and nurses out of their own pockets. If they paid them at all.

> One night that sticks in my mind was when this family, in very poor shape, came running and wanted my help delivering a baby. They couldn't get hold of the doctor. They didn't even have electricity. So, I delivered that baby by lantern. It was a sad situation. I don't know if I should say this... but anyway, they named the child Ella. I was told later that she became a prostitute.

Well, she wouldn't have become anything if Ella hadn't brought her into the world "free gratis" as Jimmy Banks would say. Ella went on to become one of the first nurses hired to work in the then-brand-new Prince Edward Hospital, the "Protestant hospital." Later, she managed the Sherwood Hospital for patients with special needs. In between, Ella worked alongside the famous Dr. George Dewar.

> After I had graduated, soon after, a school chum of mine was expecting and she wanted me to special her, which I did, and Dr. Dewar was the doctor. In those days, they didn't have any X-rays so, when the baby was born, Dr.

Dewar was examining the lady. He looked up at me and he said, "Miss Edwards, there's another one in there." Two girls. I can still see the grin on his face. Anyway, within the last six months, those two girls came to see me. I was really delighted to see them. They're in their 70s now. Very nice, very nice.

Not sure if the twins were named Ella and Georgina, and not sure if either Dr. George or Nurse Ella were paid. And for the record, that was not "young" Dr. George from O'Leary, but his uncle, "old" Dr. George who had his surgery in Bunbury behind where the No Frills store is now.

Seems appropriate somehow.

Playing and Fighting Hockey and Fires

Oscar Campbell and model of rumrunner Nellie J Banks he built.

They lived miles apart and probably had never met, but Oscar Campbell and Gordon Stewart had much in common besides putting out fires and playing hockey. Oscar was born in 1912, a life-long firefighter in Borden and the fire chief from 1949-1973. He was also a star hockey player with the Borden Nationals back in their heyday in the 1930s and '40s. Oscar bought his first pair of new skates thanks to a keg of rum.

> One time when the rum came ashore down here, I sold a keg of rum and I bought new skates for $45. That was a lot of money. The shore was full of it. A rumrunner from up west was bringing it in in one of those American dories. There were two men in each dory and one dory upset, and they had to throw the liquor out of the other dory to get the two fellas in. The kegs all went adrift and came down to our back shore. Five-gallon kegs. At that time, I got $30

179

for the keg. It was in the fall of the year, and there was a lot of kegs out under the lolly you couldn't get at. When I went down to the shore, the boys had a keg with the head broke in and an old broken bottle drinking out of it.

"Lolly" sounds like how you'd feel after drinking boat rum out of a broken bottle, but is actually a form of semi-congealed ice, half ice and half ice water It's a word rarely heard outside PEI and probably not used since the days of the ice boats that ran between Cape Tormentine, NB, and Cape Traverse, PEI. Oscar knew all about lolly because 1) he was a native son of Borden, which in 1917 became the link to the mainland when car and rail ferries replaced the ice boats; and 2) he was a deep-water diver, inspecting wharves and vessels in all weather so he swam in more than his share of lolly.

Oscar and his pals managed to land six kegs of rum that day, and they bought hockey gear with the proceeds, proving that liquor may be good for athletes after all.

Borden was hockey crazy when Oscar was growing up: four outdoor rinks, ingeniously lit by streetlights, a senior men's team as well as a senior women's team. The Borden Nationals travelled by horse and sleigh to many of their away games, and it was a four-to-five-hour journey to Victoria-by-the-Sea to play the Unions. After the game, bruised and sweaty, they'd head back to Borden, grab a couple hours sleep and then head off to work. The Nationals bolstered their lineup with players from across the Island.

They paid their board and gave them $7 a week. We got good crowds. We ran 13 specials out of here one winter. CNR special trains to Charlottetown, fans and players. We only paid I think it was $50 for the train, pick up enough passengers along the way to pay it. Breadal bane, Emerald — all those places. Fights. On the train, there'd always be someone drunk, fighting.

The "hockey specials" would only carry the fans of one team. If a Charlottetown Abbies' fan popped up on a Summerside Crystals' train... let's just say it was a long walk home from Emerald Junction, especially with black eyes and minor flesh wounds. When Oscar played with the Nationals, the team to beat was usually the Victoria Unions. "We'd beat them, yeah, but if you won, after the game, you'd have to beat half them again just getting out of the rink."

◆

Gordon Stewart was a contemporary of Oscar's, born in 1913. He played all his hockey in Charlottetown and, even in the big city, money to buy hockey equipment was scarce. And there were no rumrunning schooners jettisoning their loads.

> We used to use magazines for our shinpads. Tie a piece of string around them. When we played, it was very light equipment, gloves, and maybe kneepads and shinpads. No shoulder pads at all. Some fellas wore felt. No helmets, nothing like that at all. Today, it's all slash and bang. A dollar, a dollar-and-a-half for a stick. There was a skate factory over in Dartmouth, Nova Scotia, that made Star skates, just with a straight blade. And CCM made the 'Automobile' skate.[8] Cs and Ds they called them. The Stars were made in Dartmouth, and the Automobiles were made in Ontario. I wore Automobile Ds, straight blade.

When Gordon was growing up in Charlottetown, anyone wealthy enough to own a car put it up on blocks in December, and then travelled all winter by horse and sleigh. Horses were also an integral supplier of hockey pucks.

---

8   The Automobile skate was one of the first to combine boot and blade, similar to today's skates. Previously, the blades were strapped on to the bottom of boots

Oh, yeah. You know, you'd have to have an awful lot of pucks to play on the outdoor rinks. They'd go into the snowbanks and you didn't recover them until the next spring. So, a bit of horse manure was better than a puck. You didn't worry about losing it.

Gordon came from a fire-fighting family. He joined the fire department in 1934 and was fire chief from 1966 to 1988, following in his grandfather Chief Albert Large's footsteps. Gordon's brother Lou was a firefighter for 60 years. Combined, the Stewarts served for a total of 147 years as firefighters in Charlottetown.

Gordon played left wing while Oscar Campbell was a speedy little centreman. In 1931, the Borden Nationals won the Maritime championship to go along with a half-dozen Island championship trophies. Oscar once played against former Toronto Maple Leaf great and hockey-hall-of-famer Gordie Drillon after he retired from the NHL. Drillon played in two of Canada's hockey shrines, Maple Leaf Gardens and the Montreal Forum, before joining the Royal Canadian Air Force in 1943 to fight in the Second World War. After the war, Drillon scouted for the Leafs, and played senior hockey on PEI against teams like Borden and Victoria. Players such as Oscar were thrilled to play against the hockey legend. In a 2004 interview, Gordon Stewart reminisced about playing in Maple Leaf Gardens.

> I'm about the only one left on the Charlottetown team that played hockey in Maple Leaf Gardens. Charlottetown had the Abegweit team in the Maritime Senior hockey circuit. They formed a junior hockey team in 1931, and I played on a team called the Charlottetown Silver Foxes. We won the championship for the league and then we went on to win the Maritime junior championship. In 1934, they formed what was known as the Charlottetown Junior Abbies, a new team. We competed in the Maritime championship and we beat a team from Bathurst,

New Brunswick; we beat the team from Halifax, making us Maritime champions. Then a team called the Montreal Cranes came to Charlottetown and we played them in the Forum, a two-game, total-goal series. And we beat them to become Maritime-Quebec champions.

The next step was to go to Ontario for the eastern Canadian championships, and the games were at Maple Leaf Gardens in Toronto against a team called St. Michaels College. But that was our downfall. They beat us 7-2 and 12-2, so we were out of it then. They went on to play the western Canadian champs, and they won the Memorial Cup as Canadian Junior champions. And almost every player on their team turned professional the next year.

Players like Bobby Bauer played on that St. Mike's team, who became an all-star with the Boston Bruins and has his name inscribed on the Stanley Cup, and Turk Broda, who won five Stanley Cups as goaltender in the Maple Leafs heyday in the 1940s. So, what was it like for a teenager like Gordon to play against these guys in Maple Leaf Gardens?

Well, I'll tell you, the first time we went out for a practice, on this great big ice surface and seats up as high as you could see, there was about 5,000 people there watching us practice. Then, when we played in our two games, there was 12-14,000 people there each game.

Which was the population of Charlottetown in 1934-35. Playing with Gordon against the St. Michael's Majors were teammates Tic Williams, Tiger Mackie, and Pud Whitlock. Tiger went on to an illustrious hockey career in the USA playing on AHL teams like the Springfield Indians, owned by legendary Boston Bruin Eddie Shore. Tic played with an all-Canadian team in Colorado, earning the grand sum of $50 a week with food and lodgings thrown in at the best hotel in Denver. Not bad in the Depression years of the early 1930s.

Back on PEI, Oscar found himself loaned to arch-rivals Victoria. One cold night, the team travelled to Charlottetown for a playoff game. The train didn't go through Victoria so...

> We went to Charlottetown on the ice by sleigh, followed the coastline down. Loaded our gear in the back of sleighs, went down and played, then went to a restaurant and had a bite to eat, and came back after we played the game. I suppose it'd be 2:00 or 3:00 [in the morning] when we got back. No lights.

The moon and stars lit the way home. The Unions didn't always travel by horse and sleigh.

> One time, we were going to Bedeque. There was a bridge to cross and we had an old truck. We had straw in the back and a stove, and we got on the bridge and we met a horse. The horse reared and the driver hawed a little too far, and the sleigh caught the box of the truck. We went right through the railing and into the water. Hockey gear, everything all soaking wet. We went up and played the game of hockey, and came back in the back of another truck. I forget if we won. Nobody got hurt. Charlie Loven lost his skates. He played anyway. A fella down there gave him a pair of skates. Everybody we played hockey against had fun back then.

In those days, many players smoked cigarettes. They smoked in the dressing rooms between periods, and some coaches even smoked during the game behind the bench.

> I smoked mostly Chesterfields, anything you could get. They were only 25 cents a package then.

I joked earlier about how a keg of bootleg rum paid for a pair of Oscar's skates. Oscar was later cherry-picked to play for those very same Charlottetown Abbies, who were sponsored by Hickey and Nicholson, the Charlottetown tobacco company, famous for their Black Twist Chewing Tobacco. "I was paid $7 a week, and my board, and my cigarettes." A dollar-a-day and all he could smoke.

Oscar went on to work for CN Marine in Borden. There's a chance he and Gordon Stewart crossed paths when Gordon's junior Abbies took the train and CN ferry to Toronto that time. Two great men who served their communities as fire chiefs, and entertained Islanders with their hockey skills.

Gus Gregory, 2nd WW
veteran & fisherman

There was a fortune in rumrunning in those days. It was terrible the money that was in rumrunning.

Prohibition lasted until 1948 on PEI, and, in theory, all liquor was illegal except for the rum and whisky doctors were allowed to prescribe for "bad nerves."

Gus Gregory from Chepstow saw liquor being landing on the North Side by the boatload, and one of those rumrunning schooners was the famous *Nellie J. Banks.*

I was aboard the *Nellie J. Banks* about four miles off Campbell's Cove, and I bought rum on her for three dollars a gallon. A big 40-ouncer of gin cost $1.40, and $1.25 for a 26-ouncer of Old Sailor rum. $15 for a 5-gallon keg of rum, and if you wanted to buy a bottle of whisky, they charged you a dollar and a half, but if you bought a case, twelve in a case, you'd get it for $15.00. Scotch whisky.

Teacher's Highland Cream and Black and White Scotch with the two terriers on the label. Many rum boats carried cigarettes as well, minus the government tax seal, so they were cheap too – ten cents a pack. The rum boats anchored just beyond the three-mile limit, out of the legal jurisdiction of the prohibition officers and the big RCMP steamers. At night, the rumrunner would shine a lantern on the big white sail, and people would putt-putt out in their little fishing boats powered by a one-cylinder marine engine, nicknamed 'make-and-break' engines, also an apt description if you happened to run out of gas carrying a load of illegal liquor. Ben Irving went to the rumrunner one time when he was fishing lobsters. The schooner was off a little wee bit further than he figured I guess, but he kept going anyway.

For years, Roy Clow, from Murray Harbour North, was the eyes and ears of any liquor movement off the eastern end of PEI. When he was a young fella, Roy ran a little rum himself, a couple of kegs to see him and his brothers through the long winter. Years later after the war, Roy came home and became a fisheries officer. He knew the ins and outs of every harbour from North Lake to Montague.

Ben didn't have any money worthwhile, but he bought a couple of quarts and he was heading back to shore. And when he was a quarter of a mile off, the engine stopped. Ran out of gas. So, he took a big drink out of the quart bottle of rum, and then he poured the rest in the gas tank. He waited until the carburetor filled on the old five horsepower Bruce Stewart engine [also known as the Imperial, manufactured in Charlottetown] and he opened the sparkplug and put a little bit of rum in there. It had a right wicked spark, and he shut the priming cup and gave her a chuck and away she went. Ben said, 'By God, she never turned over faster in her life.' A five Bruce Stewart engine would burn rum just like you'd eat bread and molasses. He came ashore on less than half a bottle of rum. I don't know whether he drained the carburetor when he got in and drank the rest or not. He hated to part with his rum, I know that.

Like Gus, Roy was a Second World War veteran. Both were appreciative of being able to take a drink legally while in the armed forces. And, being country boys raised on the water, both were into the rum long before they joined the army.

I remember one time I was aboard a rumrunner with my brother. The limit was three miles then [later extended to 12 miles] and the rum boat sailed right in where we were fishing lobsters. I was only about seven or eight years old. My brother Stanley took a water jar and he dumped the water out of it and went aboard the schooner and got it filled with rum. Three dollars for a full gallon.

And there were some clams in our boat – oh, they'd been there for a week, all opened up, and we were using them for bait to catch the odd codfish. One of the schooner's crew saw them sitting in the basket and he said, 'Sir, could I have one of those clams?'

And Stanley said, 'Oh, you couldn't eat them, they're too old.'

'Oh yes, sir, they look all right with me.' And God, he jumped aboard our boat and grabbed that basket, and he was back on his deck like a monkey. The whole crew got breaking the shells with their fists and eating them raw. They never even peeled the skin off them. And they gave Stanley a quart of Teacher's Highland Cream for the clams.

Roy and his brother hung around until they saw a puff of black smoke off in the distance sent up by the RCMP cutter S.S.*Ulna*. The clam-eating-Newfoundlanders didn't appear to get sick.

They were all right two or three days later, still sailing up and down. Poor fellas had nothing to eat. They'd be there for months trying to get clear of a load of rum.

Another time, Roy traded two molasses sandwiches and a jug of fresh water for two quarts of rum, and watched as:

> One fella shot a gull. And boys, they put the dory overboard and picked the gull up, took it back aboard, and boiled it up for soup or stew. You know what a gull would be like to eat. They did some funny things in them old days.

An emphatic "no" to knowing what a gull tastes like, and "yes" to "did some funny things."

The S.S. *Ulna* had been assigned to the RCMP in 1932 to enforce the liquor code, specifically to stop rumrunning on PEI and in northern Nova Scotia. The *Ulna* and the other prohibition vessels like the *Scaterie* had a lot of coastline to cover, especially during the years prohibition overlapped in both provinces. That same year, the RCMP made the headlines for all the wrong reasons. Their Water Street warehouse in Charlottetown was burgled, and "six cases of French brandy, one case of Scotch whisky, fifteen bottles of whisky, and fifteen gallons of rum"[9] had been stolen. Plus "a half ton of sugar." Rum cake, anyone?

Naturally, politics got into the mix. Prohibition had been a political hot potato both federally and provincially since the *Scott Act* of 1878, aka *The Canada Temperance Act*. In July 1932, *The Evening Patriot* newspaper in Charlottetown reported: "George Leslie Jr., efficient prohibition officer in Souris, had been relieved of his office. The best men are not always wanted on that job." Fired for being a little too efficient... Gus Gregory knew George, whom is, I believe, the same George Leslie who shot and killed the last bear on PEI on the Souris Line Road in 1927. Gus knew most of the Souris-area rumrunners and bootleggers as well as the prohibition officers, and, like everyone else, he was entertained by the daily game of cat and mouse.

---

9 25 July 1932 front page of *The Charlottetown Patriot*.

There were cutters around. At one time there was three of them around: the *Marguerite*, the *Saratoga*, and the *Scaterie*. And there were prohibition officers on the land too, and I'm going to tell you a story about three prohibition officers who went to raid a bootlegger's place in Souris. One fella went to the basement, and a local man from the North Side, who was also a prohibition officer, stayed on the ground – on the main floor – and the third fella went upstairs. Now the third fella and the guy they were raiding were good friends. The bootlegger went over to a china cabinet and he took out a silver tea-pot and he passed it to the prohibition officer. The prohibition officer took a good big drink and passed it back to the bootlegger who put it back in the china cabinet. So that was the kind of work that went on.

You have to wonder how Gus was so sure of all the details of that little vignette.

Then the Mounted Police came here in 1932, and then things changed quite a bit. They weren't local fellas. There was one RCMP who came here – he's around here yet – he was an Englishman. Doug Heath was his name. Oh jeez, he would chase you all over the country to get a conviction. He'd stay out all night, watching, just to catch you with a bottle of rum.

One night, Roy snuck up on an RCMP car waiting in the shadows at the wharf in Annandale for a load of rum to come in. Roy let the air out of their back tires so his pal could safely land a few five-gallon kegs of rum at another wharf down the road. Gus fished alongside a man who put one of the first car engines in his boat. He now had the fastest boat around, and could easily outrun the cutters. He got cocky, slowing down to let the *Ulna* close the gap then he'd point to his pile of five-gallon kegs, wave, and rooster-tail off leaving the cutter far behind. These antics went on for months to the dismay of other rumrunners who complained he was needlessly antagonizing the RCMP. All went well, except for a little thing the Greeks liked to call *hubris*. One day, his engine stalled, water in the gas, and the prohibition officers caught up, seized both his load of rum and his boat, which, since it was the fastest boat around, they used to catch other rumrunners.

The boat rum was famously strong and thick, like molasses, with a reddish colour that supposedly would stain the inside of a teacup. Gus said bootleggers paid the rumrunner $10 a gallon, then watered down the rum by half, so were still making a tidy profit. Maisie Lamont Adams from French River had a brother who knew an enterprising bootlegger in Summerside who operated a fleet of rum boats out of an abandoned house.

> He rented this attic and put a telephone in it. He knew line was tapped by the cops, and when the rumrunner would be coming in to French River, he would say the ship was coming in to Tignish. And if it was coming in to Malpeque, he said it was coming in to Cavendish. This is how they operated so the cops couldn't catch them.

Maisie was a popular lady, and for the 17 years she ran the lighthouse, her tiny kitchen was a magnet for locals sharing the gossip.

> French River was full of that bootlegging stuff. And the rumrunning too. Well, I guess you want to believe they did. And there's always people who have money and didn't need to do it. They think they're pretty big. They don't want anyone to know. Ben MacLeod and Fred MacEwan, they went out to the rumrunner one night to get liquor and didn't the cops get after them. And they wouldn't stop so the cops fired guns at them, and struck Fred MacEwan in the leg with a bullet. Nobody knew just what happened for a long, long time, but Fred was laid up with that for quite a while.

And now we know... and the beauty of it all: Fred could treat his wound both internally and externally with a teacup full of red rum.

Roy Clow had a Boston first cousin who came home to the Island every summer. Jimmy Clow had done well and, naturally, couldn't help but show off a little in front of his Island relatives. You know, things like wearing a white shirt even when it wasn't Sunday. Plus, he always carried his personal shot glass everywhere he went, in case someone produced a bottle of rum. One day, Roy's father fired up the Five Bruce Stewart engine, the one that ran on rum, and the three of them headed out past Poverty Beach to get a couple of quarts of rum off the rum boat. To fool the prohibition officers aboard the RCMP cutter S.S. *Ulna*, who were diligently keeping an eye on things just inside the three-mile limit, the Clow clan jigged for cod as they chugged along.

Dad said, 'Look at that son-of-a-so-and-so watching us. We're not going to get any rum today.' Jimmy said, 'Would they bother us?' Dad said, 'Bother us? They'd tow us to Pictou! But we'll fool them fellas. We'll sail right straight out to the rumrunner.' So, we went right by the cutter, never stopped, waved at them, lovely morning.

My father said to the schooner captain, 'They can't stop us taking a drink outside the limit can they?' 'No, sir. I'll give you a drink. Come on aboard.' I wasn't old enough to drink then. Oh, I'd drink alright. I just wouldn't let Dad and Jimmy see me. I'd steal it on them when I got a chance. Anyway, they went aboard and went down into the cabin and when they came up I saw a big bulge inside of Dad's shirt, and one in Jimmy's. I said, 'How are you going to get them bottles past the cutter?' Dad said, 'Don't say a word.'

When they got back in our boat, the cutter couldn't see them over the top of the schooner. Dad took a cod-line – there was a lead sinker on it, of course, and a hook, no bait on the hook, – and he put two half hitches around the neck of the bottle. Then he did the same to Jimmy's bottle and said to me, 'You go back to the stern and start fishing. Slip this bottle over where they can't see you, and let it go down until the lead touches the bottom, and then just move it up and down as if you're jigging for cod.' So that's what we did.

And the minute we left the schooner, smoke started blowing out the stack of the old *Ulna* – she was a coal-burner – and she swung around and came up alongside us. The officer said, 'Well, you're out of luck today, boys.' 'Yeah, I know,' Dad said. 'But we'll get a few codfish anyway.' So the *Ulna* went about a mile and stopped, and laid there. So soon as they stopped, Dad and Jimmy pulled the two bottles up and took the half hitches off and opened the bottle Jimmy had.

Jimmy always carried a shot-glass with him. He was very fussy about drinking. He'd be washing out the thing out before he'd take a drink. So, he took this shot-glass out of his pocket and he dipped it overboard and gave it a slush around in the water and it slipped out of his hand. 'Well, J.C.,' he said, 'Look what I did. I lost my glass.' The sun was shining and you could see the glass going down, turning around in the sunlight. Well, I kept jigging and got a half dozen or so more fish and, in no time, we had a barrel of fish. Dad said, 'That's good enough. Start her up.' I was the engineer. I could start the engine.

So we started to shore, and they got the bottle up and were having another drink. I started cutting the throats of the fish, throwing their insides overboard, and bending their head back to cut it off. About the third fish I was gutting – oh, about a 30-inch codfish, a good big-sized codfish – I cut his throat and went to rip him down the belly, and I heard 'clink' at the end of the knife. I thought this fella's swallowed a stone. I was curious and took his stomach out to see what kind of a stone was in it, and cut it open. And what do you suppose was in it? The shot-glass. Jimmy's shot-glass was in the cod's stomach, as true as I'm sitting here.

Cousin Jimmy took his shot glass back to Boston, and also a tale about rumrunners and codfish, which he dined out on for years to come.

Telephone switchboard operators

To be sure, it was a hard time to make much money, but we made our own fun. In the Mount Royal school district, there was hardly a house that didn't have a fiddle. One particularly, Phonse Phillip – he was secretary of the school – he had two boys, Albert and Tommy. I taught them at school and they could both play for dances. They were just in grades 4 and 5. You could go to any house in Mount Royal and, with just a suggestion, get a dance going. 'Well, what are you folks doing tonight?' 'Well, nothing really.' 'Why not phone around and see if we can a few people and get a dance going.' And of course, every house didn't have a phone, and, if so, it was the party line.

The aptly-named Charlie Bell was born in Cape Traverse in 1913. He got his grade 10 in a one-room school, passed his entrance exams, and headed for Prince of Wales College to get his teaching certificate. When he was 18, he was hired by the Mount Royal school trustees to teach for the regal sum of $600, including the supplement, a year. Money was scarce, but regardless, good neighbours meant good times. And if you couldn't scare up a dance, the telephone provided another form of entertainment:

> On one or two occasions, just for amusement, nothing to do, I'd go to the phone and ring our own number, and then listen to the receivers going up to see who was talking to whom about what. You'd hear these phones clicking on the line and, of course, nothing happened, and after a minute or two I'd say, 'Well, are you getting much?' And down they'd all go.

The Costello family - six girls and two boys plus father Ephie- from Elmwood, Lot 65 PEI were musical. One daughter - Rita (Costello) MacDonald was considered to be one of the best fiddler players on the Island. Rita was playing at a dance in the old Thistle and Shamrock school one night when a fight broke out. The only way to safety was out a window with her fiddle under her arm . As they got older the sisters and brothers married and moved on but the sisters kept playing music and learned new tunes by playing to one another over the telephone while the neighbours listened in on the party line. Rita lived a long life, dying at age 98 in April 2000.

These days, our mobile phones are used the least to make telephone calls. Telephones today are message centres, fact-checkers – thanks to Google and Wikipedia – as well as clocks, keypads, portable games, and video cameras. Hard to believe it all started 150 years ago with a wall-mounted crank telephone. In 1919, if you had a telephone in Kelly's Cross, you didn't worry too much about neighbours listening-in to your conversation: there was only one other subscriber. Jessie MacKinnon had the means to "listen in" to her heart's content, not that she did. For years, Jessie ran the central switchboard in Eldon:

> When I went to work, there were 90-some phones, I think 99 phones on the exchange, but it grew bigger.

Jessie showed me the old telephone book – booklet really – with all the numbers she used to patch through.

> Two ring, two-line two, and two short rings. Two ring 11, that was John MacPherson's mill, line 2, one long and a short ring. But then see, it grew and grew and grew.

> I was paid $20 a week running the central. That was pretty good, but I'd never go through it again. Well, I suppose I would if I was younger, but a lot of sad things. Really sad. I'd get all the bad news first. I remember once, the first winter I had the switchboard, it was just before Christmas, and there were these two girls from Iona. They got killed out west. Well, the call came through, middle of the night. It was the operator in Eldon they were wanting, and they asked me if I knew the people, and I said yes. So, I didn't know who to call first. So, I called one family, and they went and told the other family. Well, then people were calling back and forth all night. I felt so terrible bad for them. Later on, after the funerals were over, I got a letter from the father of one of the girls, thanking me. I think it was the only thank-you I ever got. And lots of nights I'd be up with some stupid old drunk.

By default, Jessie was a first-responder, a job she wasn't trained for except for being a woman with a big heart living in rural Prince Edward Island in the 1940s. The switchboard operators I talked to whether in town or country were woman. I knew of only one man doing the job, but at the end of the 19th century when telephones became popular, the operators were all men. Eventually, the telephone companies figured out they could pay women less to do the same job. Once again, women were second-class citizens doing a first-rate job. The way of the world even today... So, within a few years all the operators were women, and one of those women was Eileen Young Hickox from Charlottetown:

The old, old telephone office was in half of the Hyndman Insurance building [Lower Queen Street] and, in 1932, they built the one on the corner of Queen and Fitzroy Street, and it was modernized, smaller cords and everything. I was there for eight years and a half, took a couple of months to learn the trade. You didn't get paid while you were learning, and then we got $5 a week for I couldn't tell you how long. We got a big raise then, gradually, 25 cents a month, and finally, after eight years and a half, I got $8 if I worked twice on Sunday.

When Eileen was controlling the patch panel, you could call the operator and ask for the correct time or the weather conditions. Both Eileen and I wondered how the operators were supposed to know what was going on outside when they were all but tethered to their stations, painted lines drawn on the floor keeping them in place. Jessie mentioned the drunks calling in to chat – or often, cry in their beer – were a constant irritation, but perhaps the big bucks and good times compensated. Eileen made many friends at the telephone office, and she treasured them all:

I worked every Christmas day and the other shift worked every New Year's Day. There were 32 operators, no men, at the time, and we had a lot of fun. One funny thing I remember, the switchboard ran from one end of the top floor to the other, and the doors leading into the operating room were behind the switchboard. You couldn't see people until they got right around the board. Well, this night they heard a commotion, it was just the two girls, and this night operator creeped along the side of the board and pulled the horn out and said, 'Come out from behind there or I'll shoot!' When the fella came out it was one of the policemen who patrolled the office every night to see that the girls were alright. That was a joke around the office for a long time.

Someone else who made a living thanks to the telephone,

indirectly at least, was the late, great entrepreneur and Island legend, Johnny Reid. His pals included bands like Shay Duffin and the Leprechauns, Bill Haley and the Comets, plus Maritimers like Anne Murray, Gene MacLellan and the Stomper, Tom Connors, who honed their musical chops at JRs. However, Johnny started on his entrepreneurial assent in a modest and unique way: when he was a teenager, he installed a telephone in his parents' back yard shed on Dorchester Street, bought a deep fryer and 400 pounds of potatoes, and went into the fast food business:

> It cost a cent-a-pound for the potatoes, and the fat I cooked them in cost ten cents a pound. I cooked them on a naphtha gas stove; you had to pump it up, 15 cents a gallon. The little deep fryer, with the little basket in it for making fries at home, came from the 5 and 10. And at the 5 and 10, I found a little potato cutter and that's how I made my fries. A nickel a bag for fries.

He stuck notices on the doors of every bootlegger in the east end of Charlottetown, advertising hot French fries, call this number, five cents delivered. Drinkers called Johnny On-The-Spot and he hired a boy on a bicycle to deliver the piping hot fries. Business boomed and, still on Dorchester Street, he parlayed the cheap deep-fryer and the shed into a well-equipped lunch counter called Johnny's Fish and Chips:

> I was reading the *Toronto Star* one day. I didn't buy it because I couldn't afford it. Someone gave me the paper, and I found this recipe for making fish and chips. So, I modified it after I tried it, and I used to sell 2,000 orders a week.

And there was more to come.

> I put an oven in a truck I had and we started delivering. My slogan was: *You can come and pick it up or we'll deliver it hot. Just pick up the phone and dial. We're Johnny-on-the-spot.*

He stuck a sign in the window of his new digs on Weymouth Street next to the train station: "Eat here or we'll both starve." That was the late 1950s and early 1960s, and not far behind were renovations, which produced JRs lounge and the Davey Jones Locker. A legend was born. Or created. Or master-minded. For under $10.00, you could order either steak and scallops or deep-fried Malpeque oysters with all the trimmings, or a seafood kabob – shrimps, scallops, sole, salmon, tomatoes, and peppers. Take your pick.

The telephone played an integral role in Johnny's success. Patrons at the local bootleggers ordered their fries on the pay phone in the front parlour. At least they could at his brother Georgie Reid's establishment.

Pay phones have gone the way of the dodo and the Charlottetown bootlegger. Once common on downtown street corners, telephone booths are almost obsolete. Except in Spain. Ingeniously, the Spanish have converted telephone booths into plug-in stations for electric cars. If Johnny Reid was alive today, no doubt he'd find a way to deliver hot French fries with a Tesla, and invent a snappy slogan to go with it, something along the lines of: "You'll get a charge out of our chips," or "Our fries only cost a plugged nickel."

Ok, best to leave the motto-making to the entrepreneurs, the deep thinkers, and deep fryers. At the top of the menu for the Davey Jones Locker, Johnny printed "A message from the Double 'A' corral: Eat seafood, live longer. Eat oysters, love longer."

I'll have the oysters, please.

Hattie Walsh Hughes,
Cardigan, PEI

Ah, you didn't go to the doctor at all. You never heard tell of a doctor. If you were sick, it was goose grease. Goose was popular then and not turkey for Christmas. Everybody saved their goose grease, and they rubbed it on your chest and back. It was molasses and pepper for the cough. A spoonful of that molasses thickened up with black pepper. I guess we thought it worked.

And another thing was Epsom Salts to get your bowels working. That was pretty popular. If they thought you had pneumonia, they put the mustard plaster to ya. It would be very rare you'd be going to a doctor, very rare.

Hattie Hughes from Cardigan, remembering the hard times of the 1930s when both dollars and visits to the doctor were rare. A few miles up the coast, Mary MacPhee Malone was born in 1925 on PEI's "north side" in Big Pond near Rock Barra, where she attended the one-room school. Her mother, Cecilia Hennessey, doled out the remedies:

Oh, God, the rancid goose grease with the molasses in it. You drank it. That was like a cough syrup was for your throat. You had your Christmas goose and you saved the oil. In the winter time when the kids needed a cough syrup, they'd give you a spoonful of that. It would be very rancid, so they'd put molasses in it.

Now you had rancid goose grease AND rancid molasses. Tasty.

♦

In 2018, the Canadian Medical Association declared May 1st as National Physicians' Day, and one assumes that the day also honours previous generations of country doctors. Back in Hattie's and Mary's day, if the home remedies didn't work, the doctors made house calls. The dedication of doctors was incredible. They travelled in all weather. One enterprising doctor in Murray Harbour even attached steel tracks, like the ones on bulldozers, to the rear of his Model-T Ford, transforming it into a crude but effective snowmobile.

Sometimes, neither home remedies nor a visit from the doctor was effective, as was the case during the 1918-19 Spanish Flu epidemic. Ruby Chappell was born in Breadalbane in 1914. Her family survived the onslaught of that 'flu, but:

> We had neighbours down home, Ed Ross, I think three of them died that winter. I heard my father say they were all quarantined. You couldn't even go to the wake.

How did the doctor not get sick? Ruby and others said Dr. Nelson Bovyer from Crapaud chewed tobacco to ward off the Flu germs.

> I can remember when I was a kid if we had a cold, Mother rubbed goose grease and turpentine on our chest, and put a red flannel over it. That was the cure for pneumonia and a bad cold. We never went to a doctor and we'd always get better. The old people's remedies. One time I said to Dr. Beer, telling

him about goose grease and turpentine, I said, I guess manys-a-time we had pneumonia and didn't know it. He said, 'Well, it wasn't a bad thing to do.' He agreed with the remedy, but some of the doctors would laugh at you. Thought it was crazy. Dr. Beer was great. He was in Kensington and he was the greatest doctor. He'd drive down here in the wintertime, horse and sleigh, my husband had pneumonia. He'd go to the woodstove out there, and put his feet up on the damper. Warm his feet before he'd leave for home. He and the wife came to see me a few years ago, and he asked, 'What did you do with the old stove?' I laughed and said, 'Dr. Beer, it's gone years ago.' Yeah, he was a great doctor. He'd never turn us down, come any time of the night. He'd get paid whatever he could, if it was $5.00 you gave him or whatever. Yeah, they were great.

Dr. Kenneth Beer later became a surgeon in Summerside and seventy-five years after Ruby's testimonial, his former patients are still singing his praises.

Joy Moase: "Dr. Beer was an awesome surgeon and his bedside manner couldn't be beat. And what a great sense of humour. And so compassionate and kind. Bless him, he helped so many through so much."

B.J. Forbes: "He performed several surgeries on my hips when I was a kid. I've had to see several orthopaedic surgeons in the past few years. They have all marveled at his ingenuity."

And Shelley Reeves McKenna remembers him this way: "Dr. Beer lived next door to my grandparents, the Hockins. He was also my surgeon when I was two months old. I had three surgeries that saved my life. I was given less than a one-percent chance of surviving. I also have a bird's eye maple clock made by him."

In 1941, when Mary Adams Ramsay was born in the New London lighthouse to Canada's first female lighthouse keeper Maisie Lamont Adams, Elton Woodside, also known as "The Flying Farmer," flew Dr. Beer out from Summerside. They landed on the beach but were a few minutes late: Mary had been birthed by local midwife and R.N., Peach Duggan. Yet, he remembered them years later when both Mary and Maisie were special guests at Dr. Beer's and his wife's fiftieth wedding anniversary.

In Murray River, Dr. Lester Brehaut was also run into the ground treating Spanish Flu patients. To conserve his energy, he hired young Milton Buell from Abney to drive him around in the Model-T while he catnapped in the back seat. Milton was only 14 or 15 at the time. You didn't need a driver's licence back then. One day, they ran out of gas in a district that Milton wasn't familiar with, not surprising since Milton didn't make it into Murray River maybe five miles from Abney until he was 10 years old. Milton said he felt bad waking the Doc up, but Dr. Brehaut got out of the car, stretched his six-foot-plus frame, looked around to get his bearings, and said, "Wait here." He walked a half mile to a farmhouse and returned with a gallon jar of moonshine. He poured the 'shine into the Model-T, and Milton said, "The car never ran better."

Even today, a ruptured appendix is nothing to sneeze at; but before penicillin, it was often fatal especially if the rotten appendix wasn't removed immediately. In 1932, when he was nine, George Wotton took sick. Dr. Nelson Bovyer diagnosed it as appendicitis and decided to send George to Charlottetown for treatment.

> I was a child in the Victoria school, and I had to be rushed to the hospital right away. That could only be done by car and there were only two cars in the district. My dad had one and the schoolteacher had the other. My dad was away [delivering the mail] with

the car and couldn't be reached, so the schoolteacher was the only one. He had to close the school in order to rush me to the hospital.

When we got to the Bonshaw Hills, he started to complain about a pain in his side. When we got to the old Infirmary, out opposite the Exhibition Grounds, they operated on the teacher for appendicitis an hour before they operated on me. The team of doctors and nurses that operated on me did him first because he was in such bad shape. Isn't that a strange story?

Uh, yeah, some might call it fate, because you have to wonder what would have happened if they hadn't already been halfway to the hospital when the schoolteacher, Malcolm MacKenzie, took sick. They both recovered. In another twist, Malcolm MacKenzie married George's sister, and was later the Island's deputy minister of education.

Kismet in spades.

♦

As Ruby Chappell mentioned, in the days before universal Medicare in Canada, people paid the doctor what they could out of their own pockets. Some doctors were paid "in kind," which might be a couple of hens, half a pig, or, as Clayton Ballum, who drove Dr. J.A. Stewart from Tyne Valley on his rounds, once quipped:

I can see people here walking down the road who were brought into this world for half a cord of wood. The doctor'd get the other half when the next baby was born.

Ella Willis was born in 1910 in Hampshire. In 1934 she was a nurse at the Prince Edward Island Hospital on Brighton Road when it opened. Later, she was the Director of Mental

Health on PEI, but in the interim, she took whatever nursing jobs were available. Like many doctors, she wasn't always paid for her services:

> The doctors in my day were not that well-off. It was a terrible strain. One of the doctors, one of the most popular ones in Charlottetown, that man died a pauper. His son had to pay off his bills just because the doctor wouldn't take money from somebody who he thought couldn't afford it. That went on a great deal, more than ever has been publicized. Doctors suffered because their patients were so poor. He certainly did. I know that for a fact because I knew his son quite well.

Folks claim Dr. Lester Brehaut went so far as to order his billing books and any outstanding bills owed to him to be burnt when he died, one of many reasons why he was considered a saint in the Murray River/Murray Harbour area.

In Souris, people felt the same love for their legendary doctor, A.A. Augustus MacDonald. Dr. Gus, as he was affectionately known, was also a Member of the Legislative Assembly, elected four times as an MLA in Kings County. However, several people told me they never voted for him, not because they didn't like him, but "because he was more valuable as a doctor than a politician."

Dr. Gus was the attending physician when Grace Ryan's mother died of tuberculosis in Priest Pond on the north side. Naturally, the doctor was worried young Grace had contracted the deadly disease too:

> He was the epitome of a country doctor, and he put in a lot of years. He used to give me a quarter to shut my mouth and listen to him. He gave me a quarter every time I went to see him, every three months for quite a few years until he decided I was healthy enough that I wasn't going to die. Maybe my father would have to give him back the quarter, I don't know. He'd say, 'You be quiet, Grace, and don't cry.

I've got a quarter here and you can go get ice cream.'
And to get to Souris and have ice cream, well. You
know there was no such thing as ice cream in my
neck of the woods. You could get five cones for a
quarter.

Grace survived, didn't get diabetes, fished tuna, planted her
crops by the phases of the moon, and gathered Irish moss.
Her father had a trapline and, one day, Grace decided he
wasn't getting enough money for his furs. So, at the age
of 12, she took over the bartering and made enough extra
selling his furs to buy a washing machine. A life well-lived
and saved. Grace was also a poet and wrote this tribute to
Dr. A.A. Gus MacDonald:

Oh, the old-fashioned doctor, how we loved him in
his day,

As he drove around the country in his slow and certain way

Though the skies were raining pitchforks or the
summer boiling hot,

Wherever he was wanted, he was always on the spot.

He was a country doctor and his methods were not
new

But no matter what the trouble, he knew just what
to do.

To the highest flights of science, he made not the
least pretence

But he had the large equipment of solid common
sense.

We leaned on him and loved him 'til his wonderous
heart was stilled

And he lay at rest forever in the graveyard on the
hill.

Money Poor, Family Rich

The Hattie and Harry Hughes family of Cardigan

We were probably starting school before we realized there should be a mother or a woman in the house. At that time, the only three places you went were school, home, and church. I think I was in school and heard the other kids talking about their mother, and then we started asking Daddy, and he'd say, 'Oh, we'll talk about that someday.' He never wanted to.

Like her father Edmund Walsh, Hattie Walsh Hughes was a rock-like fixture in Cardigan. Hattie's Mum was Alice MacLean who died when Hattie was only three. Edmund took over, becoming both mother and father.

I can remember him carrying me up to bed just like I used carry my kids up. And I remember how poor we were. We never had a bed. Just a great big tick of straw on the floor. Every fall when they threshed the grain, they always filled this big tick up full of fresh straw. And that's where we laid. I don't remember having blankets; it was coats and buffalos and whatever we'd have over us to keep us warm.

But the one thing I remember and the thing that made me what I am, is the great love my father had for us. When he carried us up to bed, he got on his knees alongside that tick and I can see him yet, bend down and to kiss us and start praying. Every night. Every night. Yeah, it was really cold them winters. He'd get up and get a fire on, and carry us down and sit by the oven door and put our feet in the oven to keep us warm.

Hattie was the second youngest of four children: two older brothers and one younger. Her dad farmed and he kept an eagle-eye on his beloved kiddies. Any work he took off the farm to earn some much-needed cash was always close to home, out back in the lumber woods, or cutting ice off the nearby fish hatchery pond for 50 cents a day.

He worked at odd jobs around, like when they were building the fish hatchery. He worked there with the horse and cart. After a storm, he'd be shovelling snow off the tracks down at the station in Cardigan. And I can remember he'd grow a crop of potatoes or oats. He'd bag the oats up and put it on the cart, and he'd take all us kids to the store to sell it. We went everywhere he went. Everywhere. We went to the fields when he went to plough, and we sat under a tree until he was done. Or if he was harrowing or whatever he was doing. So, he'd put the grain in the cart and put all us kids on, and we'd go down to John A.'s store. We didn't know what was going on, but when we came home, we'd have tea and sugar and molasses, but we'd have no bags of feed any more. Bartering.

Oats were a constant theme in the Walsh house. Traded for molasses to put on their porridge every morning. Later that field of oats played an interesting role in the history of the Walsh family.

Hattie was born in 1930, the second year of the Great Depression, so Edmund wasn't getting much for his 100-pound bags of oats or his 75-pound bags of potatoes.

> The poverty was unreal! We didn't know we didn't have money, I guess. Molasses and molasses and porridge. Porridge and more porridge. I didn't have toys to play with. I never saw a doll. But we didn't feel poor because we didn't know many other people, and the ones we did know were pretty much like ourselves. But at school, we were kind of pushed off to one side, all right, in some classes but in most we weren't. Mrs. Leigh Allen was a saint to me in school. Every day at dinnertime she'd say, "Come on now, Hattie, we'll go down and put more water in the soup." She'd always take me down to her house for lunch. Yeah.

The Walshes had a few milk cows, and a henhouse full of laying chickens; they killed a pig every fall to go with the daily plate of boiled turnips and potatoes, so there was always food on the table. Porridge, at least. And more importantly, they had a house full of love.

> But with all that we went through, it was the love and respect that held us together. I'm sure.

Christmas was a hard time for many families in the Dirty Thirties. Hattie and her siblings made Christmas tree ornaments out of the tinfoil that lined the bright yellow King Cole tea packages. A big treat was an orange.

> After my mother died, the first thing that happened was a great big rush of nuns coming out to the house, wanting to take us to the orphanage.

Unbeknownst to the children, as a widower, Edmund was under constant pressure to farm his kids out to two-parent relatives, or worse, pack them off to St. Vincent's, the Catholic orphanage in Charlottetown. Fat chance. "Daddy wouldn't have anything to do with that!"

No doubt some of those evening prayers implored God to help him keep his family together.

> So, anyway, the nuns were going to come this day to take us. At least, we had a feeling in our minds they were, between hearing Daddy talking and some of the neighbours talking about it. We got a feeling they were coming on such-and-such a day and we were going to be gone. So, anyway, it was a lovely hot day in the summertime, and Daddy said, 'I think you should go hide today, kids.'

> So, we went up back of the house into a grain field and we stayed there all day. Yeah. I remember this car came, and these women with these black dresses. That was the nuns after us.

Cloak and dagger in a field of oats. But the kids must have been terrified. Big black car, big black dresses... The nuns poked around and left, and life returned to normal. Hattie's aunts in Charlottetown made frequent visits to help out when they could. Life wasn't easy, but Hattie, inspired by her father's faith and determination, rose to the occasion.

> Oh, he was a real saint. Yeah, he was. Daddy always made the bread. I can remember that Royal Yeast Cake just as if it was sitting there now. He'd get me up on the chair showing me how to do it. I was making bread standing on a chair at the table when I was five years old. I don't know what the bread tasted like, but I guess we ate it. I don't know.

> Everybody had chores to do. We all had a little stool when Daddy would be milking the cows in the barn. Everybody sat on their little stool while he did the milking. And then we all went to the house with the buckets of milk. We followed him around like chickens after a hen. I'm sure that's what it looked like.

Hattie learned how to bake bannock, and she made soap out of rendered beef fat. They cooled their milk and butter in the brook. Edmund got a rural mail route, and Hattie and the boys helped with that. Every summer, they all picked blueberries and sold them at MacDonald's store for half-a-cent-a-pound. There were salmon in the river to gaff with a pitchfork, and, for entertainment, chicken raffles and card parties to attend. Hattie said they were "Money poor, but family rich." And luckier than some.

> There was another poor family up on the hill from us, but the father and mother were both there. It seemed like they were poorer than us, because I can remember her coming down to our house crying. She couldn't get the kids to bed because they were hungry, so Daddy went and got a piece of meat out of the barrel, and some potatoes and molasses, and put it all into a box for her to take home. A cold, snowy night. Yeah. So that's the way we grew up. The good old days. I'm sure they were, because we felt like a million dollars.

Hattie finished school. She fell in love and married Harry Hughes, and passed her father's love on to their 10 children. Eventually, Edmund came to live with the Hughes family. His grandchildren summed him up in one succinct phrase: "He was a lovely man."

But let's give Hattie the last word on this remarkable man who, against all odds, managed to keep his little flock safe and, more importantly, together.

> I don't begrudge one hour of that. We were happy, and I don't remember anyone getting into a fight, and I can't remember Daddy ever getting cross. There was never any anger around our house. It's all great memories.

Hattie died in 2018 at the age of 88. She left behind 10 children, 21 grandchildren, and 19 great grandchildren. And a legacy of love.

You Can't Drive a Pig

The Venerables acting company. Mickey Place centre, back row.

All animals are equal, but some animals are more equal than others.[10]

Tamworth, Red Wattle, Chester White, and Gloucestershire Old Spot hogged the past, but farmers now prefer fast-growing pig breeds like Yorkshire, Berkshire, and Hampshire. One thing they all have in common: a British connection, just like George Orwell, who made the pig the "most equal" animal on the farm in his 1948 satire *Animal Farm*. He also made pigs the smartest barnyard animal to the eventual uneasiness of everyone else, Farmer Jones of Manor Farm included: "Remember also that in fighting against man we must not come to resemble him. Even when you have conquered him, do not adopt his vices."

---

10 George Orwell's Animal Farm.

Roma Mulligan was born on a farm in Freetown in 1917. She knew her porker pals had lots of little grey cells.

> Pigs are smart people. I could write a book on pigs. When my husband got sick, we sold the cattle. I had to live so I went into pigs. The cattle were gone from the barn and it was awfully cold, but so many nights I got up and went to that barn with a lantern, and I'd be so frightened because the barn was creaking. I was terrified something was going to come down from the loft. I'd be so scared. But anyway, these pigs and I got along fine. I'd open the barn door and I'd say, "How's my girls today?" Well, they'd all start talking. They'd all chirp up and they were all so perfect like you couldn't believe. So don't tell me pigs are stupid.

Never. Not me. If the pigs are talking and chirping, we're halfway to the nightmarish predictions of *Animal Farm*. Such was Roma's bond and relationship with her pigs, I'd go so far as to call her a pig whisperer, which she may come by honestly. Her family name was Curley. Perversely, one of Roma's jobs when she was a girl was helping her father butcher the pig in the fall. She hated the whole process, from the hit between the eyes with the 10-pound maul to the scraping of the intestines to save the fat so her mother could make soap. Roma said she closed her eyes. And thought of England or at least English pig breeds.

Mickey Place used a different adverb to describe the pigs he encountered when he moved from the U.S.A. to his mother's family farm in Alexandra, PEI, overlooking Governor's Island in Hillsborough Bay. Mickey was born in 1909 in Lynn, Massachusetts. When he was nine years old, he had his eyes opened wide by the transition from urban life – bacon and pork chops wrapped in wax paper by the butcher – to rural life – herding animals onto a flat-bottomed boat.

> Judsons had a big scow and, in the spring of the year, they used to take cattle over to Governor's Island, plus young horses and pigs, and just leave them.

They had to go over once in a while to water them. In the spring, they also had a lobster factory there to can lobster. It was one of the big days of my youth when they'd take the cattle over because my chum was Douglas Judson, and we'd get other kids from around too and play cowboys. Oh, it was a great day. You had to round up the cattle and get them on the boat and go over with them. Then in the fall, we'd get them back.

Now it's an easy job getting them on the island but it was quite a job rounding them up to get them off. They were there all summer and they were quite wild. You'd have to run like anything to round them up and get them on the boat. A pig will look every which way and eventually he'll run outside the boundaries of the people who are trying to herd him. It's the most awful job. All you have to do to get a bunch of cows to go on a scow is get one to go and the others will follow. The same way with sheep. But with a pig? No way. They're far too independent. And they're smarter than you think they are, too.

Mickey, meet Roma. Mickey's final words of porcine wisdom: "There's one thing I have learned: you can't drive a pig."

Mickey went into the banking business and wisely kept clear of pork futures. He was also a talented actor and, along with Bill Weale and Mae Ames, was a long-time trouper with The Venerables.

♦

Just down the road from Mickey's family farm, Mac Irving in Cherry Valley raised pigs to sell at the old Davis and Fraser meat plant, later Canada Packers, in the east end of Charlottetown. In the wintertime when the bays and harbours froze over, farmers like Mac took advantage of the shortcut to town over the ice with their horse and sleigh:

Cold day, a cold trip, cold work. It's always cold out on the ice, you know. No shelter. If you had a good smart horse, you'd get in in an hour, maybe an hour and 25 minutes. You'd go across the ice here to Pownal, you see, and then take the road from there, from Tea Hill to town. Oh, the hills were terrible in them days, yeah.

Mac remembered when the highways crew actually lowered the steep road at Tea Hill. Then in the 1950s when they upgraded the "back road" into what's now the Trans-Canada Highway to Wood Islands, he said they took out so many twists and turns the road was shortened by over a mile. You might say the old road was like a pig's tail. I would. Mac didn't. He did say this, however:

In them days, we used to butcher the pigs [at] home on the farm and take them in to the pork factory. You'd have to haul them on a wood sleigh. Then, they took the pigs alive.

Hauling half a ton of live pigs over the ice was a feat of strength and ingenuity, but factor in a ton or more of horse-flesh plus the weight of man and sleigh, coupled with the ever-present danger of going through the ice and:

People went through the ice, oh yeah, there was lots of that. There was an Irving man out here who drowned off Pownal wharf one time. He was coming home from town and had two women with him, and the horse went through the ice and he couldn't get him out alone so he started off walking to get help. The horse saw him going and whinnied. The man felt so bad he went back, and the horse pulled him in through the ice and he was drowned.

The horse drowned, too, of course.

These days when we mention pigs and cows and horses, we think farm, but at one time people in towns and villages also kept animals in their back yards and sheds. Kathleen Cameron was born in 1897 and lived most of her long life in Summerside:

> Oh, yes, we had a barn for the horse. In fact, at one time we had a horse, and a cow, and a pig, all in that barn right in downtown Summerside. Then the law came in saying you can't have a pig and you can't have a hen. You can't have anything like that. You never have hens and chickens now. You don't raise pigs to have for your own pork in the wintertime. I don't believe you can have a cow in the town now. A lot of people had a cow, the well-off people too. We'd raise a pig to kill in the fall. I remember the pig being killed and the poor pig's squeal. Ahh, the poor little pig. Almost a pet. Every fall, my father would have a pork fattening for the winter. It got good feed. What lovely meat.

> The pig was killed in late November, scalded in boiling water to remove the bristles, and then cut up into loin roasts and spare ribs. The offal was ground up and squeezed into the cleaned intestines to make sausages, and the hams and bacon were cured in secret recipes. And, in an interesting twist on Santa Claus' lunch, on Christmas Eve, Kathleen and her eight sisters and brothers always left him a pork sandwich. Rudolph and his mates took note of the snack and were well-behaved the rest of the night.

♦

"We got into the swine, a boar and everything, and started raising little weaner pigs." Gladys Bryan was someone else who loved her pigs. Gladys and her husband Heber ran a mixed farm in Howlan in the western end of Prince Edward Island.

We struck it good then, too. I looked after the little fellas and Heber looked after the sows. The winter was the worst, getting out to the barn. I'd have to follow Heber and he had long legs. I'd say, 'Heber, now come on, just take short steps or I can't follow you.'

In blizzards and on days the snow drifted, they clung to the rope they'd strung from the house to the barn, because one thing every farmer knows, the animals have to be fed, regardless.

There wasn't always enough teats to go around, so I bottle fed a lot of times. I remember one sow had fourteen little pigs. Well, she didn't have enough titties to feed them so one little fella was left out, and I said to Heber, 'We can't do away with him, he's a cute little fella.' So, I called the vet and I got a formula to give the little pig, and you know, every morning and evening I went out, that little fella knew my voice. He'd leave the group and come right over.

One morning I went out, and the mother was trying to get down, and he got stuck under her and she crushed him. I could have cried. Ahh, the dear little fella. I didn't have a name for him but I'd say, 'Come on, dear, come on, dear.' He knew my voice so well. That was a sad ending.

Like Roma and Kathleen, it seemed Gladys could love her pig and eat it too.

◆

The patron of swine herders is Saint Anthony, a third-century monk, and, in his honour, it's still traditional in parts of Europe to name the smallest pig in the litter, the runt, Anthony. However, assuming his mama doesn't accidentally roll over on him, even Anthony grows up to be a 300-pound porker.

"I can remember when we killed the pork, or the pig, Mum corned a lot of it, cured it." Grace Swan was born on a farm in York in 1920.

> Mum liked to have fresh pork, so she used to fry a lot of the pork, cook it in the oven, and then she'd put it in crocks, layer after layer and pour the fat over it, and you could take that out and it was just like fresh pork. She kept it in the cellar. That'd be corned pork, like corned beef.

Neighbours in both town and country tried to stagger the pig killing so to be able to share the fresh meat. Even with the pork chops par-fried and preserved in gallon crocks, there was still a mountain of pork to deal with.

> And then she'd cure the hams in a pickle, and after they'd been in this pickle for so long, she'd take them out and dry them, hang them up. I remember a little girl coming to visit one day and she saw the hams hanging up and she asked, 'Are you people having pig or cow for dinner?' That was about the size of it – pig or cow.

Before electricity and refrigerators, many farmers kept roasts of pork and beef in the barn, buried deep in the oats or barley bin where the grain kept the meat from thawing and freezing during the long winter and short spring.

Nothing on the butchered pig was wasted. The lard was used to make soap and candles, and even the pig's feet were boiled up and eaten. Clarisse Gallant's mother in Oyster Bed Bridge sewed the pig's bladder up tight into a soccer-type ball for the kiddies kick around the barnyard. Down the road from the Gallants, the LeClair family in Rustico had seven sons who were veterans of the Second World War. The youngest son was too young for that war, so signed up to fight in Korea instead. Leonard LeClair remembered the tough times of the Great Depression in the 1930s:

Mum used to keep chickens and eggs, and we used to have a cow and we had a horse for a while. Mum used to go to the barn with a great big rag and a bucket of water and wash the pig. She'd keep that pig just as clean as anything. She used to look after that pig so well. The pig jumped up one day and knocked her down in the pen.

Since Leonard's mum made her own soap, in a bit of irony that I think would have tickled George Orwell, the pig was being lathered up with lard from last year's pig. So, what happened to the cleanest pig on the north shore of PEI? "We killed the pig." Survival of the fittest, not the cleanest. Leonard said times were so bad his father made the kids' bootlaces out of dried eel skin, so that pig didn't stand a chance.

Let's give George Orwell's pig the last word:

Man is the only creature that consumes without producing. He does not give milk, he does not lay eggs, he is too weak to pull the plough, he cannot run fast enough to catch rabbits. Yet he is lord of all the animals.

Charlie Scranton Order of Canada

Food is an intrinsic part of life, and often underlines holidays, birthdays, and other special occasions. The smells and tastes of food are triggers to pleasant memories, or unpleasant if you ate the carob/soy/turnip cake once offered up at one memorable birthday party. I had just turned 50. I cried for two days, and no one's forgotten my favorite cake since.

But, just in case, it's chocolate butter cake, strawberry jam between the layers, with peanut butter and vanilla icing, people. Hold the turnips, please.

Take Thanksgiving. While not as big a deal in Canada as in the USA, nonetheless it's a holiday feared by poultry everywhere. For centuries, families have chowed down on goose or duck or chicken with a side dish of cranberry sauce.

Born on a rocky farm in Guysboro County, Nova Scotia, in 1916, Charlie Scranton seized the opportunity to make a few dollars when he was 10 years old.

I started with ducks. My aunt used to raise ducks. A great lady for ducks. Anyway, she gave me three duck eggs. I bought them home and put them under an old hen and they hatched out. We got three ducks out of that setting. But the next year, I went on my own raising ducks and I got up to 65. I'd get a sale for them at the hotel in Guysboro, and, of course, I'd have to kill them and pick them doggone ducks' feathers. There'd be a lot of pinfeathers I'd have to take out. But that's how I started in the poultry business.

And then I got into chickens and hens, and got delivering eggs and poultry around Guysboro, one heck of a lot of work. Make a profit of seventy-five cents a bird.

Chickenfeed. Charlie decided to expand his poultry empire. He bought a bicycle and an old incubator and started hatching out baby chicks. He'd deliver the balls of yellow fluff on his bike, muffled "cheep cheep cheeps" trailing behind him as he bounced along on Guysboro County's gravel roads. And what goes nicely with poultry and all the trimmings of a Thanksgiving dinner?

My father went to the States and worked in Cape Cod building cranberry bogs. But his parents were anxious for him to come back home because the younger brother had also gone to the States and it was looking like he was going to stay there. So, my father became a fisherman, farmed and fished, the worst jobs you could ever possibly do because you'd fish all morning and come home dead tired after doing a day's work on the water. If it was a windy day, you wouldn't get home until near dinnertime.

He fished lobsters, about 150 lobster traps, and salmon, and in those days, salmon was good. They'd be 15-18 pound ones. I think the biggest salmon he ever caught was 28 or 38 pounds. Over three feet long. Those were beautiful salmon. The Atlantic salmon — the taste of them was like nothing else. Best in the world. I ate many of them. Ten cents a pound for salmon. But then along came the pulp industry in Guysboro County. The runoff covered all of the beds that the salmon used to spawn in Salmon River: the bark off the pulp wood covered the salmon beds and there were no salmon anymore. Fewer and fewer and fewer salmon. I quit the salmon fishing before I left for PEI.

Charlie said the smartest thing he ever did was move to PEI in 1940. Disappearing salmon stocks was only part of the reason. He had inherited a farm that grew "nothing but rocks," and since he had gone to agricultural school majoring in – wait for it – poultry, he decided his chicken-sexing and caponizing skills were better suited to pastoral PEI. And he was right. Islanders loved him, and he acquired many new friends as he criss-crossed the Island testing poultry for the federal government. Charlie was honoured with a Doctorate of Laws from UPEI and the Order of Canada from Ottawa. Not bad for a guy who started off peddling and pedalling bike-loads of baby chicks, and wound up the auctioneer at the annual Easter Beef Show.

♦

Food tastes vary. "Pease porridge hot, pease porridge cold..." A porridge made from peas doesn't excite me at seven in the morning. Like my grandfather Joe, I like regular oatmeal, boiled for 20 minutes then cooled until a thick rubbery crust forms. Mmmm... cold rubber smothered in milk and molasses. Berni Hughes Campbell from Bedford, PEI had sixteen brothers and sisters so her mum had to be a good cook. Or a strict disciplinarian. "Eat your rubber!"

During the Second World War, three of Berni's brothers fought overseas:

> My brother Joe went in the Canadian Navy and my brother Pat had gone to the States. He went with

the American Navy and my brother Fred was in the Air Force. And they all came home. My mother sent them parcels and letters, and she'd make fruitcakes and send molasses cookies and things that they loved. The boys used to send money home, and she took that money and saved it. When Fred got out of the war, he moved to Kingston, Ontario. He met this girl and got married. He had a fair amount of money to start in [Queens] University.

♦

Mothers and sisters and grandmothers have been sending comfort to their loved ones at war since war began. Addie Hamm in Bunbury sent chocolate cakes and fudge to satisfy her two brothers' sweet-teeth while they were fighting in the First World War. Her mother even sent apples from the farm because one brother complained the apples in France weren't as good as the ones at home. I bet their wine's not as good as ours either.

Berni had a simple comfort food: soup.

> She used to make the greatest soups. Saturday was soup day. And then if she cooked ham, she'd make dumplings. And we always ate our dumplings with molasses. Did you ever hear tell of that? I did that for my children, had molasses on my dumplings, and when they'd have them someplace else, they'd say, 'Well, that's not what my mother does – she gives us molasses.'

The natural reaction is to assume Berni is stretching the truth, but, like five of her sisters, she became a nun. She also studied to become an R.N., and her first posting was in the kitchen of the old Charlottetown Hospital, the "Catholic hospital" back when the hospitals were denominational, baking 35 pies at a time.

I got a lot of compliments on my cooking there. Thanks to my Mum. At home Mum would say, 'Who wants to help me?' Georgie was always outside and Patricia would clean, so I was left to cook. And when I went to the novitiate, it's funny, I was picked out to cook and I was always sent to the kitchen. I loved to cook. I'd make thirty-five pies, and jelly rolls. Sixty-four eggs, four great big pans and the jelly rolls would never crack when I rolled them. It was because of all the beating – we beat the eggs separately. The doctors used to make a point of coming for my jelly roll. Dr Sopor – every Saturday, you'd hear the big feet coming across the floor – he had huge feet. I'm sure they were that long... looking for the jelly rolls. I can still see him yet.

He needed the calories to keep those feet moving. Berni wound up in a convent in Texas working as an operating room nurse in a Dallas hospital. She came home to PEI one summer, met a man, fell in love, got married, and raised a family. I'll bet her children are as kind-hearted and as handy in the kitchen as their mum and grandmum. Bets are off whether they put molasses on dumplings.

◆

Angus Johnston knew a thing or two about idiosyncratic tastes in food. For years, Angus was known as the Meat Man in southeastern PEI. Angus was born in Little Sands in 1913 and was only 16 when he took over the reins of his father's truck wagon and started going door-to-door peddling meat out of Murray River.

He [Dad] came home one morning from being around the village and said, 'Angus. I can't go to Murray Harbour with this meat. Do you think you could get clear of it?'

'I'll give it a try, Dad.' So down I go to the Harbour

with the horse and wagon. One place I went was Alf Chapman's. 'Would you like some meat today, Missus?'

'No, we buy all our meat from Albert Johnston.'

'I'm his son.'

'Oh, we'll take a piece of meat then.'

I was that happy, I was singing hymns all the way home from Murray Harbour to Murray River.

His father's good reputation spilled over to Angus. He sold the wagon with its load of roasts and steaks and necks that day, and the Meat Man was born.

Sold the works. Great people. Great people. And I remember selling the first beef tongue. It was to a lady in New Perth, a Mrs. Moar. She said to me, 'Have you got a beef tongue?'

'No but I'll have one for you next week.'

'That'll be fine,' she said.

Twenty-five cents. Before that, a lot of the tongues went for [silver] fox feed. Five cents a pound.

Hmmm... I've got $20.00 worth in my head.

◆

The New Perth Moars were originally from Orkney, windswept islands off the northern coast of Scotland. My ancestors came from there as well, and I've read stories about them being so poor they'd dangle on ropes over 100-foot cliffs just to pillage a few gull or puffin eggs. Beef tongue was probably an undreamed-of-luxury. I doubt they ate much molasses, still a staple in every Maritimer's larder. Ours anyway. Well, mine. My wife grew up in Ontario and Virginia, and wouldn't touch molasses with a ten-foot pancake, but my brothers and I ate molasses on our bread, pancakes, and porridge. Mum made molasses cake and molasses cookies, but one thing we never poured molasses on was vegetables, unlike Greta MacLennan Grigg's father.

Angus MacLennan, a farmer and carpenter from Port Hill lived to be 86, so he must have been doing something right:

> I bet there was more molasses eaten at our house than any other house because we all liked molasses. I can't eat a biscuit or I can't eat cheese without molasses. Especially cheese. Dad put molasses on everything – he even put molasses on potatoes, especially if they were boiled potatoes.

On French fries, it's the PEI version of poutine.

Our ancestors brought particular tastes in food across with them from the Old World. They also brought over codes of morality and civility that remained in the family for generations. For example, swearing was one of the worst sins in our house when I was a kid, especially for my strict Presbyterian great-grandmother Mercie Henderson who lived with us. She'd *tsk tsk* at my attempts at swearing when I was learning to talk, unique words I'd heard from neighbours, or so my mother also named Mercie claimed. More than once, I tasted a mouthful of soap.

Edison Nelson knew what I was talking about. Edison was born in China Point in 1914, the year the First World War broke out. His mother died at his birth, so he was raised by his grandmother Huggan, who had two sons who fought in the war. Fortunately, they made it back home as "returned men."

> I was brought up at my grandmother's and she had three boys, two were in the army and, when they came home, they were always around. When I got to be three years old, they learned me to swear. And she used to put that Coleman's Mustard on my tongue. That dry Coleman's mustard, my God. They'd get me

swearing and she'd get the mustard, so they learnt me then to go upstairs and there was a hole cut in the ceiling to let the heat up from the stove. They showed how to shut the door and put a chair against the door knob, and I'd put my head down through that hole and yell down, 'Get the mustard, Mum, I'm at it again!' And it wouldn't matter if I stayed there for two hours, she'd nab me when I came down and I'd get the mustard.

What a hotdog.

Sharing... In The Barefoot Days

The Thompsons of Ponds, Pictou Co, NS

Sharing: sometimes we do it for love, other times out of necessity. In the bygone days, it meant sharing a bed with siblings, or sharing the chores around the farm. Kathleen Henderson Jelley had nine siblings. Kathleen was born without the sense of smell; accordingly, one of her daily chores was emptying the chamber pots. She was also the youngest in the family, and that usually meant she wound up with the smallest piece of pie or cake. Aunt Deannie, my father's twin sister was also the baby of the family, and from her experiences growing up, getting the short end of everything, she made sure her kids shared birthday cakes and butterscotch pie sliced equally to within an atom. The kid who did the cutting was the last to do the choosing. The wisdom of Sara Lee...

Harold Ross was a Second World War veteran. He was born in Ellerslie in 1920 and, when he was a boy, the week before Christmas was exciting for two reasons: the imminent arrival of Santa Claus, plus it meant the long-anticipated trip of the year to the bright lights of town.

> Christmas time, my sister and I, and father and mother used to go to Summerside. They'd go down to Holman's, and they'd buy everything they needed for the winter. So many bags of flour and bags of sugar and tea. And my sister and I would get 25 cents. That was the payoff for the year. Twenty-five cents. Old Santa Claus used to be up on top of Brace MacKay's store with a big bag of candy kisses. He'd pelt a handful down onto the street, and it was like feeding the chickens or pigeons.

When Roma Curley Mulligan's great-grandfather and two brothers immigrated from Ireland to Freetown, they only had enough money to buy one horse, which they shared from farm-to-farm. Years later, her grandfather and his brothers all chipped in to buy and share manure spreaders and hay loaders.

In the 1940s, Souris brothers Waldron and Roy Dingwell didn't even bother to keep it in the family: they swapped their new truck back and forth with the neighbour's new car.

> The people who lived across the road from us, we always went back and forth see, and they got the new car, a brand new Model-A. And we bought the new truck. We got that at Poole and Thompson's down in Montague.
>
> If anybody wanted to haul stuff, they took the truck. And if anybody wanted to go on a Sunday drive, they took the car. We'd swap. It was common back then. We always worked together back then. There was never any money involved. And that old truck when we got her first, there was no cab on it. Just the engine mounted on the chassis. It was the funniest

looking thing, with the two big headlights. The cab came afterwards.

The Dingwell boys hauled everything from 80-pound cans of milk to the creamery to 45-gallon barrels of marked gas to local farmers. They were young, making a go of it, and they liked to party. Being on the road all the time, they knew the location of every house party and country dance.

Barn dances were going on back then and it was usually on a Monday night. The rest of them had no way of travelling, so they'd all pile in the back of the truck and away we'd go. It's a wonder somebody didn't get killed. They'd all be drinking, and coming home, you'd have to gather them up. What a time. Today, you wouldn't be allowed to do it. We'd go to a dance and dance all night and come home, get called down to the wharf, perhaps a barge-load of gravel had come in, and take a load of gravel out to Bayfield or somewhere. Just have time to change our clothes and go to work. It was just good old-time clean fun.

Speaking of music and neighbours, the MacRae sisters and their brothers – ten kids, Mum and Dad plus Uncle Wilfred – all lived in the New London lighthouse. Jack MacRae was the keeper when he wasn't off fighting: he was a veteran of both the First and Second World Wars. Every fall, new neighbours from New Brunswick sailed into the bay in big white fishing schooners. The Caraquets had arrived to the delight of Mary MacRae Brander.

That was a big deal for us to see the Caraquet vessels coming in, all under sail. They'd come in on the weekends and anchor right outside the lighthouse. We were supposed to give those men oil. All lighthouse keepers were supposed to furnish them with oil for their lanterns on the boats. Free, out of big barrels. That was the law. We'd have ten 45-gallon drums of oil to keep the light burning. Then they'd come in in the evenings and entertain us with mouth organ music. And there was one man who came from Quebec, LeClair was his name, and he settled in Rustico. He just died a few years ago. He was a Caraquet. Claude was his first name, a very friendly man.

The Caraquets fished cod off PEI's north side, and they came into New London Bay to dig clams to bait their hooks. And to swap jigs for kerosene oil. When Jack MacRae headed off to Burma to fight in the Second World War, Claude and Maisie Adams took over the New London lighthouse.

In 1943, Maisie's daughter Mary was born in the lighthouse, the same year Claude died of cancer. Maisie took over his duties and became Canada's first female lighthouse keeper. She always said if it hadn't been for the kindness of family and her French River neighbours, she never would have survived raising three children, and running the lighthouse and range light on her own. Her brother Donald supplied eggs and beef, and one neighbour contributed a baby pig who tried to swim across the gut to the Cavendish sandspit, but was beaten back by the tide. Months later, Maisie had a party, and everyone shared the wayward pig.

◆

MacKenzie King "Mac" Dixon was born in 1926 in South Melville where his family ran a flour and grist mill. The Dixons shared the DeSable River with two other mills, one woollen and one a sawmill. They also shared their dinner table with nearly everyone who came to get their wheat or oats ground. Thanks to Mac's grammie and mum, everyone got a meal, as did their horses, but when it came to sharing their radio, a Deforest Crosley that ran on big batteries, the Dixons drew the line.

My grandmother was an invalid. She had fallen and broken a hip, so the family banded together and we got her a radio, one of the first radios around. We were just lucky to have it. It was a radio without the speaker – the loud speaker – it just had earphones. I can remember there was always a row over who was going to get these earphones when a certain pro-gramme would come on. At last, we took them apart and each person would have one. Well, that was ok. But after supper, we'd have to wait until my dad was heading out to do the evening chores. He'd say, 'Just one more minute. I just want to hear this. Just a min-ute now and then I'll give it to you.'

That would be "Amos and Andy" from New York. I forget how many different batteries it took. A batter-ies and B batteries, and seven tubes. One day, some-one made a mistake and hooked the battery up the wrong way and bang. Seven tubes gone. Well, there wasn't that many dollars around to buy tubes in those days. We had to do without a radio for a while, but anyway, come hockey time, we found the mon-ey somewhere and got it going again. Foster Hewitt... oh, yeah. Saturday night, that was our night to howl. Oh boy.

A scene re-enacted across Canada a generation later when television arrived... the Saturday night hockey game was still a thrill, and the Thompson boys were allowed to stay up and "howl" like the Dixons... Murray Westgate in his ESSO uniform, the same Foster Hewitt, the voice of *Hockey Night in Canada*, "up in the gondola," still calling the games. Memories shared by Canadians from the Atlantic to the Pacific to the Arctic.

Every community had one house with a radio that ran on batteries, and maybe a flour and grist mill, grinding flour and animal feed. In 1926 in Murray Harbour North, when Roy Clow was nine, his dad became seriously ill. One cold December morning, Roy's mother got him out of bed early and asked him if he thought he could take a load of wheat to Dan MacRae's mill in Heatherdale. Roy hitched up the mare, and was gone before daylight.

I said, 'Sure,' I thought this was great: get a trip to the mill. I took old Nell, the old mare, my favourite, took her and a wood sleigh, and away we went to the grist mill. I thought if I went early, I'd get the grist done in a hurry. So we got up to Dan MacRae's. I went down the hill and around the corner and, Lord God, I looked and there were horses and sleighs everywhere. Everybody was there with a grist, and I cursed and swore to myself.

If you don't think nine-year old Roy cursed and swore, then you didn't know Roy.

Anyway, I went down and Dan came out, and he knew me because I'd been there before. 'What are you doing, young fella!' He was an awful nice fella, Dan MacRae, and he had gold teeth and white hair full of dust from the wheat. He had no cap on and he looked like Santa Claus.

He said, 'You've got a grist, Roy.'

I said, 'Yeah.'

He said, 'You're coming back to pick this up later.'

I said, 'Oh no, I can't come back. I have to get it tonight.'

'Oh my God,' he said, 'You're gonna be late, but I'll do the best I can.'

Anyway, he got through the other fellas and then through mine about an hour and a half before dark. So, I got it loaded on the sleigh, and I walked beside the sleigh to give Nell a break, and it was a slow old trip into Montague.

It was too late to head back to Murray Harbour North, so Roy decided to spend the night with his older sister in Montague.

I stayed there for the night and I left before daylight. I got home after dinner. I was seven hours, I guess, or more, on the road. That was a long, old drag. We shared the flour around. We gave Elmer Millar's wife part of a bag, and Fred Millar and Dave Millar shared the flour. Some of them wanted some shorts, and some wanted some bran, so I shared it around. That's what we'd do. Share with all the neighbours."

In those days, when someone said, "Eat my shorts," they weren't quoting Bart Simpson. Grinding wheat produces flour, bran, middlings, and shorts. Shorts and middlings were used for cattle fodder, but also to make biscuits and my favourite breakfast cereal, cream of wheat.

Warren Leard in Coleman milled the best cream of wheat ever, so popular that he was never able to keep it in stock even if I phoned ahead and asked him to stash some away for me. Someone else always ferreted it out before I got there. Talk about eating my shorts.

◆

"This is an old song from the 1920s called 'Barefoot Days.'" When he was a young lad growing up in Charlottetown, the late Hughie Trainor took in the vaudeville and minstrel shows that played the Lyceum Theatre.

Hey, barefoot days when we were just a coupla kids,

Hey, barefoot days, oh boy, the things I did...

Hughie loved to share his rich baritone voice and to eventually perform on the same stage was a dream come true.

We'd go down to Shady Nook with a bent pin for a hook

And we'd fish all day and fish all night,

The jolly old fish refused to bite.

And then we'd slide down someone's cellar door

And we'd slide and slide until our pants got torn

And then we'd have to go home and get in bed

While mama got busy with the needle and thread.

Oh boy, what joy, we had in barefoot days,

Oh boy, oh what joy, we had in barefoot daa-ays.[11]

"That brings back memories, yes, indeed." Hughie performed for love, not money, but was rewarded in other ways. He met his future wife backstage at the minstrel show. After he sang the night they first met, he took her to White's restaurant for a dish of ice cream and cake. Ten cents. This was during the Second World War, prohibition was enforced even though Charlottetown was awash with British pilots, navigators, and ground personnel accustomed to having a couple of pints at their local pub. The C.O. at the RAF base, where the Charlottetown airport now sits, had read the men the riot act, warning them that the 65 bootleggers in town were strictly off limits. As was the one whorehouse. Whole blocks of King and Dorchester Streets were *verboten*, and were patrolled regularly by MPs from the airbase.

Mr. White came to the rescue. He was originally from England and empathized with the aviators – nicknamed "pigeons" by the local residents – and he had an unwritten rule: anyone in uniform who ordered a "pot of cold tea" received a potful of black rum instead. Mr. White's kindness made him a very popular guy with the pigeons. What he lost in tea sales was more than compensated by the warm glow of satisfaction resulting from the act of sharing. And putting one over on the MPs.

---

11   Billy Jones, "Oh, Boy! What Joy We Had in Barefoot Days," 16 January 1924, secondhandsongs.com/performance/864928.

The Cummings and Annie (Cody) Henderson family,
Freeland, Lot 11, PEI

A beleaguered father looked around the supper table one evening before saying grace: "Heavenly Father, keep us alive, there's ten for eatin' and food for five."

I have 28 first cousins, all on my father's side of the family. Not bad for a bunch of Presbyterians who believed dancing led to sex or was it the other way around. Regardless, I was put to shame by a woman from the Morell area who had 83 first cousins, and, when I picked myself up off the floor continued, "That's nothing. My father had 94 in a family of 12." Subtract four from that twelve: one for him, two brothers who were priests plus a sister who was a nun, leaving eight siblings to carry the load, averaging eleven and a half kids per family. The half kids only ate on weekends. But there was a reason that families were so big back in the bygone days. No, not because people were randy. Well, maybe. A better reason than a lack of self-control was a lack of birth control, plus people lived on farms 70-80-90 years ago. And extra mouths at the dinner table meant more hands on the hoes.

We used to say the Hardys were like the ants:

'Says the *ant* to the cricket,

I'm your servant and friend,

But *we ants never borrow;*

We ants never lend.'

Quoted by Kathleen Henderson Jelley, born in 1913, and who grew up on a farm in Freeland Lot 11 in western PEI.

The Hardys never borrowed anything. All our other neighbours would come for the lend of a shovel or the lend of an axe or borrow bread, but not the Hardys. I remember going to the Hardys to dig potatoes because I had the catalogue out. If we went to Uncle Josh's or a neighbour's to work, Dad didn't want us to take money. Never. He thought we should be doing a good deed instead of taking money. And that's what he and Mum did, all the good they did; they brought us up that way.

The Hardys – "we ants never borrow" – had a lot of boys. They never had to hire for anything they had to do, because they had Everett, Wilber, Ivan, Cecil, Elmer, Jimmy, and Frank – seven boys – so they had lots of help at home. But one year when the boys were all out fishing, only Wilber was still on the farm. He asked us to go up and pick his potatoes, and I got the catalogue out. I think he paid us 50 cents a day, and I got material for a skirt. I suppose it was the first skirt I ever had.

Kathleen was the baby of a family of 10, plus two children who died young. Her eldest brother Jim had moved to Boston and her mother Annie wrote to him before Kathleen was born to ask what to name the impending baby. He wrote back, "Call her Enough."

♦

The Deighan family in Summerside boasted 20 children. Father Ernie and the oldest son Charlie were both railway-men, driving steam, and later diesel locomotives. Another railwayman, Charlie Fraser, worked alongside the Deighans, and he claimed they ate a 50-pound bag of potatoes for supper. Charlie and his wife Rose lived in the west end of Summerside near the tracks, and they also raised a big family. Rose was a transplanted Newfoundlander and had met Charlie during the Second World War when he passed through on his way to Europe:

> We had 10 children. I was alone most of the time and I did all the business, picked up his paychecks and cashed them, because he wasn't home.

Charlie fired, and later, drove the western freight up to Tignish and often was gone for days at a time. A railway-man feared running out of food more than he was afraid of 20-foot snowdrifts.

> I packed big lunches for him. One of those great big picnic baskets, you know, with the two handles on it. I would pack that with everything: bacon and eggs for his breakfast. Sweets. And there'd have to be bread and something for sandwiches, because he had the bunkhouse and, as long as he had the food, he could make up his own.

Rose said she spent half her life baking homemade bread, rolls, biscuits, cakes, cookies.

> And that's why he's got diabetes today. I fed him too well.

So, while he's out working, you're sitting home taking it easy.

Oh, yes. Now, how easy can it be with 10 children, now you tell me. We could watch from the living room window when he was on the western freight and, as soon as

the kids heard the train, they'd be all out waving at Dad going past.

When Charlie was promoted to engineer, he made a couple of stops on the way back to Summerside:

In the fall of the year, you know what he used to do? He'd buy potatoes and 100-pound bags of turnips and carrots, and he'd slow the train down here at the crossing, and he'd throw them out and the kids would go up with their sleighs and bring them home.

Enough for a couple of meals according to Charlie Fraser.

♦

Gordon Dockendorff's ancestors emigrated from Germany to Maine in the mid-18th century. In 1792, a generation later, the family left for Prince Edward Island.

They had very large families. Jacob the First had 14 children and his son William had 12. Jacob the Second had 11 and Jacob the Third had 17. That'd be my grandfather.

The Dockendorffs settled in York Point across the harbour from what is now Victoria Park. In the wintertime, people heading to Charlottetown cut through the Dockendorff farm by horse and sleigh, dodging children, to cross on the harbour ice.

In Pownal, a few miles to the east of Charlottetown, the Jones family farmed and later were station agents at Hazelbrook. Susan Jones Andrews' mother was one of 15 children and was related to the well-known Jenkins family on the 48 Road:

My mother's name was Dorothy Jenkins before she was married. She was a relative of the 21 Jenkins in Mount Albion. Robert Jenkins was the father, but he had two wives. So, my mother was a first cousin of them all. Twenty-one. They had a great time.

The Mount Albion Jenkins family was, like the Dockendorffs, originally German, descended from Nicholas Henkell and Anna Otto, who possibly changed their name to Jenkins to avoid paying child support. Kidding. They didn't have child support in those days.

◆

One of the smartest people I ever met was the late Arthur Hughes. We met by chance one August day in the poultry barn at the Dundas Fair where I was trying to figure out the difference between a Rhode Island Red and a Plymouth Rock. The Rhode Island Reds have US licence plates.

There was 15 in our family, but there were a lot of big families in those times and, of course, they depended on the family to do most of the work. Each youngster had their own job to do: one to look after the hens, another fella to look after a couple of sows, another fella took care of the cows. My job was mostly the horses.

Arthur told me Dr Toombs in Mount Stewart charged $3.00 to bring a baby into the world. Arthur knew hens, horses, and every other barnyard creature, and lamented the changes he'd seen in farming over his 90-plus years. Mixed farms evolved into monocultures, bringing an end to the bucolic days of endless pastures swarming with wild flowers and bees.

◆

Up west in Cape Wolfe, Ralph Cooke went fishing with his father when he was 11 years old. The Cookes lived on the shore, fished lobster, cod, herring, and hake, and were subsistence farmers at best, but Ralph still knew a thing or two about the bees... and the birds thanks to their neighbours. He showed me a photograph of the Riley family, all crammed into a Model-T Ford:

> That's Bernard Riley and his wife – they had 15 kids. See them sitting in the back seat? Dad used to laugh. He was a very private man, my father, and Bernard and Teresa had that car, and they'd go in to O'Leary and they'd park. Even 10 years after they were married, they'd be necking right in broad daylight. You know, that was a no-no in those times. Or, you might see them down a back road. Parked.

With 15 kids, no wonder they took evasive action. Jill and I only had two kids and a dog, but we gave up sneaking around early in life, and took up wind sprints and ice baths instead, never knowing of the opportunities the back roads in O'Leary offered. You know the old joke about big families: We were so poor, we slept five to a bed... I never slept alone until I got married.

◆

Rose Deighan mentioned how hard she worked. It was wash day, six days a week for the mothers of those big families, no electricity, never mind filling a suitcase full of baked goods for Charlie. I'm the oldest of six boys. Our mother gave up a good job in a bank when she got married in 1951, and, fool that I was, I remember telling people my mother didn't work.

Louis Cantelo from Seven Mile Road near Cardigan was born in 1904, two generations before me, but he had a much better appreciation of just how hard women worked.

They did all the work in the house and they helped out in the fields. They pitched grain and milked cows. They were really busy women, and then they'd come in and spin wool and knit half the night.

Like my grandmothers, both of Louis' grandmothers- Martha Acorn Creed and Mary MacKinnon Cantelo - were midwives. My grandmother delivered me. Money was very scarce at that time, and they'd have to pay the doctor perhaps $15. And they wouldn't have to pay her anything. Money was scarce and we were fairly poor, so my father drove all the way down to Sturgeon and brought up my grandmother. It was in the wintertime and, coming down, the sleigh went into a rut and she fell out. My father laughed, but she didn't think it was very funny. That was my grandmother Martha Creed, she had been an Acorn. The women at that time did an awful lot of the work men do today. She died at about 70 years old, in 1923. I remember I was just coming home from the west [on the harvest excursion train], and the word came up that my grandmother had died. I happened to be the first home. I had to hitch up the horse right quick, and get my mother over there as fast as I could, 17 miles of a drive. I think she just wore out, working hard. She raised 12 children. That's a lot of work.

Martha Acorn Creed, one of the unsung heroes of Canadian history: midwife, mother of 12, made her own soap, sewed all the kids' clothes, spun wool, and grew and spun flax into linen. Not many "me" days for that woman. Incidentally, the Acorns were also of German descent. There seems to be a pattern emerging. And like the Henkells, Johann Eachorn changed his name. The Eachorns/Acorns settled on PEI in 1782, and produced 14 children, 132 grandchildren and 222 great grand-children, proving that nuts, like apples, don't fall very far from the tree.

♦

A constant worry for parents from pioneer times in the 1700s through to the Second World War was the fear of losing a child to illnesses like diphtheria and smallpox or even appendicitis. War also claimed more than a fair share of young men. Leonard LeClair was one of 12 children born to Prosper and Julie LeClair in Rustico. He showed me a photograph of himself and seven of his brothers who enlisted in the armed services and had gone off to fight overseas:

> This is Clarence. He went to the States when he was a young man, and he joined the American army when the Second World War broke out. There's another brother, he was in the States too and he joined the army, too. This is Reuben and this is Francis, he was in the Navy and this fella, Furlie, he was in the Navy. And Eugene was in the Navy. There was seven altogether, and the last fella, his name was Eric, he was too young to join the army when the war broke out. He went to the States and later he got in the air force, and they shipped him off to Korea. We all came back, yeah, we all came back.

Imagine the family reunion when all eight boys... boys? ... men made it home to Rustico:

> My father, he was, well, crying. At the house, crying, yeah.

Every son had been sending a dollar-a-day home to their mum. Leonard and six brothers had all worked as bellhops at the Queen Hotel on Water Street in Charlottetown, but after the war, Leonard landed a new job in the butter department at Central Creameries on Fitzroy Street. He once found a man's coat in a cream can, and another time, instead of saying so long to the oolong, a tea bag somehow made it through the inspection line. That day's butter was decorated with tiny black flecks.

A few black specks on his buttered bannock wouldn't have bothered Ernie MacPherson. Ernie was born in 1899 in

Dunblane, and he lived to 108. In his youth, Ernie crossed the Strait to work in mainland lumber camps, and he survived the 1918-19 Spanish flu. Several of his campmates somehow contracted it, even though they were far from civilization, isolated 20 miles deep in the woods. In the 1920s, Ernie finally came home to stay on the family farm:

> We grew Sebagos and [Green] Mountain potatoes, and Keswicks and [Netted] Gems. And some lighter Blues and some darker Blues. That's what the people lived on, blue potatoes and herring.

Ambrose Monaghan and his 10 brothers and sisters also lived on blue potatoes and herring. Ambrose was born and raised on a farm in 1913 in Kelly's Cross:

> I was right at the foot of the pack, the last born.

As in all big families, Ambie saw a lot of hand-me-down clothes, but said there was an upside too:

> When it came to hand-me-downs, after five or six times, there was nothing left to hand down so you got something new. So, it worked both ways.

Estelle Soloman Bolger wore more than her share of second-hand clothes. Estelle was born in 1909 in Georgetown where her family ran a variety of businesses, from a bakery and a barbershop to a hotel where sailors in port from around the world bunked up and paid 10 cents extra for a hot bath. Estelle was taught the barbering business by her father. Eventually, she moved to Summerside where she met and married fiddle player and harness-maker Lenie Bolger from Foxley River. The Bolgers were noted not only for their music but also for their big families, and for nicknames like Earring Johnny:

> He had a daughter, Bea, Beatrice, and she had 19 children. They all lived.

Another brother, Gabriel, had 17 children.

He said it'd break your heart to see 14 slices of bread going off the plate at once.

A swipe or two of black-flecked butter might have halted the sliced bread migration or maybe not.

By Christmas, they were on their second pig.

Estelle said it took four pigs to get them through the winter. I'll always remember a man from Bass River, Nova Scotia, telling me that you knew you would make it through another winter if by January "you still had half your hay and half your pork." And all your children.

Dutch Courage

Bert Tersteeg, musician & 2nd WW survivor

Time will say nothing but I told you so.

Time only knows the price we have to pay;

If I could tell you I would let you know.[12]

We were occupied by the Germans. They just ran over the country, first of all with the bombardments, bombing several places, and one Sunday morning, we went to church and German airplanes came over and they bombed my neighbourhood. My wife's house was right there. They nearly flattened her house with those bombs. As a matter of fact, my wife's mother got hurt that Sunday morning. So that was the first real notice that the war was on. The

---

12   Poem excerpts are from W. H. Auden's "If I Could Tell You." Collected Shorter Poems: 1927-1957. London: Faber & Faber, 1969.

Dutch army was defeated in two or three days, but everything was sabotaged already.

Islanders remember Hubertus "Bert" Tersteeg as a talented, sharing, and much-loved musician and educator. He was born in Utrecht in 1928, a city famous for its Medieval centre and the 18th century Treaty of Utrecht, the peace agreement between Britain and France. However, the Nazis did not believe in peace or treaties – including the Treaty of Versailles and the Geneva Convention – which they signed, then later disregarded as they invaded other European and African countries. On May 15, 1940, when Bert was 12, the German military entered the Netherlands the day after they blitzed the city of Rotterdam and threatened to take similar action with Utrecht. In the subsequent years, life for Bert, his family, and other Dutch citizens in the Low Countries changed dramatically.

> My oldest brother had to go to Germany. He had no choice. You had to go when you turned 18, so we lost him. He had no choice. He worked in a factory there. The food disappeared. It became a fight for food. My father nearly got caught. The Germans used to go to the farmers and take a pig or cow in the field. The farmer wasn't allowed to sell it to us, but what they did do was kill it and cut it up in the field. But if you were caught by the Germans, you were going to be shot on the spot. But my dad, in the middle of the night, slaughtered a cow and brought it home – most of it – and a couple of days later, we had one of those run-ins with the Germans. They stepped right into our house when we were eating, and they asked what kind of meat were we eating. Fortunately, it was sheep. If it had been cows' meat, we would have had it!

If we should weep when clowns put on their show,

If we should stumble when musicians play,

Time will say nothing but I told you so...

Meeuwis Ferdinandus "Fred" Dejonge also knew something about hiding food from the German army. Fred was born in Hoek in the southwestern corner of The Netherlands, and was six years old when the Second World War began. His childhood world on the family farm came crashing down. The youthful game of hide-and-seek became a dangerous game of cat-and-mouse: hiding food and guns from the Germans:

> First of all, the homing pigeons had to go. If you had homing pigeons, you had to take them to the village to be killed. Then the rifles and shotguns. They took all of them. People hid the rifles, took them all apart, and put them in a hollow log. I never knew, of course, but on our farm my father had a hollow log with four shotguns hidden in it. There was a very active re-sistance during the war. The Germans would have loved it if we had played ball with them the same as the Belgians did.

A little post-war sniping is reasonable from a man whose country suffered five years of brutality and indoctrination:

> From grade four and up, you had to take two hours of German, as stubbornly as possible.

◆

And what of Bert Tersteeg? A year before D-Day and the Germans' retreat from Utrecht, a German officer heard Bert playing one of the many instruments he had mastered. He offered Bert a fully-paid four-year scholarship in Berlin. Bert was not only a musical prodigy, he was also a loyal Dutch citizen, and a good athlete and footballer. He joined the underground instead.

I was the runner on the square where I lived. I was a very fast runner, as skinny as a rake, but I could run because I played a lot of soccer. I used to stand at the gate of the square, and I could see who was coming down from the bridge or up from the other side. If I saw Germans, I'd run home like crazy and switch off the British radio station, [to] which we were listening, because that was not allowed. The only real news about the war we got was from Britain; the rest was all in German and, of course, was all propaganda. If you were caught listening to British radio, you'd had it.

Suppose the lions all get up and go,

And all the brooks and soldiers run away;

Will Time say nothing but I told you so?

If I could tell you I would let you know.

♦

Thanks to hidden radios and the BBC, the Tersteegs knew the tide had turned when they heard of the Allied invasion in Italy in 1943, and then six months later the news of the D-Day landings.

On my father's birthday, June 6. And by that time, we knew the Germans were retreating, moving back, back, back, so we knew it wouldn't be too long before the war was over. The first six soldiers I saw were Canadians. Oh, they looked so big. A couple of Jeeps, and we ran up, and one gave me a chocolate bar. A half, because he had already eaten half. I must have been so skinny by that time, so he gave me the chocolate bar. I didn't know what I tasted. Food from heaven. Wow.

When the Allied Forces landed in Normandy, they began

the arduous push to liberate Northern Europe from the Nazis. By early September 1944, the Allied forces, under the code name "Operation Market Garden" and led by the Canadians, had entered The Netherlands.

However, the Allies faced fierce resistance from the German army on several fronts.

Ironically, the winter of 1944-1945 became known as "Hunger Winter." The Germans cut off food and fuel supplies to the country. Food became an obsession. The Dutch clung to life eating potato peelings and tulip bulbs. Anything. Bert trapped rabbits. He said that by 1945, there wasn't a rabbit left in the country. Thousands of people – 18,000, to be exact – died of starvation. Canadian and American soldiers were horrified by the gaunt survivors who greeted them with skeletal-yet-wide-open arms.

Now, different aircraft were flying low over Utrecht. Bert described the scene:

> It rained manna. They threw baskets of food down from airplanes. They actually did. The British and the Swedes, and anybody who had spare food actually parachuted all that stuff down. It was divided up and immediately the farmers started to work the fields again. Within a couple of years, we were back to normal, having learned a little bit more appreciation for food. Oh, yeah. There was nothing left by the end of the war. No rabbits. Absolutely nothing. I have seen-and I'm not proud of it – but in the city, I saw a man drop dead in front of me, his belly swollen like this. Starvation. And at that time, I was 16 or 17 years old. Not a nice sight, I'll tell you. Nope.

The winds must come from somewhere when they blow,

There must be reasons why the leaves decay;

Time will say nothing but I told you so...

While some areas of the Netherlands were being liberated, the war continued to rage around Fred Dejonge's village. One day, he heard a strange sound overhead: a V-1 rocket. The sound of the rocket stopped suddenly and the flying bomb dropped out of the sky onto the streets of Antwerp, Belgium, about 60km from Hoek, NL. In retaliation for the Normandy invasion, Hitler was unleashing revenge on civilians, and was testing the unmanned rocket, later nicknamed the Doodlebug by the British, on Belgium.

Fred remembered the arrival of the Allies in the Netherlands when he was 11:

> They landed on June 6, and by September 22, the Canadians were at my place. The Germans disappeared in one or two nights, before the Canadians came. One morning, I woke up and they had taken all the barbed wire off the fences. All of a sudden, in the middle of the afternoon, I saw so much commotion and the Canadian army was there. Generosity and feasting. I slept in the house, but I don't think I ate a meal in our house for the next 10 days. They wanted fresh milk, fresh eggs, fresh potatoes, and they'd give you three times as much as what they wanted from you, but, oh boy. Cans of pork and beans were everywhere. For three months after the war, you'd find a can of pork and beans. Nobody bothered to pick them up. There was lots of food then.

Young Fred might not have appreciated the cans of pork and beans because the Canadians brought treats a little closer to a boy's heart and stomach:

> Chocolate bars and cookies. And candy. I liked the Canadian soldiers. Very much so. They were adored.

Lloyd Gates was one of those Canadian soldiers. He has returned to The Netherlands several times with other veterans, and said they were treated "like rock stars" every time, just as they were in 1944. Fred said the Canadian soldiers had adopted a little dog in France, and it had followed them across northern Europe. It was the fattest dog he'd ever seen. And the Canadian soldiers also taught Fred some English words, none of which can be repeated here without this book getting an "R" rating.

♦

Eventually, Fred and Bert immigrated to Canada, and became valued residents of Prince Edward Island and citizens of Canada. Their moves across the Atlantic were inspired by their Second World War heroes: the Canadian soldiers who fought their way into The Netherlands and ended the suffering caused by the German army. Fred farmed first in Ontario and then in Millview, PEI.

In a way, Bert farmed as well. He arrived in Canada to play music with the Canadian Army. He began the music program at St. Dunstan's University, and helped start both the New Brunswick and Prince Edward Island symphonies. He went on to chair the UPEI Music department where he nurtured a generation of young Island musicians and educators: Perry Williams, Frank Nabuurs, Dave Shepherd, Alan Dowling, Chrissy Blanchard, Bob Nicholson, Dale Sorensen, Rowan Fitzgerald, and on and on. Quite a legacy. He also played in the orchestra pit for *Anne of Green Gables.* You don't get more Canadian than that.

♦

And what about Bert's 18-year-old older brother, who, in 1940, had been transported to Germany to work in an armaments' factory?

We didn't know if he would ever be back; a lot of young fellas never came back. At the end of the war, he walked from Germany, over Belgium, back to Holland. It took him five weeks to get home, but he made it. I remember the excitement.

I'm not sure if his path home took him through Hoek, but if so, he might have found the odd can of pork and beans lying around. And some very happy people.

Strong Back and a Weak Mind

Ray Brooks, beekeeper

Blue potatoes and fish... Gus Gregory from Chepstow believed a feed of MacIntyre blues and salt herring would cure anything. Gus was born in 1917 and, when he was a young lad, thought any farmer growing more than five acres of potatoes was a gambler. Or a fool. What was he going to do with all those potatoes anyway?

It was a roll of the dice. Some farmers grew only what they could eat, plus a few bags to sell in the spring. Often, the spring left-overs were hauled to the nearest starch factory. I'll always remember Colin "Doctor" MacDonald – "Doctor" because he was the son of Dr Roddie – from St Peters saying that farmers dreaded hearing the local starch factory firing up, because it meant low prices for potatoes that fall, so there would be tons left over to boil into starch.

Potato acreage increased especially after the Second World War when more farms had tractors. Ray Brooks in Murray Harbour grew four to five acres of potatoes. His mother cooked for the men working at the starch factory next door. Ray bought his first tractor in 1946 immediately after the war and rationing ended:

Massey Harris three-plow tractor. That was a good little tractor.

I asked if he liked it better than the horses.

Oh, yes. I did, though you couldn't talk to it. I had awful sore feet and I had a terrible job following the horses, so the tractor was quite a help.

Some people traded in their horses on the tractor.

We didn't. We just kept our horses until they were gone. Let them retire. Put them on the grass in the summertime. But we'd use the horses at potato-diggin'. It was a great way to dig potatoes. Just dump them in the cart and then dump them into the cellar. You'd be a week pickin'. Five or six pickers, have them for a week.

So you'd have to feed everybody?

Oh, yes. A little girl came here one morning. She wanted to know if I'd give her a job pickin' potatoes. I said, 'We've got enough pickers in the field now.' She was only a little kid, and she was crying. She never had a coat and she wanted to earn enough money to buy a coat. 'Well,' I said, 'You go back and if you can keep up with the rest of them, you can go to work.' Well, she kept up with them all right. And she got her money and she got her coat.

Ray Brooks, what a guy. His father used to fertilize the fields with a slurry of pig and cattle manure, ribbon kelp they raked off the beach after storms, cod and hake guts from fishermen on the shore, and black mud from a swamp out back. The first beater-digger on the Brooks farm was made from old car parts. Ray said it beat the potatoes out of the rows so hard they flew all over the farm.

And you might wonder why that little girl wasn't in school. Picking potatoes was so important back then that school was abandoned every fall so children could help with the harvest. Some were paid. Others helped neighbours who returned the favour at threshing time. As a girl, Florence Dixon picked her share of potatoes. She was born in 1914, at the beginning of the First World War:

> Two weeks in the fall. Paid 25 cents a day. I thought I was making a lot of money. We always had lunches sent out to the field morning and afternoon. We had dinner wherever we were pickin' potatoes. Of course we came home for supper. Irish cobblers and Green Mountain and some of the old-fashioned blues. My father always grew some MacIntyre blues.

To have on Friday with salt cod.

> Yes, or herring.

When you were four years old, there was a very bad 'flu epidemic.

> My father almost died. It was in the fall, and the neighbours came and harvested the crop. Wonderful.

During 1918-19, the Spanish 'Flu killed more people than the First World War. Their lungs filled and they drowned.

Cobblers and Green Mountains were the early-crop stand-bys, and everyone grew a couple of drills of the blues. Some old varieties, wonderfully-named varieties, have faded away: Early Rose, Calico, Jenny Lind, Dakota Red, and Star. Star was a pulpy, starchy variety, well-suited for making starch. PEI had a half-dozen starch factories at one time, dependent on culls and cheap potatoes.

OK. The potatoes are picked and ready to sell. If the pickers were only getting 25 cents a day, the farmer must have been raking in the big bucks. Or not. Vernon McCarville was born in 1915, grew up on a farm in Thistle and Shamrock, and remembers both the good times of the 1920s and the Great Depression of the 1930s:

> They called them the Roaring Twenties. In the '20s, my father sold an animal hide – a bull – and got

$127 for it. A similar hide ten or fifteen years later down here at John P. Smith's, I got half a cent a pound. A 98-pound hide and I got 48 cents, and my father got $127 in the '20s for the same thing. Nothing was worth anything.

You couldn't give things away. Potatoes were six cents a bushel [50 pounds] and it cost nine cents for the bag. So, it didn't pay to put the potatoes in a bag. That's how bad it was. I remember this fella asking a potato dealer 'What do you think potatoes are going to do at six cents a bushel?' The dealer said, 'They're going to go up.' The farmer said, 'What makes you think they're going to go up?' The dealer replied, 'Well, they can't go down.'

You couldn't give up. Another year, there was a big crop and you had to bury the potatoes; dug a big hole and buried them all. You couldn't sell them at all. And for six cents a lot of people didn't bother, you see. They just got a machine and buried them.

Vernon said if someone from the city had showed up at the farm, he'd have given away those potatoes. But if you needed free potatoes, and many people did, then you didn't have the gas to put in a car. Not that you had a car in the first place.

When we were kids, we played in an old car with cloth windows that sat rusting below the byre behind the barn, surrounded by rotting mounds of thirty-year old manure. The hens laid eggs in the back seat. It was a Star car that my grandfather, Joe Cunningham, bought in 1929. Within three months, the stock market crashed on Wall Street, a long way from Avondale, Pictou County. However, following the logic if a butterfly farts in Australia, there's a tornado in Tennessee, Joe could no longer afford to run the Star car. He parked it out of sight from the road, and it never moved again.

The potatoes are picked. We didn't get any money but, like

Vernon said, you can't give up, so let's take a load down to the Murray Harbour wharf, and dump them into the hold of a schooner. Captain Hubert White came from a long line of sea captains and schooner sailors. He hauled thousands of tons of PEI potatoes and turnips to the mainland in his schooner, the *Francis D. Cook*:

> My home port was what I called my favorite. It seemed like every weekend you were away, tied up to some coal pier. Through the week, maybe you'd be somewhere interesting, but on the weekends, we were stuck. Slept on board, ate on board. Oh, we lived pretty good and we picked up a lot of things on the go. We'd get to Sydney and there'd be fresh fish, halibut, so we didn't do too-too bad that way.

> We'd go down to Canso with a load of produce, piled up on the deck and everywhere. All kinds of vegetables – pumpkins even – and potatoes in the hold, and retail it at the wharf. See, down in Canso, they couldn't grow anything. It's all rocks there. We had our customers and every year we'd go. Then we'd go in the spring, too, and peddle from one port to another, and when we got to Sydney, we'd wholesale the vegetables.

> And then load coal for back to Charlottetown. A. Pickard and Co. [coal merchants] and Large too. Pickard's had their own wharf [where the Delta Hotel is now]. And it all died a natural death. Oil took over. Now you couldn't afford to buy a bag of coal.

The Power boys did the unloading at Pickard's wharf. Next to the wharf was Frank Clarke's big produce warehouse, next to it the railway tracks and old PEI Railway engine house. Cross the railway bridge going east and it was farms all the way to Murray Harbour.

There were at least 20 other captains sailing out of Murray Harbour back in the 1930s: Captain Royal White, the Chapmans, Captain Thomas Trenholm, and Captains George

Dunn and Hedley Penny. It was a foggy day in Freetown if one of them came back to PEI with an empty schooner:

> We used to go all around Nova Scotia ports, to Sydney, and to Halifax a little, the Magdalene Islands, too. The *Francis D. Cook* carried 75 tons, so we lived off the schooner for years. We carried herring for lobster bait, coal on freight, salt, produce, gravel.

Gravel?

> For the government roads. You were allowed to take it off the shore then. We loaded it off the beach, but now you couldn't take it. Over at Cape George, Ballantyne's Cove [Antigonish County] is about 25 or 30 miles by water as you go towards the Canso Strait. We'd boat it off the beach into dories. They always said all you needed to haul gravel was a strong back and weak mind. A dollar and a quarter in Charlottetown. We were giving them the gravel and hauling it for a dollar and a quarter. Then they had it cut down to a dollar a ton, so what we were doing was just surviving on that.

Wharves across the Island are infilled with Nova Scotia rock and gravel. At $1.25 a ton in a 75-ton schooner, the crew would split $93.75. My back hurts thinking about it.

New Glasgow, NS was a coal port popular with the schooner men. They'd tie up at the wharf next to the downtown bridge, sell their load of potatoes and cabbage, and then load up with Stellarton coal. There was a big bakery in New Glasgow, and the men would buy empty sugar bags, thicker and superior to flour bags, for five cents a bag. They'd head back to PEI just before the Christmas freeze-up and surprise Mother with the sugar bags. New underwear all around and curtains for the parlour. PEI was a breadbasket for these coal towns. My grandfather Joe had a Pictou County farm. He grew rocks.

Speaking of rocks, you might guess a place nicknamed

"The Rock" might also be a market for PEI produce. On the Charlottetown waterfront near the Buntain and Bell wharf, Wellington MacNeill had an office and a corral. He brought wild western horses in by rail from Alberta. The ones he could get shoes on, he sold cheap to Island farmers; the wilder horses that he couldn't shoe were fed to his silver foxes in Tea Hill, or went back into the railcar and were shipped to Europe for human consumption. He also ran a thriving business buying everything from cattle to hay to turnips to ship by C.N. freighter to Newfoundland. Bus Gay is Wellington MacNeill's nephew, more like a son. He told me this story about his entrepreneurial Uncle Well, his entrepreneurial and *tobacco-chewing* Uncle Well:

> Ford Wilson... he's dead now. He used to drive the truck for Uncle Well. He looked after that truck perfectly. Did he ever. It was a big truck with a staked back on it. So anyway, one day Uncle Well couldn't get to town, so Ford went out and picked him up. They picked me up too, of course. On the way into town, Uncle Well spit on the floor of the truck. Jesus. Ford stopped the truck and said, 'Look MacNeill. Don't you spit on the floor of this truck.' Uncle Well said, 'I own this truck.' Ford said, 'OK, take it. I'll walk home.' That's the type he was.

Did he get out?

No. Uncle Well calmed down.

Well MacNeill was a larger-than-life character. There wasn't a farmer in Queens or Kings County who didn't recognize his black Dodge when it rolled into the barnyard. It was covered in red mud and had a spittoon on the floor. Could have used one in his truck too. His reputation preceded him: he reputedly could estimate within 50 pounds the weight of three steers standing in a field. He carried a big wad of cash in his hip pocket. One farmer told me $10,000, another $50,000. Bus Gay says it was somewhere in the middle. Regardless, peeling off the tens and twenties always impressed the farmers.

He held court at a shoeshine and barber shop in downtown Charlottetown every morning. He bought and shipped everything. Honey. Chickens. Eggs. Pigs. Live pigs. Ford Wilson rarely let anyone touch his truck. Or spit in it. We know Ford wasn't afraid of the boss, so you can bet he wasn't afraid of the boss's son Alfred, wearer of natty suits and driver of fast cars, either:

> About 11:00 in the morning, Alfred came down to the wharf and started giving orders, but nobody would listen to him. Some vessels were in loading and he went to Ford Wilson and says, 'Ford,' he says, 'Ford, take that truck and go pick up some weaner [25-50lbs] pigs.' Ford says, 'You're not my boss. I'm not gonna move until the boss tells me. But if you want to take the truck and pick up the weaner pigs, you go ahead.'

> Alfred hopped in the truck, and away he went out and picked up the weaner pigs. He got back and there were three pigs in the truck. Tailgate came off. Lost the whole works except for three. They were all over the place.

Bus Gay is a chip off the old Well MacNeill block, a genuine character. We don't see characters like them anymore. In the 1940s, Bus would fly down to New York City to visit an aunt and uncle living in Manhattan. He'd take in a few shows, check out the big bands – he liked the Dorseys – and spend a week parading around town. To pay for his room and board, before he'd left PEI, he'd gone to the henhouse, grabbed a dozen eggs, and that night Aunt Margaret would whip up omelettes made from fresh PEI eggs.

I don't know if he brought back five cent sugar bags.

Cold Water and Flour for Supper

Dougall Dunkie MacDonald, 2nd WW veteran, Pictou County

When the Second World War ended in 1945, life did a 180-degree turnaround: from killing and rationing to peace and the halcyon 1950s of conspicuous consumption. Optimism reigned. Babies were born. Dougald Dunkie MacDonald, born on a rocky, unproductive farm in Baileys Brook in the hills of eastern Pictou County, saw things differently. He was born in 1918, the year the First World War ended, the war that was supposed to end all wars. A baby born in England at exactly 11:00 on the 11th of November 1918 was named Pax to celebrate the Armistice. At the age of 21, he was killed in the Second World War.[13]

After fighting in the war, Dougald went home to Nova Scotia. He was 27. He landed a job at Trenton Industries Ltd, for-

---

13 Guy Cuthbertson, Peace at Last: A Portrait of Armistice Day, 11 November 1918, New Haven, CT, Yale UP, 2018.

merly the Eastern Car Company, in Trenton, N.S., building railway cars. Pictou County's coal mines and steel plants were booming. The Sobeys empire was expanding, and the taverns and banks were packed when the shift whistles blew on Friday afternoon. But things didn't change overnight:

> I came home from overseas and, oh God, things were tough, I'm telling you. One fella came to work with me, and at lunch time on his first day at the car works, he was sitting there, and I said 'Did you forget your lunch pail, Bob?'

> 'No, Dougald, I didn't,' he said, 'I had nothing to put in it. I promised my two girls that if they went to school today, I'd try to get a loaf of bread for supper. They had nothing to eat yesterday, just water. So, I got them to go to school today.'

Dougald rubbed his big hands together as he reminisced:

> Well, I saw a lot of hardships in the war, and I hated like hell to see it at home. We were only making $4 or $5 a day, and he'd have to wait two weeks before he got his first pay. So, I put my hand in my pocket and took everything out. $4.85. I said, 'Here Bob. It's all yours.' He took a piece of chalk and started adding up what he'd get: a loaf of bread, and so many slices of bologna, and a quart of milk, and so on. And he said, 'Boy, we're going to a good supper tonight!' And when he got paid – I'd forgotten all about the $4.85 – he tried to give it back. I said, 'I didn't loan it to you, Bob. I gave it to you.'

Dougald said they had lots to eat on the farm and cheap, fresh fish down at the wharf in nearby Lismore. He grew up in a Gaelic-speaking Highland Scottish community where no one ever went hungry; where food and labour, as well as the old stories and folklore, had been shared for generations. Atlantic salmon, eggs, turnips, and beef were bartered at D.D. MacDonald's big general store in Baileys Brook. D.D. stocked an icehouse to keep the salmon cool before shipping it off to Boston on the train. If you couldn't pay up front, he kept a running tab in neat little account books with thin tissues of carbon paper between the pages.

◆

Helen Cudmore's family provided the same service for their customers in Oyster Bed Bridge. It was where neighbours and friends gathered after supper to smoke a pipe and share the day's news. Helen's Dad was well-liked and knew everyone who came through the door. He thought he could trust everyone… but not so:

> There was one gentleman my Dad got very suspicious of. He used to scare my brother and I when we were in the store. He never wanted us around. Dad found out later he'd been stealing from the till. Dad went upstairs and made a little hole as big as your thumb in the floor, and he'd send us upstairs after school to watch this guy. We caught him. We caught two that way. Dad just gave them a talking to.

Helen said it wouldn't have been so bad if the thieves had stolen food because they were hungry. They stole just to steal. Her dad figured one man didn't even spend the money he stole at Cudmore's store since he never bought anything; he was just one of the loafers who came in at night to sit around and spit tobacco into the pot-bellied stove.

Gladys Bryan tells a similar story. She was born in 1918 in Elmsdale in the western end of PEI. In the Depression years of the 1930s, her father moved the family to Saint John, NB . He'd jumped at the chance to hire on as a stevedore on the waterfront. It didn't pay much and some weeks, there weren't many ships to unload. Gladys and her siblings went to bed hungry. Hunger, said Gladys, sometimes makes people do desperate things:

> One awful sad thing I can tell you about. Perhaps

I shouldn't, but I will. Our next-door neighbour was out of work and he had two or three kids. He went down to the corner store. He was just standing around and he spied a small bag of flour, and he picked it up and he took it home. The man who owned the store noticed him so he called the police. They went to his house and they looked in the window and here was the man's wife taking the flour and mixing it with cold water. That's what them and the kids were eating.

So, the store owner said to the policeman, 'Let's get out of here. I'll send them up a supply of groceries.' Imagine now. Well, you couldn't punish a man for doing that could you? They didn't have a bite in the house to feed his kids. That was about the saddest thing in my life... feeding the kids cold water and flour.

Gladys had a couple of unusual food connections: when she was nine, she caught T.B. from an infected cow's milk on her grandparents' farm in Alberton. And she was, I believe, the only person I knew from her generation who saw lots of bananas when she was growing up, thanks to the vessels returning to Saint John from the Caribbean:

Great big banana boats coming in. One thing they did, any big stalks of bananas that looked spoiled, they just threw on the wharf because they couldn't sell them in the store. A lot of people would go down there to pick up those bananas. They got a lot of food that way. The stevedores must have realized that, rather than throw food in the water, people needed food to eat.

After the Second World War, bananas supplanted apples as the world's most consumed fruit, but at one time, it was a real treat to find a banana in your Christmas stocking. One man told me Santa brought him and his sister a banana each one year. His sister immediately ate hers, but he saved his so he could tempt her with it later. After a week, he went back to his sock drawer to retrieve the hidden banana. It had rotted into a mushy black blob.

Banana and peanut butter sandwiches were never a favourite in our house when my five brothers and I were growing up. We preferred grilled brown sugar sandwiches, the browner the sugar and the whiter the bread the better. Dentists loved us.

MacKenzie King Dixon, on the other hand, probably never ate white bread in his life. Mac was the third generation to run the family's flour and grist mill on the DeSable River in South Melville. Oats, barley, and wheat were ground into meal, whole wheat flour, shorts, middlings, and bran.

> When my dad was running the mill, people came from all down the south shore as far away as Rocky Point, and that was a fair drive with a horse and wagon. They even came across from St. Peter's Island. In those days, every person, every customer, who came with a grist of wheat always got their horse fed. And themselves fed. That was thrown in. No charge for that. My grandmother told me that she fed as many as 14 in a day. Of course, that would be two meals – dinner and supper. That was part of the deal. You'd wonder how they ever made a living out of it but, apparently, they did.

The bottomless teapot... and how many biscuits and loaves of bread did that poor woman bake? One year, Mac and I recorded an April Fool's day prank to run on CBC radio. The gist of the gag was their mill was being targeted by a herd of hungry moose who were breaking down the doors, and eating the cream of wheat. There has never been a moose on PEI. Mac told a story we concocted about a big bull moose knocking himself out cold while being chased out of the mill. Mac's dad invited all the neighbours over for a moose barbeque. When asked, Mac said the meat tasted like chicken. Mac was such an honest guy that an hour after we recorded the fake moose story, he called me at home worried people might think he was a serial liar for playing along with me. I assured him that since he'd been a straight-shooter for 85 years, people would forgive him for one April Fool's joke. CBC ran the fake story and three people called in with moose sightings.

♦

My old pal Roy Clow tells this story about pigs and capelin.

> Schools of capelin maybe two feet deep. Once it got dark, the capelin came right in to the shore. We'd take a Lunenburg dory and we'd wade alongside the dory and bail the capelin into the dory until it was loaded.

Capelin are a small, oily, herring-like fish. Every fall, Roy and his pal Dave Sorrey from Murray Harbour North fished capelin in the Northumberland Strait for cash:

> Dave and I would bag them up – we'd get 10 or 15 bags – and I had an old Model-T Ford truck then. We'd take them the next day to Southport selling them to farmers for pig food. Pigs loved them. They'd eat them like bananas. We sold them awful cheap – 90 cents a bag, 200-pound bags. One farmer had a piggery with 50 pigs and he used to buy an awful lot of capelin. He shipped his pigs to Canada Packers. Anyway, they stopped buying pork from him. He'd fed the pigs capelin too close to the time they were butchered and the meat tasted like fish something awful. So, we lost that business.

I don't know why Roy thought pigs loved bananas. But come to think of it, who would have thought pigs liked capelin? That's something for today's foodies to ponder: banana-infused pork, a variation on the peanut-butter-and-banana sandwich. Then again, why bother? The pork would probably taste like Mac Dixon's moose meat – chicken.

Horses and Tractors Just Don't Mix

Horse vs tractor Dundas PEI

When the Second World War ended in 1945, steel and rubber destined for the war effort were plowed instead into modernizing farms across the country, tractors instead of tanks, and more tractors meant fewer horses. For many farmers, the decision to replace the team of horses with a tractor was fraught with gloom, akin to trading in one of the family.

I had my father's love of horses. Our horses would never drink in town. No, they wouldn't drink the town water. No, sir. They'd just put their nose down to the bucket and shake the bridle, no drinking in town. I remember I had the horse and sleigh in one day, and the man at the livery stable said, 'I couldn't get that mare to drink.' And I said, 'No. She'll not drink in town.' No siree, she wasn't going to do anything like that.

Elizabeth MacEwen was born in 1909 in New Dominion, PEI. She and her brothers practically lived with the family's horses, and didn't begrudge lugging a bucket of well water for the horse when they went to Charlottetown. To save a few cents, many farmers took a bag of oats for the horse when they travelled to town. One thing they didn't bring back to the farm with them was the by-product of those oats: manure. Horses produce around 15 kilos – 35 pounds – of manure every day. Not only were country horses dropping off a few pounds of manure every time they came to town, but there were dozens of town horses adding to the mix.

Robert Farquharson was born in Charlottetown in 1913:

> Everybody had a horse. Slovens and jiggers, dump-carts, and those four-wheeled express wagons, they were on the street all the time. That's why, particularly in the lower end of town, the houses were fairly close together, but there was room between the houses for a wagon to drive in. And the horse manure – there were a lot of sparrows around at that time. And a lot of used oats.

Farmers could park for free around Queen Square where the post office, library, and market were located, and where city and country folk mingled and socialized. There were fish peddlers and Roop's Meat stall, a bowling alley, a theatre, and a water fountain. A row of jiggers or slovens lined Richmond Street for anyone needing to hire a heavy-duty, low-slung wagon to deliver hay or a load of eighty-pound milk cans.

♦

> By God, I was pretty young – they put me to work pretty young, yes. As soon as you were able to drive a horse. They'd put you to work following the horse in the field, like harrowing.

Mac Irving was born in Cherry Valley in 1902. Of course, most horses never saw the bright lights of the Big Potato. They worked on the many mixed-crop farms across the Island where young boys and a few girls learned to handle horses as soon as they could untangle harness.

> Some farms had five or six horses; smaller farms would perhaps only have a team. And they generally kept a horse for driving. There was no cars then, you know, never heard tell of. Everything was done with horses. They'd have a good, smart, blood horse to do their driving, going to town, going to church, going to the store. Going any place they wanted to go.

Growing up on a farm was the same for John Campbell, born a generation after Mac Irving on the other side of the Island, in Grahams Road, on the road to New London.

> I ploughed with a team of horses and a single plough when I was 14 years old. They claim that anybody who ploughed an acre with a single plough walked 14 miles in the day. I ploughed with two horses and did that until the spring of 1950 when we got our first tractor. A 22-Massey, 30 horsepower. The tractor cost $1,495, and we traded in a horse and five fat cattle, and we paid $100 to make up the $1,495. So that bought our first tractor.

The irony is obvious, probably more so to the bartered horse. And if you're a horse, stop reading now. It's just going to get worse. Mac Irving again:

> They often traded a team of horses for a tractor. Lots of people, yeah. I bought my first tractor in 1956, but generally kept a team of horses after that. Didn't do very much with them, but you had them in the wintertime for going to the woods and hauling in hay and jigging around. Hauling out manure, that kind of a thing. Yeah. It's not very many years ago since most people quit the horses altogether. I don't think there's a work horse around here anywhere for miles.

It finally came that everybody had a tractor, yeah. There were a lot of fox ranches then, and if a horse got old and wasn't much good you could sell a horse for $15 or $20 for fox feed. A sad end for the horse. You'd feel bad you know, a lot of people would... taking them to the fox ranch... but then... well...

Mac trailed off and couldn't finish. Later, he told me he didn't think the horses were put down in a cruel way before being chopped up for the silver foxes. He hoped so anyway.

Like many farmers, Mac had a hard time squaring the reality of farming with a tractor and his love of horses. Some horses, the smaller, sturdier ones, the ones that could fit down a narrow coal mine, were shipped across to the collieries in Nova Scotia. My cousin, who grew up in Stellarton, in coal-rich Pictou County, told me the horses lived down in the pits for 364 days a year, and were only allowed up into the sunlight for one day. She remembered seeing the horses galloping and frolicking in a field across the road from the mines, blissfully unaware how short-lived their freedom would be. The only consolation was that if there was an explosion or cave-in, the standing orders were to bring the horses out of the coal mines first.

The Francis family in Fortune Bridge made their living off horses, building and marketing wagons and sleighs for three generations. The Francis cutter was called "the Cadillac of sleighs," and was considered untippable on unplowed and rutted winter roads. Lorne Francis was the last to run the old firm. After the War ended and tractors became popular, his father Harry wisely had both sides covered: he also became a dealer for International Harvester. In 1946, Harry sold 21 tractors, not all to farmers. A local rumrunner bought one to haul five- and ten-gallon kegs of rum up from the shore. It didn't always work out as planned.

I can remember when I was going to school, one Sunday, a cousin of mine and I went back on our farm, which ran down to Rollo Bay shore. A couple of weeks before that, somebody – nobody knew who for sure – brought in a load of rum. Hundreds of kegs of rum all buried in the sand in Rollo Bay. And the tide came the wrong way and washed the tops clear. So the farmers down there all got some kegs out of it. They got rich all of a sudden. They used to joke after about them lighting their pipes with two-dollar bills.

At this point, anyone under the age of 40 is probably scratching their head and asking what in the name of Susan B. Anthony is a $2 bill?   Answer: a Toonie, only much lighter...

The farmers hauled the kegs home with horses, and the bootlegger with the tractor, although "nobody knew who for sure," was left high and dry. Dry in both senses of the word.

♦

At the beginning of the 20th century, cars were banned for five years on PEI, and then partially banned for five more. One reason cited was the beloved horses didn't like the noise of cars nor the smells of oil and gasoline. Horses and the internal combustion engine were like chalk and cheese: incompatible.

For years, Sheldon and Florence Dixon ran a big general store in Tryon. When he was a young lad – he was born in 1914 – Sheldon saw his first car, a 1920 Maxwell, owned by Wendell Beaton from Bonshaw. Mr. Beaton had rigged the muffler of his Maxwell – the make of car legendary comedian Jack Benny supposedly drove with his sidekick Rochester – to make a loud banging noise whenever he passed a horse on the road.

He was one of those guys who used to like playing jokes on people. So, he had cut a hole in the exhaust pipe and put a "cut-out" in it. That would make the muffler back-fire whenever he wanted. One Sunday afternoon, he came up and took us for a ride. We went up through Albany and around down through Cape Traverse. He'd say, 'I see a horse and wagon coming down the road. When we get up close to that horse, you step on that gadget on the floor there, under your feet.'

So, we got pretty close to the horse and wagon, and I stepped on this cut-out and he stepped on the gas. By the time we passed the horse and wagon, it was making quite a racket. I suppose the poor old horse never saw or heard tell of a car before, and he got such a fright, he took off into the woods, broke the shafts on the wagon and threw everybody out of it.

Mr. Beaton obviously never heard the old axiom "Horse sense not horse play," but he certainly made a strong case for continuing the ban on cars. But the tide of cars- and tractors- was unstoppable. The 1950s were hailed as the age of modernization. Even Mac Irving bowed to the might of the bright red tractor and bought one in 1956, long after he'd memorized this ode.

The Tractor

This Iron Horse demands no oats, he never needs the vet, he doesn't care how hot it is, and he never fears the wet.

A botfly never teases him, the colic never pains,

the steering gear directs his course, better than voice or reins.

In winter he will hibernate if there's no work to do, a shed that's dry is all he asks, he wants no hay to chew.

But if there's grinding to be done, threshing or sawing wood he'll do as much in a day as ten good horses could.

True. One tractor did replace a team-or-two- of horses. Indisputable facts. But there's more to life

than facts. There's heart and soul, and love. Mac
Irving has the last word:

I had different favorite horses. There's not much to
tell about them. They were just horses, you know,
and you liked them, and you'd feed them extra. You'd
like to get on their backs to have a ride, when you
were young. Yes.

Tommy and Pearl (Sweet) Duncan

I never was married until I was 48. I come home from the States, and I had this farm and I started in batching and I said, "Well this is no good. I can't get along this way.

Tommy Duncan was a century baby, born in 1900 in Mill River. He was good with horses, maybe not so much with the opposite sex. But he knew he didn't want to spend the rest of his life talking to his Clydesdales, so he decided to sweeten the pot.

So, Pearl was teaching school. She just lived in the next house over here, and I said, "Well I'm going to try my luck." So, by golly, I got her. I courted her some. There was quite a bit of difference in our ages. I robbed the cradle.

Eighteen years difference to be precise. But they had known one another all their lives... more or less. We were in the Duncan's kitchen, Pearl making tea and cutting into a block of cheddar, Tommy rocking in his well-worn chair. They had a story to tell.

I went in to see this baby and I asked Pearl's mother would it be all right if I picked the baby up.

When Tommy was 18, his mother asked him to harness the driving mare. She wanted to pay a visit to Mrs. Sweet down the road who had given birth to a bouncing baby girl.

"I was six months old," said Pearl.

Tommy continued, "'Oh yes, pick the baby up.' So, I picked her, gave her a kiss."

"His mother said 'Kiss the baby,'" corrected Pearl.

"So, I kissed the baby, and 30 years later, I married her."

"It took a long time," laughed Pearl.

Call it kismet or true love, but Tommy and Pearl were meant to be together. Not, however, without a bit of controversy. One day in the summer of 1948, Tommy and his father were out in the potato field when they ran into mechanical problems.

> My father sent me to Summerside to get a part for the potato sprayer and he gave me $15 to pay for it. I went up the road here to Pearl's. The bus stopped there and she got on the bus and I got on the bus, and we went to Summerside, got married, and spent the $15. We didn't come home for near a week.

While the minister was being paid, the potatoes went unsprayed.

> When we got married, the minister said, 'There you're all set now. Do you have the ring?' And, by golly, I didn't have a ring! And I didn't have the money to buy one. And I wish you could have seen the damn old suit I was married in.

Pearl chimed in, "Didn't have a licence. I didn't have a dress. We eloped."

Tommy's parents hadn't a clue what happened and, when he arrived home days later, "They gave me hell." Naturally, a new bride was quite a shock, "because all good hay-making weather and nobody to help do the work." Oh. Right.

The hay. Well, someone was rolling in the clover. And what about the $15?

> Boy, lookee here: They wanted to know if I got the part. I didn't have no part. Hell, I spent the $15.

Five dollars went to pay the minister. Another dollar to buy bus tickets to Charlottetown to see the horse races. The bus was so crowded, Tommy had to sit at the back and Pearl at the front. They passed the bus going the other way and got off in Kensington and headed back to Summerside. They rented one of Groom's tourist cottages on the outskirts of town where Tommy decided to try his luck in the outdoor shower. He made the rookie mistake of taking his towel in with him and came out looking like he'd spent the night under a potato sprayer. They laughed at off, and were still laughing when I interviewed them 50 years later. Tommy lived to be 100, Pearl to 89, happily married for 53 years.

◆

Eloping meant they missed out on a shivaree, that age-old custom when neighbours show up on the wedding night to create as much noise and confusion as possible. The newlyweds grit their teeth, grin, and bear the shenanigans, and are expected to serve their "guests" food and drink.

Marguerite Bell from Tryon was serenaded with a shivaree in 1925 when, at the tender age of 17, she married Victor Howatt.

> We went to school together, boyfriend and girlfriend. We used to go to the rink together. They had a car – his father bought a car. He ran a lobster factory and he took cans of lobster into Charlottetown and bought a car.

An interesting twist on bartering. I wonder if the car was green and turned red in the heat.

We got married in Bedeque. Reverend Fitzpatrick.
Our two mothers stood for us.

So Victor's mother was his best man?

Kind of.

They borrowed Dad's lobster-mobile and headed for the
eastern end of the Island.

Montague. We didn't stay. We didn't have that much
money, so we had to come back the same day. We had
a shivaree: everybody comes and you're supposed to
bake things and they wish you well. They made lots
of noise and ate all the apples in the orchard.

Their marriage was a bowl of cherries. Without the pits.

Ruby Whitlock from Hunter River was also married at 17,
and she also had a shivaree. Ruby fell in love with a Welsh
immigrant named Anthony Newport. They were married
in December 1933.

Mum made a cake. There were shivareers outside
so she had sandwiches and things made to pass out
to them. And then we thought we'd come to town.
James Brown was a friend of ours and he had an old
car so James and his girlfriend said, 'We'll take you
to town.'

Good plan: escape the raucous apple-eating shivareers with
a relaxing jaunt over the Bonshaw Hills.

There was no pavement. It was just clay roads and,
in December, it was rutted out. Just wheel tracks frozen hard. You tell the rest of it, Anthony.

Well, we got to town anyway and went to a restaurant. And then coming home, we had a flat tire on
the rear. And we had to push the car up every hill.
She wouldn't pull herself up the hill. It was all right
going downhill. We were just young people and
didn't know too much about cars, but if we'd taken
a tire off the front and put it on the back, we'd have

been able to drive home. But it was a lot of fun. That was our honeymoon. The next day, we went back to work.

In their eyes, it was all worth it because it had been love at first sight for both Ruby and Anthony, but, like the drive to town, there were a few bumps getting there.

Anthony's brother Aubrey was working for an old farmer called Bob Silliphant. Bob'd spent many years in Mexico and he'd married a Mexican girl, but his first wife used to get me to scrub ceilings and do the floors for her. So, I met Anthony's brother and he walked me home a couple of times. The farmer used to say, 'Take the lantern to take her home.' So, he'd light the lantern and walk me home.

Anthony was born in 1912. When he and younger brother Aubrey landed on PEI in the early spring of 1928, neither of them owned a pair of long pants. Like their parents, the cold, and then the mud a few weeks later, overwhelmed them. Out of necessity, the brothers were close, to stay warm if nothing else.

Anyway, I went up there one day and Anthony was there. I'd never seen him before. That was it. Yup. Love at first sight. His brother didn't like it too well.

In the tradition of jilted lovers the world-over, Aubrey considered the French Foreign Legion. The rough sail across the Atlantic from Britain fresh in his mind, he instead joined the R.C.M.P. and was stationed far from the red soil of his adopted PEI, leaving big brother Anthony to court and spark Ruby. Anthony said:

We went together five years before we got married. I had to stay at home until I was 21 before I could get permission. Well, I didn't ask for permission to get married, and we would have gotten married before, but Mother was so adamant against marriage.

Ruby: She wouldn't come to the wedding! None of his family was at the wedding.

Anthony: Because I jumped the ropes. By 1933, I was 21, all right, but if I'd left getting married until I was 35, they'd have thought it was alright.

Ruby chimed in: Yeah, because that's the age they were when they got married. Thirty-five. So they thought he should wait until he was 35. My parents didn't give a darn. It was one less to feed. And when Mum saw the engagement ring on my finger, she said to me, 'You're not going to marry that damn Englishman are you?'

Englishman! Grounds for divorce in Wales. For the record, Anthony was born in Gwent. He and Ruby stayed happily married for many years, raising their family on a farm near Hunter River. Anthony was a Second World War veteran, worked in the last starch factory in PEI, and even reconciled with Aubrey, proving blood is thicker than Island mud.

◆

Food is front and centre at weddings. One old British wedding custom Anthony might have known was to whip up a bowl of cream while slowly adding oatmeal. Then add sugar to taste and put in a shallow pan. Drop in the wedding ring. Family and guests each take a spoon and eat from the pan. The person spooning up the wedding ring will be the next to marry. In my family, we bake the ring in the wedding cake. The person biting the ring will be the next person to visit cousin Ronnie, the dentist.

In these days of foodie-ism, many couples plan their honeymoons around visits to restaurants so they can take pictures of their meals to share with the world. Jumpin' Jack Proud and his bride had simpler aspirations. In the 1930s, when Jack was a young lad, his father – P.J. Proud of Proud and Moreside, Charlottetown blacksmiths – knew the car was here to stay. So, he started repairing automobiles to augment the building of wagons and sleighs. Jack was a chip off the old block in many ways.

My mother and father were married on Christmas day in Clyde River. I don't know what happened when they cuddled up under the buffalo robe, but it wasn't me. They put the reins over the dash and the horse took them home.

My brother and I used to buy wrecks after the war and we'd fix them up. I had a Mercury that had burned in a fire and a Monarch that was good in the back end so I welded the two of them together. I was teaching Phys-ed at the vocational school in Saint John and we got married on Christmas day. My wife said, 'What a crazy day to get married.'

'Well,' I said, 'You're getting a crazy guy.'

Crazy like a fox:

I sold that car for $900 — the guy had just come back from working up north and he had some money. My wife and I were going on our honeymoon, so we took her car. We took the back seat out and put a box spring and mattress in there. There were very few motels or hotels in those days. We toured all over — Louisville, Kentucky, all over the country — and first night we got as far as Bangor. All the restaurants were closed so we had nothing to eat. There was a little country store still open, so I stopped and went and got two bananas and a pint of milk. My wife always said I only got one banana, but I'm sure I bought two, and that was our honeymoon breakfast.

They say newlyweds need a lot of potassium.

Moonshine and Nightcrawlers

Ralph Gallant, moonshiner
& horse whisperer

Iron bars, concrete walls, a thin mattress, and a feeling of despair. My wife is right: time to renovate our bedroom.

Prince Edward Island once had three county jails. People still call the Queens County Jail, the "1911 Jail." Both it and the Prince County Jail in Summerside had an apartment for live-in jailers and their families.

The son of one of the Prince County jailers told me when his parents went out for the evening, they'd go down to the cells and ask an inmate to babysit. One of the former jailers told me a story about a man who tried to break into, not out of, the Prince County jail, confirming stories the late Ralph Gallant told me 25 years ago.

Ralph was a Second World War veteran, born in Duvar, PEI in 1922, the son of Rufus Gallant who was well-educated, trained horses, and loved selling rum:

> He [Rufus] had five years of Prince of Wales College and they wanted him to be a school teacher, but he wouldn't because he didn't like teaching school. He had one room in our house where he kept books and

he did a lot of people's bookkeeping. My father always had a pocket full of money even when times were hard in the '30s. The people living in the next house were starving to death. The Old Man sold red rum that he got from the rum runners.

The rum came in five-or-ten-gallon kegs, was extremely strong, and had a reddish tinge that some who drank it claimed could discolour a teacup.

He'd get it by the five-gallon keg and I used to steal it on him. I'd get the Old Woman's jam bottles and fill them up when the Old Man wasn't around. I got lots of kicks in the arse for doing that, I'll tell you. I used to be with him all the time so after a while he said, 'Ralph, you should be able to do that now, give me a little help while I'm doing something else, balancing books and stuff.'

Fella would come in wanting a gallon of rum. So, jeez, I was happy then because I could get a little more rum. I had a few of Mum's jam bottles hid in the barn so I'd fill a couple of them up with the red rum. So, this time the Old man said, 'There's something wrong. Ralph, you didn't spill any of that rum?' I said, 'No.'

'Well,' he said, 'I think I went in the hole with that last keg of rum.' I never let on anything and we're sitting down around the table eating, and he said, 'I never made any money on that keg of rum. There's something wrong.'

The Old Woman said, 'Rufus, I'm missing a lot of jam bottles from the barn.' She used to put all her jam bottles in cases and if I took one out, they'd be an empty spot there. Rufus was a bookkeeper. He was good with numbers. He put two and two together, and I'm telling you, I got a good kick in the arse over that.

Eventually the missing rum and the kicks in the arse led to a falling out between father and son. At 15, Ralph took to the road. Two years later, he forged his army enlistment papers, and went overseas to fight in the Second World War with the North Nova Scotia Highlanders or the North Novas. While on leave in England, he bumped into his father where the "Old Man," now actually an old man, was a drill instructor training conscripts. Five years had passed since they'd seen one another. Fittingly, and perhaps a bit ironically, they reconciled by going to a pub and sharing a few drinks of rum together.

The two men shared more than a stubborn streak and the love of rum. Rufus had also passed on his talents for making moonshine and training horses. Ralph eventually put both those skills to good use. After the war, Ralph moved to Minto, New Brunswick, to work in the coal mines. He fell in love, married a coal-miner's daughter named Amelia Bachand, and he and Amelia started raising what eventually became a family of 14. In time, they moved to PEI, and Ralph set up a moonshine still:

> I got caught at the still making moonshine. I got a year in Summerside jail. I lost a car with 15 gallons in it taking it to Joe Borden in Summerside. They took the car and everything. It was six months with no fine and six months with a $500 fine so I had to do six months regardless.

Loyal wife Amelia was Ralph's regular visitor at the Prince County jail:

> I'd call in every day and bring him his supper.

Ralph was given certain perks that Amelia didn't appreciate:

> Sometimes I'd walk in there and he'd be so ungodly drunk. So drunk.

It turned out one of Ralph's perks was being allowed to set up a production line to make beer. In the jail.

One day I got mad at the jailer and I told him, 'What in the name of God are you running here anyway?'

He said, 'You better keep quiet. First thing you know, I'll put you out of here.'

I said, 'You go ahead. I'm going to have you up on charges. This is nothing but a dive here. Me coming in every night and him drunk like that. Him and all the other fellas.' They used to make it right in the kitchen.

Ralph insisted they made it in furnace room, but for some reason that didn't placate Amelia. The coal-miner's daughter had her steam up. She went to the judge who had sentenced him and begged to have husband let out, "because he's becoming an alcoholic in jail." It was no secret that both the jailer and Sheriff Bob Dewar had soft hearts. Ralph said he simply took advantage of the situation:

We had some beer working all the time. They had a great big barrel of molasses and we used to drain the molasses out of that. I was allowed to go to the store to pick up things, cigarettes and tobacco, and I'd get yeast cakes. I'd fill 10-gallon jars and put them behind the furnace, and when it worked out, we'd drink it. Something like malt beer, only stronger. A lot stronger.

You never know when your moonshine-making skills are going to be required. Or your horse-training skills:

Sheriff Dewar – Bob Dewar – had four trotting horses, and I used to look after his horses for him. He used to take me home to sleep at night. He'd tell me, 'Don't go anywhere. I'll pick you up in the morning.' And he'd come pick me up at my house.

The first stop was the jail, only because Ralph had to check on his home brew. Then off to the Summerside race track. Katherine Dewar, an accomplished author and historian, grew up in Summerside, and is the daughter of Sheriff Bob:

286

My father was a very fair man. He was very just. He always saw the good in people. The worst kind of character in the world and he'd find something good about them. I think he had this feeling that if you were good to people and trusted them, you'd get good things out of them.

Sheriff Bob sounds like a character you'd meet on Sesame Street...but trusting convicts?

I'm not sure how many people that jail could hold, 20 maybe, and there was a yard outside with a fence around it. A wire fence that people could put things through and I think half the time, the prisoners roamed around the yard, so it was a relaxed jail at the time. They didn't have what I would call "bad" people there. A lot of them were moonshiners from up west who weren't really bad people. They were just enterprising entrepreneurs out to make a few bucks.

A pretty good synopsis of the situation. Obviously, Katherine had inherited her dad's faith in humanity. You might wonder, as I did, where the money to buy cigarettes and yeast cakes was coming from. As Katherine pointed out, these guys were entrepreneurs, so Ralph found a way:

The Queen came over that year – the last time the Queen came over – so I got a month off my sentence. I only had three more months to do, and my father came down from Duvar and said, 'Ralph, I'm going to bail you out of jail.' I said, 'You're not. Don't do that.' He said, 'Why not?' I said, 'Five hundred dollars is too much and times are hard.'

I was working at the racetrack with the sheriff, and we were making beer. Old Hughie Daly was the jailer and we used to pick nightcrawlers. We'd send out to the bootleggers and get a quart, and we'd be out on the lawn of the jail picking nightcrawlers with flashlights. We'd sell them to the lawyers. The lawyers used to get us to pick them. Hughie let us go out because he could trust us. We wouldn't run away. We would never think of running away. They had trust in us, eh.

Sounds like an episode of *Hogan's Heroes*. Sheriff Bob's trickle-down effect: trust and ye shall be rewarded, sometimes with nightcrawlers.

When I interviewed Ralph, he had tubes down his throat, a constant feed of oxygen for his lungs. He had black lung disease from working half his life in coal mines. Yet, both he and Amelia said they'd live their lives the same way all over again. Ralph was extremely proud of Amelia and said she had kept the family together, making the kids' clothes and always planting a big vegetable garden even while they traipsed across Canada, from mine to mine, New Brunswick to Alberta, and back, and finally to Prince Edward Island. Ralph was also gratified to have reconciled with his father, and, after 14 children of his own, had a greater appreciation of Rufus' travails when Ralph was a lad.

♦

Katherine Dewar loved her dad too, and has fond childhood memories of tagging along with him every chance she got. As well as being Sheriff, Bob Dewar ran a car dealership at Reads Corner. Like her dad, Katherine loved cars, luxurious cars, fast cars. Sometimes he'd be required to take a prisoner who had been sentenced to more than two years across on the ferry to Dorchester Penitentiary in New Brunswick. He'd curl up in the back seat and nap, letting the prisoner drive his big Buick:

> He always liked big cars, nice cars. My favourite was a Buick Riviera with white leather upholstery and mahogany, real wood. And it was fast. The only time I ever got caught for speeding was in that car. I was

going up west and I pulled out and passed a car, and
Basil Stewart [later long-time mayor of Summer-
side] was behind me. He was a student policeman
that summer in St. Eleanor's. So, he nabbed me for
speeding and my father was totally embarrassed.
'I've warned you not to speed with my cars.' See, he
was sheriff and it was an embarrassment. So, my
father took the ticket, but the funny part was, Bill
Maxwell was the chief of police in St. Eleanor's and
was also one of my father's deputies. Dad gave him
the ticket and the money to pay the fine. Bill Maxwell looked at it and tore it up.

I bet a few nightcrawlers crossed palms...

The Art of Listening In

It was quite an event. Everybody listened to everybody else. We knew what everybody else on the line was doing. You have to believe it was entertainment.

Being entertained was Ella Willis, R.N., born in Hampshire in 1910. Go back 70-80 years and, not only did most people not have a telephone in their homes, but the nearest one was probably in the local general store or doctor's office.

Crank telephone

If you did have a telephone, you shared a party line with five or ten, or sometimes as many as 20 other families. Not people, families, which meant back in the days of large families, as many as a hundred "listeners-in," aka eavesdroppers, aka Nosy Parkers or Rubber Neckers.

On PEI, party lines, and the art of listening-in existed into the 1980s:

> We all listened in. I remember listening to a young man and a young woman who did their courtin' and their lovin' on the telephone. I got a great kick out of it. I wouldn't miss it for anything.

Hester Linkletter was born in 1907 at the beginning of the silver fox boom on PEI. Her father raised foxes and had two telephones: one in their house and the other in the fox pens. With fox pelts sometimes worth thousands of dollars, vigilance was essential when the foxes were breeding or kitting. Hester saw many changes in her 104 years, not the least of which was the transformation of the telephone from unique to ubiquitous. We still listen-in, only it's now unavoidable.

Alexander Graham Bell, Ding Dong to his pals, answered the telephone with "Ahoy." That salutation didn't catch on, but the invention he patented in 1876 did. In fact, he was asked one day if the telephone might be successful. He thought for a minute and replied, "You may think me cocky, sir, but I can see the day when there will be a telephone in every town in America." As brilliant as he was, little did he know. Today, there are almost 8 billion cell phones in the world. That's not counting the traditional land lines still used by old people. Like my wife... ok, and me. I need a land line to call my cell phone when my wife loses it. Ok, when I lose it. Moving on.

♦

Clayton Ballum from Mount Pleasant was a Second World War veteran and a farmer:

> The first telephone I remember was the one that had the two batteries, B batteries. You opened the little door and there were two batteries hooked up. It had a crank, eh, and once the telephone started ringing, everybody who had a telephone on that line would listen. You got all the messages you needed, eh, people listening in. They knew who was sick and who died and who had a baby. One woman said, 'I can hear you, Harry. You're breathing heavy today.' Another woman said, 'No, it's not Harry. He went

across the fields a while ago.' Yeah, they knew all the answers.

When Clayton was born in 1916, the Mount Pleasant Rural Telephone Company had two subscribers, so it wasn't hard to figure out who was listening-in.

My grandfather Joe Cunningham thought it was called a party line because of the entertainment he derived from listening-in on everyone else's conversations. Naturally he was outraged if a neighbour listened in on one of his three annual phone calls. You know the old chestnut about the farmer haggling on the telephone over the price of a calf with a cattle buyer. The price offered by the buyer froze at $10, yet the old farmer stubbornly insisted on getting $15. Finally, a third voice, that of a neighbour, piped up, "You'd better take the $10, Joe, veal prices are down and it's the best you're going to get." Every time Tommy Olding, the central operator, rang the Cunningham number – 22, two longs and two shorts – Joe went into a tizzy. Nobody phoned anybody unless it was bad news. I inherited Joe's DNA, because to this day, I won't answer the phone unless call display warns me who's calling. And if it's the bank or the doctor's office: God love us, we're all dead. I run and hide in the woodpile, almost certainly bad news.

◆

At one time, one of biggest telephone exchanges on Prince Edward Island was the Hillsboro Telephone Company across the river from Charlottetown. It served Bunbury, Southport, Tea Hill, Mount Herbert, and the surrounding area. The central switchboard was in the MacKinnon farmhouse in Crossroads. Lettie MacKinnon, one of my Island heroes, was the operator. Lettie was a typical farmwife, milking cows, making hay, as well as doing all the household chores and raising a family, but she was also a midwife and ran a birth house. In fact, she was in such demand as a midwife, she decided it was more productive to set up a maternity house rather than spend days away birthing babies, away from the switchboard that loomed in the corner of the parlour, sprouting wires and cables like an alien.

Lettie's daughter-in-law, Queenie Mutch MacKinnon, no slouch herself, claimed Lettie was the strongest woman she ever knew.

> She was independent, and she was very forceful, and she was a terrible worker, strong, hardy, and there was nothing she couldn't do: pitch manure out there in the barn, clean out pens. She could do anything, lots of things I couldn't do.

Queenie married Lettie's son Bob and moved onto the MacKinnon dairy farm and into the family house:

> You'd go to bed at night and be asleep, and all of a sudden you just never knew when, you'd hear a noise at the door and everybody was up. In the summer-time, the doctors would usually get here, but in the wintertime, sometimes they'd only get part way.

The roads weren't plowed and, more often than not, old Dr George Dewar wound up stuck in a snowdrift on his way out from Bunbury.

> It was certainly a busy time, with the telephone all the time too. There was a lot of paperwork with the telephone. You had to keep track of every call that went through. You wrote a ticket of every call on the Mount Herbert line, or on the Alexandra line, or the East River line – that was back of Mermaid – or the Hazelbrook line. They all came in here, five lines, the Charlottetown line too, to the Hillsboro telephone office. It used to be just a small telephone. Then they changed it around and put in a new system, and it covered the whole wall, a switchboard that had an electric ringer on it. She never complained. She thought she was making money. It was more love anyway, a work of love. She enjoyed it.

Every line coming in was a party line with dozens of families hooked up to each line, so plenty of eavesdropping entertainment:

> Probably 30 or more on each exchange. We remembered most of the telephone numbers, and never had to look them up. We knew everyone's telephone number back in those days. I can still think of people's numbers. Russell Driscoll's was 1 ring 22 and Austin Coady's from Hazelbrook was 4 ring 13. You'd plug into the number 4 line and dial one long ring and three short ones. There was one number back on the East River line that was 34 – that was three long rings and four short ones. And everyone on that line would hear those rings. So, it was public telephone, see, and you'd get a lot of listeners usually. There was nothing private about the telephone in those days.

And the beauty of it all was back in those days you paid by the call, so the person making the call and providing the entertainment was also paying the shot. Sweet. No wonder my grandfather loved it.

Queenie said it was inevitable that some people complained:

> Some people would get grumpy and say, 'I can't hear, there's too many people listening in on the line.' But anyway, everybody put up with it, but they always praised Grammie for her wonderful service. She was always available in the middle of the night, and there were always calls. It used to be from nine to nine and then it was 24-hour service, but we didn't get any extra pay when it changed over. At one point, it was $10.80 a month, and then it went up to $12. In 1952, it went to $30 a month, and then in 1961 it went up to $60 a month.
>
> And that was the most she ever got. Two dollars a day. Grammie thought that was excellent money. She thought she was doing really well when she got that $2 a day for looking after the telephone. But

after all it was just a sideline to all the other work that was going on here. Maternity patients coming and going. She thought it was kind of a hobby, not a real job.

A hobby on the good days maybe, but it was a real job when she was the first – as she always was – to hear bad news, like when there was a fire:

There were lots of fires. You'd get up for an emergency in the middle of the night. The switchboard was always open. You'd tear down here in your bare feet. We didn't have a furnace keeping the house warm. Wood stoves had to be kept going back then. They'd call here and we'd plug into all the lines, and ring everybody down each line, a long long long ring, and everybody came on to see what the emergency was. And people always got up and went to see if they could help with buckets. It wasn't fire engines that came then, just neighbours, neighbours with buckets did the best they could. But anyway, those were the good old days.

The woodstove Queenie mentioned caused many of those fires. Ausline Smith Axworthy from the Bungay Road in Wheatley River remembers one fire in the 1920s:

There were no telephones. I can remember when we were going to school, my aunt lived up on the Glasgow Road in Ebenezer, and my brother and I went up there one weekend with the fella who hauled the cream, Gordon Houston. Anyway, that night, it was a dreadful windy, windy night. We were out closing the barn doors. Around 9:00 or 9:30 we had come in, and before we went to bed we looked out the window and there was fire flying out through the yard. We went out and all the barns were on fire. We went across the road to Archie MacLeod's store and we watched the fire from there, and the poles at the road were burning. It was an awful fire.

Macleod's store had a telephone, but ironically there was no way to reach central and get the alarm out, because the telephone poles were on fire and the wires down.

♦

Lulu Thomson was born in 1909 on the Dock Road in Elmsdale, and she recalled a similar story, a house fire and no telephone to call for help:

> Our house burnt when we were only small, and they had a hard time to get us out because it caught fire from the flue. Mum and Dad got us all out, and we went and stayed in the barn, slept on bags of hay, horse rugs with hay underneath them, then a horse rug over the top of us until we got another new home built.

The new house was built with the help of folks near and far, repaying old debts to the Thomson family. Lulu's Mum was a midwife who always baked a few extra loaves of bread to give to neighbours, and her father was a blacksmith and carpenter who rarely charged for the coffins he built, some of them half size for children who'd not been lucky enough to escape a house fire. The Thomsons didn't have a telephone, and Lulu didn't have electricity until 1973. It didn't stifle Lulu. She lived to 104 and on her 103rd birthday, her daughters gave her a jigsaw and a drill – electric this time – so she could continue making footstools and wooden knick-knacks.

Like Lulu Thomson, Mary Stuart Sage was a force to be reckoned with, her determination and independence increasing as she aged. She inherited her iron will from her father Hector Stuart who served in both the First and Second World Wars. Between wars, Hector operated a sawmill, built boats, and ran a general store in Wood Islands. The store had not one, not two, but three telephones:

One east, one west, and a ship-to-shore telephone for vessels on the water.

Mary also had an overactive imagination:

> When I was a child, there was always a hum coming from the telephone wires, and someone told me one time not to lean against the telephone poles because the wires would take me right into Charlottetown. So, one day I leaned against the telephone pole, and I was scared I might end up in Charlottetown.

Isn't that called a teleporter in the sci-fi movies? With cell phones running off tall towers and masts these days, I'm not so sure we even have telephone wires anymore. I'd look, but I don't want to get too close. Just in case.

Doin' What Comes Naturally

Louis MacDonald, Cornwall, PEI

Every year on October 1st since 1991, we celebrate International Older Persons' Day. I'm all for it, especially now that I fit the bill. But the folks in this chapter would scoff at being recognized for doing just what came naturally in the bygone days. These people took life's difficulties with a grain of salt and a sense of humour. Take for example Louis MacDonald, born in Cornwall, PEI in 1911.

Two of many interesting things about Louis: one, he played hockey with the Cornwall Meteors, the rink's boards and clubhouse constructed out of lumber salvaged when they tore down the old Cornwall cheese factory; and two, Louis's dad George kept a diary:

> I come home from the rink one night fairly late and I decided, I don't know why I hadn't done it earlier, I decided to look up my birth year, ya see. Well, I turned to the back, naturally, and I expected a long ledger like the *Book of Kells* in Ireland, but there wasn't anything there. So, then I went over to July, my birth month and there was nothing there. Well, I figured that it was such an event that, you know, it was too much to put into writing and, out of

curiosity, I went to my birthdate, July 21st.

Well, it started out: 'Saved two loads from such-and-such a field and raked about ten or twelve rows, raked another field.' Six lines describing the hay business and the seventh line was wonderful, it said, 'Finished the hay today 21st July.' And the eighth line, do you know what it said? 'Young son born to-day, everybody well.' The hay got seven and I got one.

Things picked up for Louis: one of his first memories was being dressed up in a velvet suit and hat like Little Lord Fauntleroy. His dad George was a canny old Scot. At Christmas, when all the family was home savouring Mum's goose and pudding, all the boys headed out on Boxing Day to cut, haul, and block the next year's firewood. As Louis said, even his brother the priest had to help.

Let's head over the old railway bridge to Bunbury where Adelaide Hamm was born in 1902 on the family farm. Here's one of her earliest memories:

Of course, I don't remember about the day I was born. Shouldn't ask me anything about that because I don't know. But one of the first things I remember was my brother Frank, he was a year and a half younger than me, and, of course, I was always looking after Frank. One thing I remember distinctly was one day a chicken died, perhaps a couple of days old. We had never been at a funeral, so we decided we'd have a funeral. We were burying him out under birch trees at the front of the house. Of course, we didn't know that Mom was in the dining room watching us through the window. Comes the time for the burial, I wanted to sing the "Doxology," Frank said 'No, we'll sing "MacCarthy's Wagon."' And it went:

MacCarthy held the reins,

The reins held MacCarthy,

Liquor filled the brains

It made them light and hearty.

Muloney toddled off behind

And sure I let him lay,

There was a roar and racket

When the mare she ran away.

Off she went, off she went,

Be damned I wasn't worth a cent,

The seat was just as hard as flint

Behind MacCarthy's mare.

So Frank sang that, and I just happened to look up and saw Mum watching us, hurting herself laughing. So, we buried the little chicken to MacCarthy's Mare. Ahh, dear, dear, dear.

Addie lived to 101. She had two brothers in the First World War – Frank and Charlie. They made it back, as did the seven or eight other "returned men" from Bunbury who had enlisted. A Duffy man lost a leg and for years, sat in a little compartment running the old railway swing bridge over the harbour. Addie told me that in the parcels they regularly sent through the Red Cross to her brothers along with the fudge, chocolate cakes, and woollen mitts and socks, they also sent apples from the Hamm farm. Charlie wrote back the Bunbury apples were better than the ones they'd been eating in France. His daughter Jean Hamm Down had the letter and passed it on to her daughter Janet Down MacQuarrie.

Addie Hamm was a smart, strong, independent woman. When I asked if she had anything to do with the horses on the farm, she snorted derisively, "Sure I had something to do with the horses. Certainly!" and she told me about a little trotting mare named Nell. One day while Addie was running errands in Charlottetown, she met two ladies:

There was a woman- her name was Adelaide, my name was Adelaide and her daughter was named Adelaide- so that was unusual. And when the mother told the daughter who I was, 'Oh,' she says 'I remember seeing you years ago driving a horse up town and you'd be holding on just like this, and the horse would be going for all he was worth.' I never thought there was anybody watching what was going on.

I asked Addie if she used to take the horse and buggy to town.

Certainly. I was 16.

And you didn't worry about the horse taking off on you?

Poof! No, I loved it when she'd go good and fast. I used to pick up a cousin of mine in town and we'd go drive around the [Victoria] Park, you know. Of course, I'd let the horse go as fast as she wanted to go, and if she didn't want to go fast, I'd make her go a little faster. So anyway, when I came home, the horse was a little bit warm. It was in the summertime. And Pop says to me, 'The next time, you won't get the horse, you'll go walking.' So after that, I learned to let the horse walk the last mile home so she'd be cooled off by the time we got home.

Since time immemorial, parents haven't been able to keep up with their sixteen-year-olds. If it wasn't Nell the mare, it was Jimmy the Dodge Dart.

We can't celebrate seniors without mentioning another incredible Island woman Blanche Landry Bennett born in Summerside in 1922. Blanche is a Second World War veteran; her first time off the Island was to join the CWACs [Canadian Women's Army Corps] in Halifax. There, Blanche met and married Murray Bennett, a sailor who was serving in the Royal Canadian Navy. After the war when Murray transferred to the RCAF, they packed up the kiddies and travelled all over the world to wherever Murray was stationed. Blanche has a sharp sense of humour, no doubt honed by being the youngest of seven children born to Tillie and Joe Landry. Her dad Joe was what we'd now call a "character," a rugged individualist who, like many of his generation, rarely saw the inside of a hospital:

> First time in the hospital, [he was] 102. My sister found him on the floor. He was unconscious. He had a bleeding ulcer, and we took him to the hospital. So, he had to be operated on and he'd never been in the hospital before.

I said, "102. And he lived to be 104?"

> Uh huh. And so, we were all there and the doctor said we can't even give him a sedative to go into the O.R., because they had no record of any kind of medication that he'd ever been on. And he went in and they did the operation. They brought him out, put him in the bed – I can see him yet – and when he came to, he was just like you and me. And the next morning, out of the bed, down to the solarium and smoked his pipe.

> On his 100th birthday, my sister planned a big party. He was just sitting at the table playing solitaire, and we said, 'Jeez, Pop, aren't you getting ready for the party?' 'Ah, I'm not going to no party,' he said. 'Oh,' we said, 'You kind of have to go.' He said, 'No. Murray, want to go fishing at French River?' Murray said, 'Well, yeah, but we better go to the party first.' Pop said, 'Nah, the heck with the party. Let's go to French River. The smelts are running. We can drop in after.' So, they went to French River and fished.

Joe Landry smoked a pipe and chewed tobacco – Hickey and Nicholson Black Twist made in Charlottetown, twisted leaves of cured tobacco soaked in liquorice and molasses called "figs." So sticky every general store had a fork on the counter to dig the figs out of their wooden caddies. Chewing a fig of tobacco was an acquired taste, something Blanche never tried. But Lillian MacNevin MacEachern did when she was a young girl. Lillian was born in 1915 in Victoria-by-the-Sea where her dad, Miner MacNevin, ran a big general store, which is now the Island Chocolates Company building.

> They had a great big pot-bellied stove in the store, so that was a great place for the old gentlemen to sit around and tell stories and chew tobacco. That's the 'loafers.' Hickey and Nicholson. In fact, I stole one of those figs from my dad's store one time when I was tiny. It was back of the counter, you know, there in a box, big, long twist, and I always watched these men. They used to sit out in front in the summer on a bench in front of the store. I could watch them spitting; you know, they wouldn't spit on the sidewalk, but they could make it go over the sidewalk onto the street.
>
> So, one day I was at the store with my dad, and when I was going home, I thought I'm going to sneak one of those out. So, I pulled it out and I can remember as plain, and went out the back door with this big fig of twist. I went around the front of our house, climbed up on the gate there. Of course, I expected it to taste like liquorice, you know, but that wasn't the point. I wanted to spit! So I chewed off some and chewed it, but I couldn't spit. And it didn't taste like liquorice at all, so what was I going to do with it. I couldn't spit at all. So anyway, I took it and I buried it in my mother's flower garden, because I knew that sometimes she used to get that and steep it for fertilizer for her plants. So I thought, well, if I park this in the flower bed, the flowers would really grow. But I was so disappointed that I couldn't spit like those men did.

Probably just as well Lillian didn't take up tobacco. In the 1930s, she became a pretty good hockey player with the Victoria Union Sisters. They played their games along with their male counterparts – the Maritime champions Victoria

Unions – in the huge barn-like natural ice Victoria rink run by another Union Sister, Kathleen, and her husband H.B. Wood. Just down the road was another men's hockey team more noted for their unusual name than their skating prowess: the Hampton Do-Dads. That didn't win them many games, so they decided to change their name. Cecil Ferguson played left wing on the Hampton team:

> The Hampton Haymakers. It was the worst team there ever was. There wasn't a hockey player in the whole damn works of us. Never won a game. The first night we played, we were getting ready to go and all hell broke lose in Hampton. Canton's store was on fire. We went there and we hauled water up on that roof and put fires out. Then went over and played hockey after that. Jeez, we were some tired.

Cecil said they didn't have pucks, so they practiced with horse droppings and flattened tin cans. I asked if he ever went down to Victoria to watch the women play hockey.

> We played them one time. They beat us.

Cecil insisted they lost because they were afraid to go into the corners with the women. They weren't afraid of hurting the women; they knew the Union Sisters' reputation. Cecil said, "You never knew where you were going to get the stick."

Ships that Burn in the Night

Phantom Ghost Ship of Northumberland Strait

It just looked like a burning ship and it was sailing along. It was very late in the season, navigation was closed, so there weren't any boats out, and we looked out and saw the burning ship. I called my brother and we watched it.

For hundreds of years, a fiery ghost ship has been haunting the Northumberland Strait from New Brunswick to Cape Breton. A fully-rigged vessel, sails and masts on fire, just as Kathryn Wood from Victoria, PEI, described, just sailing along. Then suddenly disappearing. Kathryn and her brother grew up hearing stories about the Phantom Ship: two sailors were fighting over a woman, and accidentally knocked over a kerosene lamp. The ship caught fire and the love triangle, as well as the vessel's crew, all perished. Sightings and theories of the Phantom Ship go back hun-

305

dreds of years. The Mi'kmaq called it "fire upon the water." One story dates back to the 1770s and the American
Revolution when English navy ships trapped an American
privateer in Pictou Harbour. The pirate captain refused to
surrender and either scuttled his ship or was fired upon
by the British. Either way, all hands went down with the
blazing ship.

Hugh Archie MacDonald – Hughie the Organ to his friends,
and no, not what you're thinking. For 30 years, he played the
organ for the choir at St. Mary's Church in Lismore – lived
all his life in an old farmhouse in Knoydart on the shores
of eastern Pictou County, N.S. He witnessed the Phantom
Ship – sails ablaze – many times. The sightings always
preceded a nor'easter, except for one calm, beautiful June
evening in 1961:

> The 16th of June. I remember the date very well. I
> looked out to sea and there was the Phantom Ship
> all lit up out off the coast here. I wondered you know,
> because it usually was seen before a northeast gale.
> And I thought certainly there'll be no northeast gale
> tonight or tomorrow. The sky was beautiful, a very
> soft breeze blowing from the south, a lot of stars out.
> I couldn't understand. I thought I was making my-
> self believe something.
>
> I woke up about four-thirty in the morning, and
> there was a howling blizzard blowing in from the
> northeast. The hills were white with snow... the 17th
> of June on a Sunday morning. The forecasters didn't
> know a thing about it. And a lot of fishermen lost
> their lobster gear. There was a lot of criticism. It was
> a nasty cold day and didn't tone down for a couple
> of days, that storm. That was one time everybody re-
> membered seeing it.

Hugh Archie once saw the Phantom Ship in the dead of
winter, when the Strait was frozen solid. Another time,
neighbours tried to row out to intercept the burning ship,

but as hard as they rowed, they could never reach it. They did get close enough to see people on the deck, hair and beards on fire. On Nova Scotia's Sunrise Trail a few miles west of Hugh Archie's farm, Bessie Arbuckle and her brothers had always been told it was a pirate ship.

> I always believed it, and my father believed it. I saw it one time when I was a kid. We were coming from the barn after milking. First time I ever saw it. We were scared. We saw it out in the water. It was in the fall and we came in the house, and Papa said, 'Hush- be quiet. That's only the Phantom Ship you're looking at.'

Bessie's description was textbook:

> You can see the masts and you can see flames. It's really something you've got to see to know. You can see it's aflame. You can see the burning. Both times I saw it, it was coming east.

Bessie married Leroy Murdock from Ponds. Even though Leroy had grown up just down the road in a house on a hill facing the Northumberland Strait, he had never seen the Phantom Ship. Until, thanks to Bessie, one day in 1990:

> A few years ago – I have a habit – I never go to bed without looking at the water. Even in the winter, I'm always watching. This night I was getting into bed, and I looked out and I saw it and I said, 'Leroy, do you want to see the Phantom Ship?' Because he always thought I was crazy, you know, he didn't believe it. He got up and he looked out at it.

Leroy looked a little sheepish when I turned the microphone on him.

> People laugh when you tell them you saw it. It just disappeared. Harry MacDonald [a general store-keeper in Merigomish ten kilometres to the west] saw it the same night.

The younger generations sometimes scoff at ghost stories.

Older generations seem more willing to suspend disbelief and accept the possibilities of ghosts and forerunners and Phantom Ships. Bessie has a theory why:

> The generation today, they don't know much about it, but the older people knew about it, and like my father said, 'Oh it's only the Phantom Ship.' He saw it lots of times. I don't know what it is – the younger people don't watch the water like we do. See, we were brought up by the water and they haven't got the same feelings towards the water. I think that's the big thing. We're different.

One thing is certain: for generations, the Phantom Ship has been seen all the way from northern New Brunswick to the shores of Cape Breton Island, on both the Nova Scotian and the PEI sides of the Northumberland Strait. And not just by "the older people." Cape Bretoner Kim Begin was born in 1971 in Port Hood. In 1983, she and several schoolmates were celebrating the end of the school year.

> Six girls and I were having a get-together. A good-bye party. Anyway, we decided to sneak out of the house – we were only 12 years-old and we wanted to sneak out that night to go up to a haunted house. So, we all took off to this house. I was scared as it was, and I was standing out on the road waiting for the other girls, and they came screaming down the road. We all saw something out on the water. It looked like it was burning. We weren't sure what it was, but we'd heard from our grade six teacher about this Phantom Ship but we never believed him. We always thought it was a big hoax. But when we were running along, we could see people screaming, people jumping off this really, really, big boat. It was so real. We kept running home because we were terrified. And when we looked back behind us to see if we could still see it, it was gone. We saw it for about five minutes and then all of a sudden, it was gone.

The night was clear, the ship was plainly on fire "from one

end right to the other. Flames shooting everywhere and people jumping off."

Vindication for grade six teachers everywhere, not that teacher Marjorie Dunn from western PEI needed corroboration:

> A lovely evening in June and we were sitting there talking and somebody said, 'The ship is out there. Have you seen it?' I said, 'Oh no, I've never seen it.' So sure enough, here was this three-masted ship on fire, and people on it walking back and forth. You just wondered, you know, what it was. It was red, on fire, the mast and the spars, and people on the deck walking back and forth. Or probably running back and forth. My father was with me and he'd never seen it before, but the other people in the house had. Apparently, it was a common occurrence to see it in that area.

Marjorie taught grades one and grade two, all the way up to grade ten. In 1935, her first teaching assignment was teaching all grades in the one-roomed school in Burton, Lot 7 on the western end of PEI.

> Now there was a story about the burning ship. It might have been a mutiny at one time and these people were upset and were running around. Now, if there was any truth in that, I don't know. I did see it again that same fall, early November on a nice clear night but not in the same place. I came home from a wake, and there was the burning ship right in front of us. And we watched it for a long, long time. It was all afire, red, about the size of maybe the Bluenose. It was right there in front of us, this long ship, all ablaze, red, just like a sunset. As red as can be. It was quite a spectacle.

Coming home from a wake. Hmmmm. She scoffed when I suggested that maybe she was predisposed to the supernatural. Just as I scoffed while interviewing lighthouse keeper

Manson Murchison one fall day while we were standing in a howling gale beside the Point Prim lighthouse on PEI's south shore.

> The Phantom Ship – when I saw it – I was up in the lighthouse and it was down towards Pictou Island way. I saw this ship coming up the Strait and she was really lit up. It was different to see a boat lit up that way. You look at it a second time and you'd think it was a ship afire. I went to get a pair of binoculars to look at it and there was no more sign of it. It just disappeared. That's a fact.

Manson's family had sailed over from the Isle of Skye in 1803 on the ship *Polly*, which entitled him to be buried in the *Polly* cemetery just up the road from the lighthouse at Point Prim. There are generations of Murchisons buried there, many were sea captains, their headstones recording deaths as far away as the South China Sea. Manson wasn't the only Point Prim lighthouse keeper in his family, nor was he the only one to see the Phantom Ship.

> My cousin came home one time from Charlottetown, and he saw a ship out here in the bay, all lit up, he said, as real as could be. It was so real he came down and put the light on in the lighthouse. And when he got down here to put the light on there was no more ship. So, there you go. It was gone that quick. So, it is real.

I teased Manson that he would lose his lighthouse keeper "street cred" if people knew he'd witnessed a ghost ship. He laughed and said, "Then you might as well tell everyone I saw it twice." Turns out he also saw it when he manned the Caribou Island lighthouse across the Strait near the entrance to Pictou harbour. Fool me once, shame on you; fool me twice...

Manson mentioned a story I'd heard before: on a calm night in 1966, the wheelhouse crew on the MV *Prince Nova*, one of the car ferries that ran between Wood Islands and Caribou spotted what looked like a burning oil tanker. Captain Angus Brown veered the *Prince Nova* miles off course to help out, but when they got closer they realized they were looking at the legendary Phantom Ship of the Strait. Dozens of passengers had an unexpected treat that night, a story to pass on to their grandchildren.

While teaching in Burton, Lot 7, Marjorie Dunn saw a burning oil tanker and said it didn't look anything like the ghost ship. One story she heard repeatedly was the night two local fishers tried to row to intercept the burning vessel.

> At the time, this was the talk of the district. They rowed out to see what was going on: was it really a ship on fire or what? But they couldn't get near it. The heat. The heat singed this old fella's beard so they didn't go any further. They said there were people being burned on it. The whole thing was on fire from stem to stern, masts and spars, everything. Oh, it's a real ghost ship, a Phantom Ship.

Captain Thomas Trenholm and Roy Clow, two men I loved like family, two men who spent a combined 140 years at sea, never once saw the Phantom Ship. They claimed it was a figment of overheated imaginations. They insisted people were seeing a Jack o' Lantern aka swamp gas. They said the combination of sea and sky and rolling waves, people were seeing a mirage. My father, Mr. Presbyterian, grew up in Pictou County on a farm that ran down to the Strait. He laughed at the sightings, and insisted only Catholics believe in ghosts and Phantom Ships and the supernatural. Yet, he didn't laugh when his eldest sister Patricia told us that not only did she and three carloads of the Presbyterian Ladies Guild see the Phantom Ship one night, but that she'd seen it once before, when she was a little girl. She was on the Thompson farm, standing alongside her parents and grandparents next to the barn, and they all saw it. Everyone. Even the two-year old baby nestled in my great-grandmother's arms. My father. And that, as Mason Murchison would say, is a fact.

Sweet Treats

Annie Cody Henderson midwife

I have a sweet tooth. Actually, a head full of sweet teeth. And Christmas is the holiday that begs me to overindulge. There's too much of everything: presents, relatives, and especially too much rich food. But who has the self-restraint to turn down slabs of fruitcake, both dark and light? Don't discriminate. Insist on extra cherries. Or those wafer-thin Christmas cookies in the shape of snowmen and elves, covered in frothy frosting with sprinkles for eyes? Yes, it reeks of cannibalism. Tough. [Chomp] Or all those boxes of chocolates... chocolate... Mmmmm.

Like many Maritime baby boomers, I was raised on Cap'n Crunch, pancakes sweetened with corn syrup and molasses, grilled brown sugar sandwiches, and six different kinds of fudge. Then we had dessert. I have five brothers. We each could and would demolish one of those Jello Instant puddings.

Annie Cody Henderson was a celebrated midwife and country nurse in Lot 11 in western Prince Edward Island. Her daughter Maude was born in 1905, and like her nine siblings, Maude was proud of Mum, especially her cooking.

And she was also a good cook. At some point, Annie must have decided to add a little protein to one of her family's favorite sweets: she concocted a special fruitcake:

> We liked everything she made. One cake she used to make, we called the cream-filled cake. She'd make a white cake, a great big long one, and fill it with cream filling. I can see it sitting on the dining-room table yet. To cool. And she used to make salt-pork fruitcake.

Yes. Pork fruitcake. Google "salt-pork fruitcake," and the Duchess of Windsor's recipe will show up. Yes, that Duchess of Windsor, the divorcee who convinced King Edward VII to swap the Crown for her. Who knew her charms extended to salt-pork fruitcake? Wallis Simpson's cake was a version of the war cakes that surfaced during the Second World War when the usual cake ingredients such as eggs and sugar were rationed. She noted in her recipe the difficulty in softening "an unrendered hunk of salt-cured fatback.[14]" Maybe she got the idea from Annie whose cake dated from the First World War 20 years earlier, as Maude explains:

> I turned 13 in the First World War, and [Annie] made this war cake. Salt-pork fruitcake. She made different ones: a dark fruitcake and a light fruitcake, and marble cake and a white cake. And ginger snaps and sugar cookies. She had seven daughters and there wasn't one of us who could make a sugar cookie like Mama. I had one sister, Alice, she could make good ginger snaps. First, she used to boil everything, the molasses and all the spices except the flour. They were thin and they'd really snap.

Molasses and salt-pork, it doesn't get any more Atlantic Canadian than that. However, I draw the line at meat in cake. And, regarding the debate whether you should boil

---

14   Wallis Warfield, Duchess of Windsor. Some Favorite Southern Recipes of the Duchess of Windsor, Charles Scribner's Sons, 1942.

the ingredients for molasses cookies, my Mum and her mother, my Grammie (also a Henderson) did. End of debate.

Atlantic Canadians must hold the per-capita-molasses-consuming record, in part because of our old trade routes up and down the seaboard to the Caribbean. "Pine down, molasses back," as sea captains like Captain Thomas Trenholm and his father Captain William would say. They shipped tons of Barbados molasses in their schooners to a huge sugar refinery in Portland, Maine, and hundreds of puncheons from Souris to Sheet Harbour. Not all of that molasses was poured onto pancakes and biscuits. Molasses is also one of the raw ingredients in making moonshine.

Greta Grigg's father put molasses on "everything," even his boiled potatoes. Eddie Easter's father poured molasses on his salt herring. Yet, somehow, Eddie's mother missed her chance to invent salt-herring fruitcake. Molasses was used to sweeten some of the old home remedies folks used to take.

> Well, my father used to go up to the wharf. Myra Pidgeon always did the skimming of the oil off the top of the big puncheons of cod livers. My father would bring home seven or eight teddies, the long-necked green teddies; 25 cents a bottle. And you got a spoonful of that in the morning whether you liked it or not.

The MacRae sisters grew up in the New London lighthouse. Their father Jack was the keeper between the two World Wars. He'd have been the keeper longer, but was busy fighting in both wars. The five MacRae sisters lined up every morning and downed a dose of cod liver oil. Many years later, they taught me how to tell if someone is taking a dose of sulphur and molasses:

> And then after that, you got sulphur and molasses. They mixed sulphur and molasses together in a cracker can, and you got a spoonful of that too. That night, you could shake your socks over the stove and it went blue sparkles just like if you sprinkled

a match, because sulphur went right through you. Right through your pores. That's true. You try it.

I'll take Mary MacRae Brander's word for it. Her sister Isobel pointed out the sulphur and molasses treatment was "to clear out the blood, keep your blood clean." Probably clearing out all that salt-pork fruitcake.

◆

"I was a hound for candy all my life." The confession of Jim Montgomery who passed his love of candy on to countless others, because Jim was a candy wholesaler, best known as "The Candyman." Jim was born in 1902, and died wealthy at the age of 101, proving that a sweet-tooth can lead to a honeyed life. At 16, Jim became a candy salesman for Sidney T. Greene in Charlottetown, peddling candy to general stores across Prince Edward Island: "I always liked candy and still do. Coconut bonbons were my favorite." The boarding houses he stayed at didn't always serve the best food, leading Jim to dip into his sample case. Often, by the time he got back home, the sample case was empty. "Eating my profits." Jim's addiction to candy started when he was a young lad, and the wait for holiday treats was overwhelming, especially at Christmas:

> I used to crave candy. There was a little corner store run by Manuel Arsenault and he had lots of candy. I'd gather an egg and take it up, and buy candy with it. He'd give me a stick of candy for the egg. Ah, dear. (laughs)

When she was growing up in Cape Traverse, Helen Campbell Herring also traded eggs for sweets. The storekeeper only paid 12 cents a dozen for her eggs, but she said 12 cents bought enough chicken bones and caramel creams to last a week. Helen was a pioneer in both radio and television. She worked alongside Stuart Dixon and Don Messer on PEI's first radio station, CFCY. Later, she had her own televised cooking show, baking everything from hermit cookies to egg souffles on live TV:

> You can't get complacent on television, live television at least. I'd get that recipe and try it out a couple of times before I'd cook it on air. If it was a soufflé, it could have flopped on me. My husband was the guinea pig. He ate all the things I made and if he said they were good, then I'd cook them on TV. I had a real oven [in the TV studio], but I didn't have very much to work with when I think about it now. It was pretty crude, but I still meet people who have my recipes. I'd get fan mail, more from Nova Scotia than Prince Edward Island.

Helen knew if her cooking had hit the mark by how fast it took the camera crew to devour the results once "cut!" was called. One favourite was a quick version of a Sloppy Joe:

> I used finger rolls for it and the filling was very popular. It was made with Kam and then a lot of ketchup and hard-cooked eggs. You heated it and served it at a party. I just made things that I thought people would have the ingredients for in their cupboard. I didn't try to be too fancy. I tried to interest women in using different herbs and spices. Cookies and cakes and casseroles. I wasn't a home economist, you see, and I told them that when they hired me, but I could talk and work at the same time.

According to the Internet, this simple, inexpensive, and tasty bun is still popular especially at large gatherings. Ingredients include Kam's cousin, the luncheon meat Spam, and Velveeta, a distant cousin of cheese. I can't mention Helen without mentioning some of her incredible achievements: she had her grade ten by the age of 13; she had her teaching certificate from Prince of Wales College and was teaching school by 16; she bought her first car when she was 18; then became a radio and TV personality, leading to the Order of Canada; and finally, a Doctor of Laws *honoris causa* from UPEI. By luck – mine – many years ago, she was one of the first people I interviewed. She endured my banal questions, and put me on the right track for which I'm eternally grateful. Dr. Helen Herring, an amazing Islander.

Like Helen, Edison Nelson was a man of many talents: store clerk, truck driver, mussel mud digger, but he was best known for building and then running his Cherry Valley, PEI service station. Ed was born in China Point in 1914. At one time, Ed sold farm equipment for a dealer who, to sell a tractor, was notorious for taking anything on trade.

> Oh yes, a lot of people would trade in horses. I sold machinery for Walter Weeks from Hunter River. He's dead now. Walter.

After the Second World War, when Massey and Harris and McCormick went back to making farm machinery, Island farmers traded in horses, cattle, sheep, anything in fact, to buy their first tractor. And one time, according to Edison, a bag of candy sealed the deal:

> When the Cockshutt 20 came out, a small tractor, it was very popular. I sold quite a few of them around here. I went down to Leo and Joe Murphy's one day, and said, 'You fellas should have a tractor.'
>
> 'Yes,' Joe said, 'We should, but we can't afford a tractor.'
>
> 'Well,' I said, 'What have you got to trade in?'
>
> 'Well, those two old horses, and an International engine that's not working.' So I called Walter on the phone and told him and he said, 'Is that all? Who else is there on the farm?'
>
> 'Well,' I said, 'Their mother, an old, old lady.' He said, 'Alright. We'll give her a bag of peppermints.'
>
> So, he never said a word when he picked me up, and he had a bag of peppermints on the seat.

He said, 'You said there was an old lady there. Those peppermints will sometimes make a sale.' So he brought them into the house and gave to Mrs. Murphy, a nice old lady, and he asked her, 'Do you like peppermints Mrs. Murphy?'

'Oh, you dear,' she said, 'I love them.'

'Yeah,' Walter said, 'We'll take the horses and the engine.'

Freddie McInnis told me not long ago the engine's still down there... And that's 50 or 60 years ago.

Mrs. Murphy got her peppermints, and the horses? Well, they were old and so probably wound up as dinner on a silver fox ranch. Who'd have thought there could be so many elements to the Murphy boys getting a tractor.

Leo used to drive the Cockshutt 20 from China Point up to Vernon River to Mass. You'd see him going by on Sunday morning.

Around the same time and just up the road, Harley Ings from Mount Herbert used to borrow the family tractor to go courtin' and sparkin'. He said the roads were so muddy in the spring and fall he needed one.

◆

During the Second World War, Father Francis Corcoran was busy studying at St. Dunstan's, [now UPEI] working his way by waiting on tables in the college dining room. There was war rationing, and any left-over sugar was pocketed and taken home to the Baldwin Road farm by young Francis. His mother made pies and cakes and strawberry jam. His thoughtfulness usually resulted in extra treats, especially at Christmas during those tough times:

Oh, yes, times were hard. During the war, there was no money and even if you had money, you couldn't get stuff. Rationing. A pair of what we called overall pants cost $1.35. You didn't get those every time you turned around. Yeah. They always tried to get something for us at Christmas. There was one year they didn't have anything. Mama didn't know what she was going to do. She was a great cook so she made some brownies, and I never tasted the like. She called them 'Santa Claus cookies.' She said, 'Santa Claus left those for you.' Oh my, oh my, oh my, they were good. She said she'd try and make them again, so she made some more. They were good, but there never was the like of the Santa Claus cookies.

Amen to that.

End of the Line

Steam engine

All my bags are packed, I'm ready to go

I'm standin' here outside your door

I hate to wake you up to say goodbye

'Cause I'm leavin' on the last train

Don't know when I'll be back again

Oh babe, I hate to go...

With apologies to John Denver, who wrote "Leaving on a Jet Plane" in 1966, just three years before the last passenger train left Prince Edward Island. Twenty years later, the last freight train rolled onto a Borden ferry leaving behind the sinuous path walkers, bikers, and hikers now enjoy as the Confederation Trail. But the lure and lore of the railway lingers:

My father, see, worked on the railroad for 40 years.

He was a section man [looking after the tracks and switches] and about every six months, he'd get a pass for one of us to go to Charlottetown or Summerside. My sister Rachael would go, and another time, I'd get the pass and go to Charlottetown. That was something. We were grown up, you know, perhaps 15 or 16 before we ever saw Charlottetown.

Ruby Chappell, even in her 90s, still pumped about her first trip to The Big Potato. Ruby was born in 1914, so that memorable journey into the city was around 1930. And before my Prince County pals take offence, to put that train trip into perspective, Ruby was just as excited about her first trip to Summerside:

I think the first time I ever went to Summerside was with Major Murray and the wife. They lived across the road from us and they had the first car that was in Breadalbane. They took us to Summerside. Oh, that was something, to go to Summerside. And that was my first drive in a car too. All in the same day... that was a big deal.

Ivan Kennedy and his father Murdoch ran general stores in Breadalbane where Ruby grew up. Since Murdock was a CNR director, he reputedly had his own private railcar, sitting at the siding, waiting to take him on a journey to Carleton Siding or Glen Valley.

Neil MacNeill headed for Charlottetown from the eastern end of the Island. Neil boarded the train at the station in the somewhat ironically named Hopefield, because it seemed hope was one thing you abandoned when travelling by rail:

It took forever to get to Charlottetown. Forever. First time I went, I was only very, very young, not even a schoolboy. My mother had to come to town and I went with her. She had to go see Kenny Martin who was a lawyer and a judge. I still remember he gave me a California apple. He said it was from California and I took his word for it.

Hmmm, Judge Martin had a well-known sense of humour. One story that lingered long after his death was the time two well-known Charlottetown ne'er do wells, one named Partridge, the other Mallard, landed in his court charged with public drunkenness. The good judge looked up and asked, "And what are you two birds charged with this time?"

Neil's train overnighted in Murray Harbour, where the ashes were raked out, and coal and water replenished before leaving early for the slow run to Charlottetown. Along the way, the train picked up students who attended the Hillsborough Consolidated School in Mount Herbert, also known as the Macdonald School, since it was only one of four special schools built in eastern Canada with funds supplied by the Sir William Macdonald. Sir Bill was originally from PEI, and had made his fortune selling tobacco products, perhaps the best known brand being *Export A* cigarettes. They weren't the only train-bound students: in Georgetown, Bernice Delory boarded the train every morning to attend high school in Montague:

> Seven o'clock in the morning. And that turned out to be an advantage because in the evening, we had to wait for the train to come into Montague. It'd be about 5 o'clock so we'd all go down to the station and get our homework done. Communally. And Montague had a curfew, so we'd come home and go to the rink or whatever was going on. There used to be cowboy shows come here [to Georgetown] to the theatre at the town hall, live entertainment, with guitars and singing, so we'd go to those shows. Or we'd go to the rink. And then go to school the next day and tell everybody from Montague what a great time we had last night. They had a curfew, so on school nights they couldn't be out at all.

Has there ever been any love lost between Georgetowners and Montaguers?

Ah, no.

As the Murray Harbour train wound its way to town, stationmaster Roy Jones was usually waiting in Hazelbrook. Roy was also secretary of the nearby creamery, which shipped butter to town on the train. Roy wasn't always the only one greeting the train. His daughter was the petite and perpetually-in-motion Susan Jones Andrews:

> He had asthma, so my sister and I used to attend the station after we got home from school when the train would come in at 4:00 in the evening. We met a lot of people. I can tell you all their names: The engineer was Frank Paquet from Souris. The baggage man was Art Coffin. The conductor was Mr. Farquharson – he just had the thumb and the little finger on one hand. He'd had an accident on the train one day and his three middle fingers were cut off. We took music lessons on Saturdays in Charlottetown. There [were] four in our family, and when we'd go to town on the train, we went free. It cost 35 cents return. That's second class.

Not only were the passengers classified, so were the stations:

> Hazelbrook was called a first-class station because there was a place for the ladies to sit and another place for the men, separated, so they called it first class. Mount Herbert was the next station after Hazelbrook, and that was called a second-class station because it only had one waiting room. Everybody had to mix together. And yes, people did keep to the separate waiting rooms.

Of course they did, because in the 1930s, people knew men and women mixing in train stations led to dancing and dancing led to... the three-letter word I'm still unable to write, let alone say out loud, even around my wife. Especially around my wife.

To his dying day, I was terrified of him.

Every morning, the Hazelbrook section foreman – *"him"* –

cruised his section of tracks on his little trolley to make sure everything was shipshape:

> We lived right beside the tracks. One day, he was coming with his trolley, so my brother and I – my brother would be about five and I'd be about ten – we went out and put some stones on the track. We wondered if the train would crush them.

Who hasn't? Some of us put pennies on the track to see what would happen. My mother told us it didn't make cents, and she was right.

> So he came in and he said to my mother, 'Any children living here?'

> And she said, 'Yes. I have four.' 'Well,' he said, 'Do they ever go out to the tracks?'

> 'Oh, yes. They wander around quite a bit, but,' she said, 'They're good children.'

> 'Well,' he said, 'I don't think they're very good, because they almost made the trolley go off the track.' He said, 'If it happens again, I'm taking them all to jail.'

> Well, I was terrified. Every time I saw that man, I thought I was a jailbird. So even the day that he died, I don't think I went to his funeral. I was scared to death he'd jump up and grab me. I tell ya!

Imagine scaring little kids like that. The man was off his trolley. And yet...

It's a wonder Susan didn't blame herself when the old Hillsborough Bridge was structurally condemned in the mid-1950s and the Murray Harbour train was rerouted through Mount Stewart. The Hillsborough Bridge remained open to car traffic, but the weight of the steam and diesel engines was too much for it. After all, it was second-hand when we bought it at the turn of the last century; the spans floated over from the Miramichi on barges. And, by coincidence, guess who was on the last train to across the Hillsborough Bridge?

> My sister and I were going in for a music lesson, and somebody saw the bridge swaying. They thought, well we better not have that train go over it again. So, Jimmy Power, the taxi-man, took us all home that night by taxi, over the bridge in car. That was the last trip over the bridge by a train. I was on the last train. I was married in 1958, so that was about 1956. That was the end of the train.

♦

Let's head east for one more Murray Harbour train story, past stations with evocative names like Village Green, Hermitage, and Roseneath, from a man best known for his big moving vans and his antique auto collection. Paul Jenkins toyed briefly with a trainman's job on the railway before settling into the family's Royal Packing Company.

> We were on the Murray Harbour line one night. It was the middle of winter, January, and my second month on the job, I believe it was. I did what they call 'overcarry a passenger.' I took him five miles down the line past his stop to the next station. He was drunk and on the floor so we didn't find out. But, you're supposed to know where your passengers are going and where they're getting off. I wasn't quite aware of this, because some conductors were very good to you when you started the job and others wouldn't even speak to you. Some became great friends and others you just worked with.

> In any event, the conductor said, 'So and so was supposed to get off five miles back.' 'Well,' I said, 'I didn't see him.' So we both had to go up and talk to the driver who, at the time, was Jim Leiteizer, who turned out later to be a good friend of mine, and a character.

And he made a big fuss about it, and then he started to smile and I could tell he was teasing me, but we backed that train up five miles and let that man off. Now if you were in New Brunswick or Ontario, the whole train crew would have been sacked within five minutes, because you just don't back a train up. But the main line between Murray harbour and Charlottetown was not very heavily populated with high-speed trans-continentals.

In another incident, Paul was involved in a head-on collision at Emerald Junction. No one was hurt, but the engines were written off. Paul was a well-known Charlottetown businessperson; Jenkins Transfer was one of his enterprises that grew from the Royal Packing Company. The Royal was started by his grandfather J.D. Jenkins, and processed and canned chicken and fish in a factory off Grafton Street. They needed big trucks to haul the raw and finished product. Later when the Confederation Centre of the Arts was being built, Paul astutely used the same trucks to nail the contract to haul cement and rebar from the railway siding near the 1911 jail.

From day one, the railway was controversial on Prince Edward Island. In the 1870s when the idea of the PEI Railway was being bandied about by politicians, many people wanted the Legislature dissolved and an election called to determine its fate. A Rollo Bay resident wrote a letter to the *Patriot* newspaper, which opposed both the railway and Confederation, claiming he was all for building a railway and suggested one way to finance it: put a tax on unmarried men. He wrote to the editor:

> From here to East Point, I can count about 50 old bachelors who are no good to themselves or anyone else. We propose to tax them at ten shillings per year 'til they get married.

I know 50 men who'd pay that and more to return to bachelorhood. All they ask in return is a few cans of J.D. Jenkins

Island Sliced Chicken, and a bed on the floor of the Murray Harbour express.

Keith and Jean Pratt on old US railway line

Prince Edward Island swarms with tourists every summer, and many visitors are looking for a family connection. It's a sad reflection on our seemingly perpetual shaky economy that for generations the biggest export from Atlantic Canada was our youth: many young people headed south to what was once known collectively as "The Boston States." The reverse flow that happening now is partly due to cheaper living- and partly due to research into family ties and gene-alogy: our Boston States' cousins want to know whence they came, and the wonderful PEI Provincial Archives provides some of the branches to those family trees.

Keith Pratt is a prime example of an Islander who went south seeking work. Keith was born in Bloomfield Station in 1910. For years, he ran a huge general store there with his uncle A.J. Pratt. In 1959, seeing the writing on the wall, Keith jumped on the train at the station next to Pratt's store and got off in Boston. He eventually landed his dream job there, driving trains for the Massachusetts Bay Transportation Authority (MBTA). Heading to work one day, he noticed a neighbour having car trouble:

> I was sitting in the car waiting for my relatives and across the street was this lady cleaning the ice off her car. Well, I looked and looked, and thought, well, I should get out and help her. But I delayed and she got it all done, and when I went over, I didn't get a very nice look. Well, that was February and I didn't see her again until the fall, when your mother went to Italy.
>
> Jean: Not my mother. My mother never ate pizza let alone travelled to Italy.

We were sitting at their kitchen table at Keith's old home in Bloomfield, and Keith was explaining how he met his wife Jean. She was listening intently to Keith's version of events, chomping at the bit to jump in to set the record straight should it go astray. Until then, we'll let Keith carry on.

> So, I was taking the train and she too took the MBTA. There was another fella who had an eye on her too and we all travelled together to Sidney Square on the MBTA. But by golly, I came home one day and I saw her across the street, running around the gate to where her car was. So, I jumped over a fence that high and fell. And she came around.

Aha, finally. Cue the Jean Report:

> We lived across the street. We always saw him but we didn't think too much of him. I came around, and there he was, on the ground. We used to see him coming home from work and he always had vegetables, because back then he worked in a place where they shipped vegetables. But the time we got on the bus [note, not the train] when my mother went to Europe [note, not Italy] he said to me, 'Oh you're the

one who was shoveling snow, blah, blah,' stuff like that.

Anyway, I wouldn't let him in the gate but finally, another time he asked me if I wanted to go to the movies. He had no car, so it had to be MY car. Well, I let him drive, and he went to back up, and he hit me on the face with his arm and cut my chin. We went to the movies and later we went to my house, and the first thing he did, he broke my Telefunken stereo. I said, 'That's great. First you punch me and then you break my Telefunken' Well, anyway the thing of it is we got together and this is it. I've been coming up here for 38 years now.

Keith gets the last word:

We fell in love in September and got married in November. We got married November the third.

Keith must have known under American law a wife can't testify against her husband. And by law, a husband is not required to clean the snow off her car. Wait, Jean has more to say:

He wanted me to go somewhere with him, and I said, 'I'm not going anywhere with you. MARRIED people go somewhere together.' So he said, 'Then let's get married.' So, we got married.

Smooth, Keith, very smooth. All those years perfecting your people skills buying Irish moss and turnips at the store in Bloomfield finally paid off. And surely Keith atoned for his early faux pas by taking the bride on an exotic honeymoon. You'd think that and I'd think that, but Keith's love in life, before he met Jean Paradisio, was the railway. For decades, he took photographs of every train and its crew steaming through Bloomfield Station. So:

We went to Quebec, Sherbrooke, and up around the White Mountains. We left Boston on a Saturday in pouring rain, and we got into snow up near White

River Junction.

White River Junction? This is supposed to be a honeymoon. What happened to Montreal or Quebec City? Oh, wait a minute. White River Junction, population 2,286, boasts not only a Greek Revival-styled fire station, but a section of ... the Central Vermont railroad tracks.

Jean was not amused:

> Do you know what we did? Stopped to take pictures of trains every time he saw one. On our honeymoon. He's brainwashed.

A year later, Jean had calmed down enough for Keith to take her back home to PEI to show off his new bride.

> Everyone was glad, yeah. She just fitted in nice. Lovely. .

And that probably put an end to Keith's trainspotting days.

> Every time a train stopped here in the morning, they'd all come in for coffee, and I'd give them English muffins we brought down from the States. It was a break for the trainmen you know, and then they'd get back on the train and go along.

If you can't beat them... thus, Jean finally stopped competing with the railway:

> Well, I had no choice... no choice.

I was only one of many people to sit at Keith's and Jean's kitchen table in Bloomfield, lured by Keith's stories from the bygone days and his skills at unravelling local genealogy for visitors from the Boston States and beyond. Washed down with a cup of tea and a toasted English muffin. Better than any honeymoon.

Keith wasn't the first nor the last to connect with a Bostonian. Hilda Hilchey was born in Flat River in 1917 into a house full of Scottish traditions and culture. Her dad, Alec Beaton, spoke Gaelic, and her mum, Annie MacLean, baked bannock and hermit cookies. Hilda's great aunt Catherine had fled to Boston around 1900 where she landed a job in a paper mill:

> She had this man friend and they were about to be married. One evening, he was coming to visit her and she just slipped out for a minute – she was back right away – but he didn't wait for her to come back. She never saw him again. Imagine. She was gone for maybe two minutes and he never came back. No wedding, no nothing. Just nothing. He just disappeared off the face of the earth. She was pretty broken up. She never married, she never did. It's a very sad story and she was such a nice person.

Still a mystery, her fiancé was never seen again. Aunt Catherine survived and came home every summer, bringing treats for her nieces and nephews, toys, candy, and fabric to make dresses and shirts.

We also had Boston relatives who either mailed boxes of clothes that had been outgrown but not outworn, or in the case of "rich" Uncle Tim and Aunt Bernice, arrived at our door every summer with a car full of exotic American gifts like stuffed baby alligators and puffy mounds of cotton bolls from Alabama. Uncle Tim wore shirts decorated with palm trees and parrots, and his aftershave smelled like an orange grove. It was hard to reconcile Aunt Bee being Grammie's sister because she had more than three dresses and didn't wear a hat with a flower on it.

◆

Ed Deveau was born in 1922. He also remembers those care packages from "up in Boston":

> There was always somebody from the family away. They went away to make a few dollars to send home, and wherever they worked, it was in a household with well-off people and they'd be changing their

clothes all the time. The Islanders would be picking them up and saving them, and the next thing you know there'd be a barrel of clothes coming home. You'd get a box of clothes in the fall. I remember my wife had people away too, and they'd get a barrel every fall. There [were] three or four girls in that family and they'd be the best-dressed girls around town [Souris].

Kay Mooney – I don't know if you knew Kay – Kay McIsaac, she wrote quite a few books. Her father was Alec Mooney, a blacksmith, didn't have a lot of money. When she had her first communion, they didn't have a lot of money to buy a special dress, so Phoebe, my wife's mother, said, 'You send her up to me.' So, Kay went up, and Phoebe dressed her all up out of one of the barrels for her first communion. She looked good.

Being the oldest of six boys, I got first dibs on the used clothes whereas son #6 walked around in rags.

For many years, Ed Deveau was a stand-out citizen in the Souris/Rollo Bay area, but was actually born in Cambridge, Massachusetts, where his parents were both working at the time. When he was ten years old, the family moved back home, as did many other Maritimers during the 1930s. Times were tough and green cards were revoked. Ed said times were tough on PEI, too, but at least your family made sure nobody starved.

♦

Too long has my heart been far away

From the Island's hills and the lanes' red clay.

Too many summers have passed me by,

From the place by the church where our fathers lie.

Kathleen Gillis pouring the tea, Indian River, PEI

Blue from the sky that reflects on the sea

As the moon's white path beckons to me.

The whispering winds in the scented pines,

On the meadows where the Indian River winds

In 1914, Kathleen Gillis was born in the shadow of St. Mary's iconic church in Indian River. Her family's travels over the years would make good reading on TripAdvisor. Her parents left the Island looking for work first in Saskatchewan and later in Boston. When she turned 20, Kathleen headed south to Boston and managed to hang on to her green card during the "Dirty '30s." However, every summer she returned home to visit and recharge her batteries, and naturally she brought presents.

Clothing ...something useful for sure. But one of the trips home I had a check done at the border and I had a false bottom in my suitcase full of cigarettes because the boys wanted cigarettes.

Kathleen worked in Boston for over 30 years, starting off as a housekeeper where she immediately quadrupled the wages she'd been making in Charlottetown doing the same job, going from $8 a month to $8 a week. Later, she worked as a server at one of Boston's busy rail and metro transit stations where she might have run into Keith Pratt having a cup of tea and an English muffin between his runs as motorman on the MBTA Orange Line, a dream job for a railway junkie if there ever was one. In 1955, on her annual visit to PEI, Kathleen wrote a poem before heading back to Boston for another ten months of purgatory. The last thing she did in Indian River that fall was pick potatoes for a neighbour. She tucked the poem away in a book and forgot about it. Sixty years later, by chance, she opened the book and the poem fell out. A few days later, I showed up with my tape recorder, and over a cup of tea and an egg-salad sandwich, she read me the poem. It was a teary drive home.

Too long have I missed the close of day
When the sun sinks into Malpeque Bay,
The sun-drenched farms and the fields of hay,
With the sounds of calves and lambs at play.

And the stove is warm with a friendly glow
That only the Island's kitchens know.
Too many years have come and gone
Since my eyes have seen the Island's dawn
With the sky all tinted a pastel rose,
And a taste of salt in the breeze that blows,

But now I know of the things I've missed
On this bit of land that the angels kissed,

For I'm back to the fields and rivers and highlands,
I'm home once again to Prince Edward Island...to stay.